NEVER AGAIN

THANK YOU!

NEVER AGAIN
A WALK FROM HOOK OF HOLLAND TO ISTANBUL

Jeremy Cameron

JEREMY CAMERON

Jeremy

Signal

Signal Books
Oxford

First published in 2014 by
Signal Books Limited
36 Minster Road
Oxford OX4 1LY
www.signalbooks.co.uk

A catalogue record for this book is available from the British Library

ISBN 978-1-908493-96-5 Paper

Cover Design: Alice Mara
Illustrations: Alice Mara
Typesetting: Tora Kelly
Printed and bound in India by Imprint Digital Limited

CONTENTS

INTRODUCTION

In 1933, Patrick Leigh Fermor, later the doyen of British travel writing, walked from Hook of Holland to Constantinople. Leigh Fermor was eighteen at the time and had a fiver (later stolen) in his pocket. In his rucksack he carried a tweed jacket, two pairs of bags (trousers), a dozen pocket handkerchiefs, his pyjamas and an army greatcoat.

Leigh Fermor had several advantages. He was brave. (He later had a heroic war, mostly behind enemy lines.) He was intrepid. He didn't mind getting covered in snow. He picked up languages in a fortnight. Everyone wanted to be his friend: he stayed with bargees and barons, the latter putting him up for weeks on end. He was seduced by beautiful erudite women. He also, apparently, didn't have anything else to do; the whole enterprise took him three years. And he wrote beautiful prose.

Most people, including me, couldn't ever write as well as Leigh Fermor. Furthermore I can't write about tenth-century history or architectural gargoyles either. In every possible respect I was unworthy of comparison with the great man. But it seemed a good idea, buried in the depths of a British winter, to set out on his trail of long ago.

I was certainly not going to be intrepid, however. I was going to live in as much luxury as possible. I was not going to sleep under hedges; I did all that when I was young and stupid. Now I was sixty two years old and generally knackered. Three times already I had failed to walk across Europe, and then I was thirty years younger. I had a bad knee. I might not last the week. When I told my sister Sarah what I was doing she immediately said: 'Have you made a will?' I thought this was unduly pessimistic; and, incidentally, I had not made a will.

Patrick Leigh Fermor died, very old, after this journey began. He would never know that someone had tried to emulate his epic feat. I carried on, however. The chance of reaching Istanbul (as Constantinople now is) looked infinitesimal but it seemed a fitting memorial to attempt it; and, like Leigh Fermor, I didn't have anything else to do at the time.

I set out at the end of November and wrote up the account every night. This is it.

PART ONE

HOLLAND

DAY 1
HOOK OF HOLLAND TO ROTTERDAM

You could hardly see Hook of Holland.

At eight o'clock in the morning it was pitch dark, the wind was blowing a howling gale and the rain lashed so hard that the dock was barely visible. Welcome to Holland.

Not much happens in the Hook. For advice about walking to Rotterdam I was directed to the tourist office. The tourist office was, needless to say, shut on Thursdays. How could I get to Rotterdam? I had been searching the map for any route out of Hook of Holland that didn't involve motorways. I couldn't find one. I wandered about aimlessly in a circle. Then, through a stroke of massive good fortune, I stumbled across a sign for a cycle path. Of course! Those good old Dutch, of course they have cycle paths. My problem was solved.

Proper planning, needless to say, might have overcome some of these initial difficulties and helped me to locate all the paths I needed. But I don't do proper planning.

The cycle path went in a big arc. I didn't care where it went as long as it went somewhere. We passed through farmland, full of sheep and greenhouses and dykes. The rain hammered down and no-one was about. When the rain didn't hammer down the wind still blew a gale; apparently it was Force Eight last night. It was cold.

Something must have happened to Maassluis. The town centre is small and relatively old, based around a piece of water, either a canal or a river. However, the vast majority of the very large town, at least nine-tenths of it, has been built in the last decade. It's modern, soulless, totally without a shop or pub or café or, in the daytime, people. I had a cup of tea and marched on, munching my cheese and Marmite sandwiches.

The cycle path came down to the river, the vast seaway that makes Rotterdam the busiest port in the world. A flotilla of barges, boats and ships of all sizes slipped back and forth. The port of Rotterdam has over six hundred 'havens' or mooring points. On the other side of the water lies

an endless line of oil refineries, masts, chimneys and smoke. On my side benches were placed at intervals for people to admire the view. They must be very hard up for a view.

Then came the docks themselves, always interesting, some now tarted up as gastropubs but most still busy with shipping. The weather deteriorated further. I had not intended to walk as far as Rotterdam but carried on because there was nothing else to do. It was over twenty miles: and then what a sight it was.

In my travelling days, Rotterdam and Djibouti were known as the twin arseholes of the world. Djibouti is one of the many places I have set out for but not reached. Rotterdam I had not even set out for. (Incidentally, I have since heard that there is a third contender for the world title—Stroessner, in Paraguay, named after the late dictator.) Rotterdam is a poor city, or at least a city with poor people in it. The road to the city centre led through nondescript suburbs, cheaply dressed citizens and shops catering for the impoverished or immigrant—cheap food, tatty jewellers, kebab bars, the usual. Multicultural, I heard it described as later. Poor, in other words. Then, suddenly, a massive collection of monstrous buildings covered the sky line.

Some of them were futuristic glass palaces, some were sub-1960s shopping complexes. All were hideously ugly. It was as if the mayor had commissioned an Ugly Contest and told all the architects to do their dirtiest. No co-ordination between buildings had ever been mooted. No theme except ugliness had ever been planned. Everything had apparently been dropped at random from the sky.

In contrast, the fine old town hall served as a marker in the centre of town. Near it, the tourist office was not only open but helpful. I bought some more maps. I still don't know where I'm going but now I might at least know where I am when I get there.

I know only two words of Dutch. One is *tulipen* which, if I have got it right, is self-explanatory. The other is pronounced 'noken'. I don't know how it's spelled and it is unlikely to be in any dictionary and certainly not a phrasebook. However, neither word is likely to be of any use to me on this trip so I had a look for some new words in the phrasebook tonight.

Some words of Dutch are not very different from other languages although when they say them it sounds as if they're about to be sick. Other words, though, are impossible. How can I possibly be expected to remember the word for 'please': *Alstublieft*? By the time I have put down the phrasebook

I have forgotten it. It is out of the question to try it in a café when buying a cup of tea. I would sound ridiculous. I shall have to be rude instead.

My watch has stopped. I shall just have to get up when it's light and go to bed when it's dark.

Later... Ok, Ok, I take it all back. Everything I said about Rotterdam is unjustified, unfair and, of course, wrong. I accidentally gatecrashed a party celebrating an award given to an investigative journalist. A woman there told me that a year ago her father died in Buxton, Derbyshire, where I was born. She also told me that Rotterdam is a vibrant, cultured, beautiful city, rebuilt after destruction in the war and then rebuilt again into the monstrosity that it is today. She loves it. So does everyone else. Only grudging losers think it is hideous.

I think it's hideous.

In Buxton she used to walk up to Solomon's Temple, the nineteenth-century folly above Burbage where my parents lived at one time. Before I was born, when my father was away at the war, my brother Michael learned to open the front gate and escaped from the garden daily. Whenever she couldn't find him my mother had to walk all the way up to Solomon's Temple to bring him back.

DAY 2

ROTTERDAM TO DORDRECHT

The new day begins with plasters: they have to be placed on all the sore bits. Unfortunately I am so stiff in the mornings these days, even at home, that I can't reach my feet at the best of times; two cups of tea and a walk round the house are necessary before I can get the socks on. That's even without walking twenty miles the day before. Putting plasters on the blisters today was a major job. I strapped myself up and set off.

The road to the river led past more of Rotterdam's sky-seeking monsters, then over the fine new bridge. Most of the day ran through suburbia--out of the city, past Feyenoord's massive football stadium, in and out of motorways. What a boon these cycle paths are. Sometimes they go in circles, their mileage signs are a bit scatty but they do get you there unharmed.

Furthermore they know a good signpost. Even I, who can get lost walking to my kitchen, would have found it very hard to get lost today. The only country to compare with them is Switzerland, where walking paths are signposted every few paces. I have to say, though, that the Dutch have the advantage over Switzerland. The Swiss always assume that you want to get from (a) to (b) by the hardest possible route, generally over a mountain. The Dutch don't, if only because they haven't got any mountains. The biggest hill so far has been a bridge over the motorway.

Despite all their cycle paths, the Dutch motorways are still festooned with a million cars. Perhaps they should make them cycle paths too. All motorised transport would be banned. Nothing could be transported except by bicycle. Heavy goods could be transported by a collection of bicycles, fanned out across the motorway. I have always thought that the world's essential problem is motorised transport. Without it there would be peace in our time and every other time. Pollution would cease. Global warming would be a thing of the past. The world would be bathed in light. Now is the time.

A heron flew, terrified, from the dyke because I walked along. It wasn't bothered by a million cars passing within a few feet, but a rucksacked walker was alarming. Later another heron stood beside a man fishing in another dyke. Presumably he feeds it tiddlers. Both seemed content. They each wore a satisfied smirk and appeared well looked after.

Another fine bridge over another waterway brought Dordrecht. The woman at the party last night said Dordrecht would not be far enough for me today. She may have thought I was hard. It was 25 kilometres or about 16 miles. My feet are sore and my legs ache.

It is easy to forget, sitting at home with an inadequate map, what these stupid ventures are really like. My last long walk, two or three years ago, was from London to Venice. Thinking that I was too old to do it in one continuous stretch, I walked it intermittently: a couple of days from Calais to Arras, then home, then return the following week and do the next two or three days to St. Quentin. A year or so later I arrived in Venice. This time, though, I am trying continuity. It's more painful.

Dordrecht is an old town, based as always on the docks, with a marina, a vast and rather unattractive church and an old, pretty main street. Groups of sightseers looked round the town centre. I did the same.

On television tonight they talked about the sixties. To do so, they brought in a history lecturer… For the sixties! Those of us who lived through it, we're history now.

If it wasn't for the sixties, of course, I wouldn't be doing what I'm doing now. So they're to blame.

Then they showed a programme about the thirties, with film of the battle of Cable Street in 1936. Now that's what to do with the fascists.

I'm reading a wonderful book, *Half of a Yellow Sun* by Chimamanda Adichie. I can't put it down but want to spin it out a bit. I read fifty books a year—no more, no less—and I am already on forty-six. If I read more than fifty it will disturb my average and may set a precedent. I like things regular. (I think there's a name for this—something about compulsive obsessive.) The next book in the rucksack is a long one, which will help spin things out, but then there are a couple of short ones. I must read less. If I get too close to the target I may have to talk to people instead.

Mind you, I know at least two people, Howard at home and Scott in Switzerland, who think it is truly contemptible to read only fifty books a year. At first they had trouble believing it. 'Fifty?' They ask superciliously. 'Fifty?'

In Spain in September I met a German woman who reads for eight hours per day. That's what she does, she reads. She and her husband are retired. He plays tennis, she reads.

DAY 3
DORDRECHT TO BREDA

The wind blows bleak and unrestrained across water. Ahead lay the massive waterway of the Hollands Diep. To my right another large channel was hidden behind farmland. I once walked beside the St. Lawrence Seaway in Canada, where huge funnels emerge between tractors and cows. This was similar; suddenly large boats appeared in what had seemed to be open fields. I was looking forward to the immense bridge across the Hollands Diep but it turned out to be merely functional: effective rather than beautiful. The wind blew everywhere.

On Portland Bill, Dorset, stands a prison called The Verne, stuck on top of a large hill, half way out to sea on an unforgiving coastline. In winter the wind blows so hard that ropes are attached to the buildings for people to hang on to. It must be the windiest spot in England. The Verne, incidentally, is the only prison I have ever smuggled anything into. No, it wasn't drugs or mobile phones, both of which are smuggled into prisons in large quantities. Climbing up the hill for an appointment with Ray, whom I had known for a long time, I picked some blackberries and put them in my pocket. When we were safe in an interview room I gave them to him. Ray said he hadn't tasted anything like them for ten years.

No-one had any idea how to walk to Breda. I had a cup of tea in a café before the bridge, another cup of tea in a village called Zevenlegs… oh, I give up, a long name beginning with a Z, and a bar of chocolate in Teeheijden. This all seemed well off a direct route but Breda arrived eventually, over twenty miles for the day and dark when I arrived.

But what a beautiful place it is! The shopping streets are old, traditional, humming with people preparing for Christmas. The lovely main square has a fine cathedral and a batch of restaurants thumping with customers. I can see no way out of the city. Why do I find it so hard to get out of places? Is it a psychological flaw? Is it Freudian? It's easy to find the way in, just by following the signs for the centre, but I can seldom find the way out again. However, we'll worry about that in the morning.

BELGIUM

DAY 4
BREDA TO BRECHT

Into Belgium.

Where were the border guards? Why don't they turn me back, refusing me entry? Where was my passport stamp? What's the matter with these people nowadays? Borders are supposed to be hostile places. They certainly are if you're non-white and entering Britain. There was a very small sign saying Belgium. Blink and you missed it. Apart from that, nothing.

It was straight, flat and wet. Was it interesting? No, it wasn't. On days like this I try to reduce the distance in my mind, and kill the boredom, by thinking: 'Mmm, five miles, that's only Westacre to Swaffham', or 'Mmm, twelve miles, only Westacre to King's Lynn'. It sounds good until I suddenly realise: 'Bloody hell! Westacre to King's Lynn, that's a bloody long way!'

In fact the best day of my life was spent walking from Westacre to King's Lynn and back. It was Boxing Day, some time in the sixties, snow was on the ground and the ice was frozen so deep on the roads that no-one went out. I walked to the old Pilot cinema in Lynn to see a double bill: *The Bofors Gun* and *Charlie Bubbles*, both excellent. Then I walked back in the dark, never needing the torch because the moon shone so brightly. I saw four cars all day. Then, when I got back home, my mother had of course cooked a substantial meal.

Those were the days.

Zundert was a jolly place. It contains the Vincent van Gogh museum. I gave it a miss. Sitting beside my bed at home is a biography of Vincent van Gogh. It is sitting beside my bed because I never read in bed. It was a Christmas present a few years ago and some day I'm going to finish it. Once I visited the Musée d'Orsay and saw van Gogh's *Sunflowers*. At least I think I did. I saw so many famous paintings that day that I'm not too sure what I saw and what I didn't. The *Mona Lisa*? *The Hay Wain*? *The Fighting Temeraire*? I can't think of any more famous paintings.

Wuustwezel was about far enough for the day but there was nowhere to stay and nothing of any other interest; for some reason it had a tourist

information office (closed of course) but it was hard to know why anyone would want information about Wuustwezel. I walked six kilometres in the wrong direction to see if there was anywhere in Brecht. I hate walking a single step in the wrong direction. No, there wasn't anywhere to stay but there was a bus to Antwerp. I'm not proud. I will return in the morning. I went to Antwerp and there, right beside the bus stop, stood one of the sleaziest hotels it has been my pleasure to stay in.

Antwerp seems like a fine sort of place. I changed trains here years ago, the only previous time I have been in the city, but all I saw then was the magnificent railway station. That journey, incidentally, was a minor epic leading from Belgium to Sweden by train. During it I thought I had gone mad when I woke suddenly and found myself surrounded by water; the train goes straight on to the boat between Denmark and Sweden.

Nigel, Jane and I were on our way back from taking a group from a children's home to the south of France. (Their lasting cultural memory was of the topless women, needless to say.) I left them in Zeebrugge to go home while I took a train to Scandinavia.

By coincidence, Ian, one of the children living in the home at that time, contacted me only a few weeks ago via the Internet. I haven't seen or spoken to him for over thirty years but he managed to find me. He has done very well in life; he was always a good lad. We talked for hours. Yes, he remembered that trip. In particular, yes, he remembered the topless women. He also remembered the trip we made the following year.

That year, I had three other staff members with me when we took the children to Morocco. One was a woman who was very capable. One was a man who was later sent to prison. The other was a man who should have been.

We will call him James, if only because that was his name. Now, this was a difficult holiday, one which in truth we should never have embarked on. One night I was taking a twelve-year-old boy to hospital with an infected leg, a tricky experience, and arrived back at midnight to find that the other staff had lost an eighteen-year-old girl; she returned next morning, having spent the night in another tent. Happily, there was no adverse outcome for either the boy or the girl but in both cases it was more by luck than judgment. Anyway, as for James…

James decided, at the end of a very, very difficult three weeks, that he needed to bring some dope—Moroccan *kif*—back from his holiday. Presumably he thought there was some kudos in doing something so unutterably insane. He didn't tell me what he was doing, of course, and it was only some months later that I discovered what had actually happened.

James decided that the best way to bring the stuff back to England was to swallow it. That's what you do.

However, he had not planned his little venture in advance and so had not brought any condoms (lubricated) with him to swallow the stuff in. He went to the supermarket, therefore, and bought some little polythene bags. Then he filled them with *kif* and, Bob's your uncle, down they went.

There was something else, however, that James had not factored in to his calculations.

Drug smugglers who swallow their goods are travelling by air. We were travelling for four days in a van back to Britain.

James got as far as northern Spain. We were staying in a campsite with absolutely no facilities whatsoever. There were no showers, no basins, no washrooms—and no toilets. There was one tap. Apart from that, you had to go off to the woods.

James could hold it no longer. He went off to the woods, relieved himself naturally and recovered his items. Then he took them to the tap and washed them. Then—because we had not yet been through British customs—he swallowed them again.

Oh, ugh.

He nearly got home after this second swallow. Unfortunately, when we reached the boat between Zeebrugge and Felixstowe, he could hold it no longer. We had still not been through British customs. He went off to the toilets and had a repeat performance.

Later, presumably, having swallowed the items three times, he smoked the stuff with his friends and told them he had brought it back from Morocco. Whether he told them exactly how he brought it back is a matter of speculation.

In Antwerp tonight I went to the cinema. The film was a load of complete hokum but I enjoyed it, if only because I knew a couple of the actors in it. Then, just off the main square, I had the best chips of my life. The Dutch say of the Belgians that they have all got square arseholes to accommodate all the chips they eat. Funnily enough, the Belgians say exactly the same of the Dutch. Whatever their biological necessities, these chips were just wonderful, worth coming to Belgium for.

It was about twenty miles again today and I have got to burst a blister tonight. Never a fun task.

Day 5
Brecht to Lier

I should be turning east, heading for Germany, down the Rhine and then branching off through central Europe like Patrick Leigh Fermor. However, a few weeks ago I was cheated out of a tennis match by a German. I know you shouldn't hold a whole nation responsible for the malfeasance of one individual but I think it would be best to stay away from the country for the time being.

Ah, a canal at last. Belgium looks much prettier from a canal.

In recent years I have realised that much of my life has been wasted: that long period before I knew about canals. On the walk to Venice I came across them in France and realised I should have been following them years before. In Britain also, as Belinda and I found on the Grand Union, they are a wonderful distraction from real life. When they are going the same way as you are, there is simply no reason to walk along roads. When they are not going the same way it is tempting to go off in totally the wrong direction, simply for the convenience. Canals have swans, geese, herons, ducks, coots, moorhens and the occasional kingfisher. Once in France on a hot day I watched a deer having a bath in a canal, simply to cool off. There are also fish, which unfortunately brings out fishermen, surely the surliest and most unwelcoming people on earth. (Why are there no fisherwomen? Presumably they don't want to be sitting out all day in November doing nothing.) Canals are straight, flat, boring and beautiful.

The plan, such as it is, has always been to take canal paths as far as Switzerland, so this is a start. A few kilometres from Brecht a canal took me swiftly to Schoten, south of Antwerp. These are big working canals, not titchy little alleys, and sizeable barges plied up and down. Both the canal and the barges were dwarfed, however, on meeting the Albertkanal, not so much a canal, more a massive seaway; boats as big as aircraft carriers cruised back and forth. I turned left and followed it for a few kilometres then turned again and made across country via Emblem (nice name) to Lier.

In Lier I am staying in the world's most discreet hotel. Several people directed me to it and I still couldn't find it; even standing outside it I couldn't find it. Eventually someone pointed out that the modest plaque on the wall quietly and almost invisibly mentioned the word hotel. The interior is equally discreet. It is not so much the place for a lovers' tryst, more a surreptitious rendezvous for Swiss bankers.

I thought Lier would hold nothing of any note. However, it has a sudden, ancient city centre. Again, having found the way in I have no idea whether I can find the way out again. In any event, plans may have to be changed: Leuven, my original target for tomorrow, is much too far. Today was over twenty miles again but Leuven would fall into a different realm altogether.

As I head south, daylight hours ought to be longer. On the other hand, as the calendar stretches towards 21 December they will get shorter. The only answer is to head south after 21 December. Until then, try to walk fast before it gets dark.

Day 6

Lier to Aarschot

It is 1 December. Where will I be next 1 December? For that matter, where will I be on 1 January?

There was nothing to write home about—or anywhere else—on the road from Lier to Aarschot.

My father once told me that he thought his children had inherited their parents' characteristics but taken them to extremes. I forget what he said about my siblings but I know what he said about me: he liked a good walk himself, but…

Sometimes you just have to bite the bullet. I'm aiming for Namur. There doesn't seem any friendly way of getting there so it's a matter of head down, stiff upper lip and think of the Empire. Anyone who has walked sixteen miles along a flat, straight road in Belgium will know the rest. The cycle path was about an inch wide and big burly old lorries kept bearing down.

I sang *The Twelve Days of Christmas*. Really, the mind is an extraordinary piece of work. I haven't sung this since childhood and, if you had asked me what happened on the ninth day of Christmas, I wouldn't have had a clue; but, singing it all the way up from the first day, it all came instantly back. Then I sang *Green Grow the Rushes, O*. Surreptitiously, because it's religious.

Then, following the religious tendency, I started on hymns. I don't believe a word of them, of course, but what wonderful tunes! Recently I have been to a few Catholic funerals and I have to say that the Anglicans have got the edge in the tune department. And the words! 'Be Still My Soul'. I know only those four words but aren't they magnificent? Then I sang *Abide With Me* and *You'll Never Walk Alone*. That was stirring.

A poster by the roadside took a different musical angle, advertising 'Balls Of Fire' somewhere this Saturday night. Is this as in *Great Balls Of Fire*? A long time ago I saw Jerry Lee Lewis perform in Manchester; great fun he was too. He was not as fine, though, as Chuck Berry, whom I saw there around the same time: the greatest performance I was ever lucky enough to be at.

After the hymns I sang Simon and Garfunkel, particularly their paean to travel and roads and buses and old times: *America*, which always recalls the vastness and emptiness of journeys in the US. It also reminds me of the conversation my parents had with a taxi driver in Denver. They were visiting my brother Michael in New York at the same time as I was walking across the country, so they popped over to Colorado to see how I was getting on. In the cab from the airport to the city the chat with the driver went as follows:

Cab driver: 'Hi, how you doin'? Where you from?'
Parents: 'Hello, we're from England.'
Cab driver: 'England, England?'
Parents: 'Yes…'
Cab driver: 'Gee, you speak English well. How long you been speaking it?'
Parents: 'Well, all our lives, actually.'
Cab driver, after a pause: 'Y'know, I never thought of that.'

Stuck in the Midwest, in that vast country of theirs, it had naturally never occurred to him that the English language had not been invented, like everything else, in the United States of America.

The complete staff of the gregarious post office in Aarschot decided there was nowhere to stay in their town. In fact they treated the very concept with something between amusement and despair. I got on a train to Leuven, a big city, and will come back in the morning. In Leuven, in a hotel on the main square, I was asked to make a decision which they thought would be a difficult one. Would I like a room with a private bathroom en suite or a room with a private bathroom just across the hall? What was the difference in price? Thirty euros! I would walk a lot further than across the hall for thirty euros. I would bathe naked in the railway station for thirty euros.

Later I was told that there was 'almost' a hotel in Aarschot—that is, there will be a hotel when they have built it.

In Leuven, thank God, at last I could get a *Guardian*. I can't really manage without a *Guardian*. There are certain necessities when it plops on to my mat every day. First I read the obituaries. I know it's a cliché that you read the obituaries as you get older but I live in fear that someone will die without my knowing about it. Above all, I'm afraid Patrick Leigh Fermor will die. I don't want to wish this on him and I have no reason to think he won't go on for years yet, but I really don't want him to slip away unmourned by me. What I would really like would be to meet him.

After the obituaries in the morning comes the sport. Today, as it happens, I had a message from Simon at home to say that Norwich City had won 3-0. All is right with the world, then. After the cheery obituaries and a comprehensive read of the sports pages I can face the disasters of the news section.

Tonight I finished *Half of a Yellow Sun* and ditched it to save weight. This is unfortunate as it was a loan and now I won't be returning it. Trying to save further weight I am also ditching some maps and the phrasebook and I have eaten the Kendal Mint Cake. In the normal course of events I have been using up the shaving cream and toothpaste and taking the glucosamine tablets. I live in hope of noticing the difference. Of course, when I have used all the shaving cream I have to buy some more so the rucksack becomes heavier again. Go easy on that cream.

DAY 7
AARSCHOT-TIENEN-JODOIGNE

Belgium has hills!

Not yet big ones. (I once had a history teacher who forbade the use of the word 'ones', which he said was a contradiction in terms.)

Radical surgery was required last night on the blisters and I even wondered for a while whether I could continue at all. To weaken the resolve further, I realised that I was in fact closer to home in England than when I started out; I could be in London in three hours. On impulse, I decided to stay for a second night in Leuven, walking meanwhile from Aarschot to Tienen then catching the train back to Leuven. It's cheating really because it means I can leave the rucksack behind.

But it was like a holiday without it. Tienen was nearly fifteen miles and I was there by lunchtime. I had a cup of tea at the station and had to choose between the sensible decision or the stupid one. The outcome was inevitable. The sensible decision was to go straight to Leuven, lie down and let the foot recover. The stupid decision was to carry on to Jodoigne today. I walked the thirteen kilometres to Jodoigne and caught the bus back.

Actually I didn't. That is completely untrue. I couldn't even find the way out of Tienen (that problem again) so I did it the opposite way round. I caught the bus to Jodoigne and walked back. This is, of course, highly dubious practice; I'm supposed to be walking to Istanbul not from Istanbul. It is disreputable to be walking in the opposite direction. However, I reckon that the object is to cover the whole distance; if some of it lies from Jodoigne to Tienen rather than from Tienen to Jodoigne, does it matter? The question should perhaps be left with a higher authority. While they're about it, they can decide whether to disqualify me for not carrying the rucksack. It's all done now anyway. It's beyond repair.

In the bar I met Derek, an academic artist from Kent with swine flu, who is here for an exhibition of the work of Husserl, whom I have never heard of. Husserl was a phenomenologist, something else I have never heard of. Derek talked of the academic principles behind phenomenology and art. Unfortunately I couldn't understand a word he said. Then he talked of Manchester, where he originates, Nottingham where he now lives and Kent. I could understand all that. We even have mutual acquaintances. Finally we moved on to the state of the country and found ourselves in complete agreement. At any rate, he didn't argue.

Tonight I have started reading a book about de Beauvoir and Sartre, written by Carole Seymour-Jones, whom I know. De Beauvoir wrote two of the best books I have ever read, *The Second Sex* and *The Mandarins*. However, her and Sartre's reputations have been steadily shredded over the last twenty years and this book apparently puts the final boot in. I shall look forward to it.

Carole's partner, Geoffrey Parkinson, is now retired but was once the most notorious probation officer in the country. He used to write a weekly column in *New Society* and two of these articles in particular brought him infamy, at least with his employers. The first, called 'I Give Them Money', was an attack on the psychodynamic approach to working with clients that was prevalent at the time; the article annoyed a lot of people and gave a good laugh to the rest of us. The second described Geoffrey's advice to his clients to commit lesser crimes: don't commit a burglary, fiddle the Social Security instead. A lot of probation officers may have advised something of the sort but most did not publicise this advice in a column in *New Society*. Geoffrey did not get sacked but it was a close shave.

It has been a week now since Hook of Holland. That's the first target, surviving the week.

DAY 8

JODOIGNE TO NAMUR

What exactly is wrong with Belgium? Yesterday the station buffet at Tienen was like a fortress surrounded by a wall of smoke. Today it's a café in Namur which plays host to some of the city's more problematic citizens. Everyone in the place is smoking. On the streets young girls are doing the same. It's like going back in time. People may forget just how horrible the public places were in Britain, and Ireland, and France, and the US, before smoking legislation came in. Not even the smokers (those scum) would want to go back to that. Conversely, some of these Belgian smokers should take a holiday in a modern country and see how pleasant it is to eat a pizza in a restaurant free from poison.

It was not, it turns out, a stupid decision after all to walk on to Jodoigne yesterday. It was a masterstroke born of genius. Namur had become attainable today after about twenty miles of wind and rain. Huge fields lined the road. I used to know the acreage of most of the fields at home (I don't know hectares) but I couldn't begin to estimate the size of these. Tractors and lorries carted sugar beet to the factories. Mud lined the roads. Frustrated drivers threatened the lives of everyone with crazy overtaking. Everywhere was waterlogged. It's just like home.

The road ran through Ramillies. Wasn't there a battle at Ramillies? Weren't we taught to remember battles and years with an acronym like a telephone number: BROM 4689—Blenheim, Ramillies, Oudenarde, Malplaquet? Or have I got it mixed up with Esmond Romilly, the 1930s poet who was killed in the Spanish Civil War?

It is consoling to have reached the French speaking section of Belgium. I now have a vague idea of what is going on and it will be very nice to ask for a cup of tea without making a complete prat of myself, which I have been doing unfailingly until now.

Namur is ancient. I know it has an old fortress and I know there was a siege in 1692 or thereabouts (can't remember who was besieging whom). I didn't know they have a Tintin festival.

The fortress seems to be up a hill. The centre of town holds a clutch of museums and an old town hall. Much was destroyed in the First World War and much more, for good measure, in the Second. It's a busy place, the administrative centre of the area and a focus for tourism.

Denis, Belinda's brother, used to work here and assures me you can walk up the Meuse from here on. The woman from the tourist office concurs. Tomorrow we shall see if they are right. Various maps of European waterways suggest that a canal leads to Sedan in France, but on closer inspection of the map the distance seems extraordinarily long, perhaps because the canal goes round in circles. The scenic route would be nice but, where it's a case of scenery versus speed, we know who wins. Patrick Leigh Fermor would have taken a barge; he was always taking barges. Or perhaps swum it.

Poor Denis will never come here again. With a leg amputated and with an unrelated cancer, I'm afraid he isn't going anywhere. I sent him a postcard which may please him. He said recently that he isn't really interested in the future of the world, but the past may be another matter.

DAY 9
NAMUR TO DINANT

Past the Town Hall, past the Citadel, out of Namur, up the Meuse and into the Ardennes. Nice place. Depressed day.

It must be very pretty here in summer. Wooded hills line the banks of the big river. Substantial houses, a few chateaux and the odd fort look out over the water. Barges ply back and forth on the Meuse, very much a working river. Denis and the lady from the tourist office were right in saying there was a path all the way to Dinant; but why do they cobble it? Who on earth wants to walk on cobbles? Is it to make you suffer? Every one of the walkers and cyclists in recent times had ignored it and so did I. I toddled along the seventeen miles to Dinant.

The main reason to come to Belgium is the beer, particularly Leffe, and near here is the Leffe Abbey. Presumably the monks made the beer to drink themselves stupid and stop thinking about sex all the time. Which would you rather have, sex or alcohol? Well, both, actually.

No such excuse affected the denizens of the café where I had a cup of tea at lunchtime. Most of them looked as if they had been there since yesterday lunchtime.

What would I normally have been doing on a Friday morning? Taking Mimi to school. I always said that I didn't want children (the very thought is terrifying) but that I wouldn't mind having grandchildren. Now I seem to have achieved that happy state. On these walks I spend far too much time being introspective, wishing I hadn't done so many dreadful things in life (though I would probably do most of them again). I try to think of good things I have done, but that isn't so easy. Taking Mimi to school on a Friday, however, is incontrovertibly, irrevocably good. Good for me, anyway.

That's the problem with having too much time to think: you can get very maudlin. It is just impossible to fill up all the day with good thoughts—or indeed any thoughts much of the time. My worst ever walking experience was crossing Illinois and Missouri. Not only could I see at the start of the day where I would be at the end of the day; sometimes I could see the next day too. It was endless. There was nothing to think about, absolutely nothing at all. It was like solitary confinement. I would go back over my life, never a sensible thing to do. Then I found that I had thought all the thoughts it was possible to think: there were no more thoughts left. What do you do when there are no thoughts left?

That's enough! This is only the ninth day and you're only in Belgium!

More cheerful news is that I have got the *Guardian* for the fourth day in a row. After the sport and the obituaries I am inexorably drawn to the part I detest, the quick crossword (I can't do the other one). Whenever I complete the quick crossword I think I'm very clever. Whenever I fail I think the compiler is stupid. I hate the crossword but crosswords are supposed to postpone dementia. I should have started long ago.

And, speaking of forts, Dinant has an absolute whopper on a pillar of rock, right above the centre of town. Spectacular indeed.

More decisions have to be made about the route. There is a danger of following a path determined by the allure of the place names: I have already been to Emblem and today went through the very seductive Profondeville. What a wonderful address, Profondeville. Also I would really, really like to spend a night in Bouillon, which is over the hill from here; staying in Emblem, Profondeville and Bouillon would have been a hat trick of joy. Local advice, however, suggested staying on the river. One thing about the river: it's not going over any mountains. Another thing is that it's very, very hard to get lost while following a river.

FRANCE

Day 10
Dinant to Givet

Last night I slept in a room above a café in Dinant. This morning everyone in the café breakfasted on coffee and cigarettes. Or beer. Where are all those urbane Belgians who fill the top jobs in the EC? Do they have coffee and cigarettes for breakfast? I think not.

It is the weekend. In the main square I was putting on my waterproofs (as always) when a carload of young people from Lincolnshire arrived, totally disoriented after driving through the night, speaking not one word of French and hoping to find their hotel. Their hotel indeed was the sole reason for coming to Dinant, not a place they had ever heard of before. Why had they come here? Because it has a Hotel Ibis.

It is a novel way to choose a holiday destination. Rather than choose a place and then seek accommodation, you choose the accommodation and then see where there is a place. It's like those people who move house to be somewhere near a Waitrose. The young woman who approached me for assistance said she had stayed in a Hotel Ibis before and wanted to do so again. I didn't tell her that the Hotel Ibis would as always be overpriced crap. Don't want to spoil their weekend. To give them credit, though, they were already looking round Dinant and thought it was lovely. Which it is.

These kids were fine but in general it pays to be cautious when approached at random and asked if you speak English. All kinds of loonies want to share a small piece of a foreign land with you, possibly for an extended period. Long ago I had a cautionary experience in Split, Croatia, and I have been very careful ever since.

It was seven o'clock in the morning in Split and I had just got off a night bus. I had failed again to walk to Athens and was not in a good mood. A thin, bearded North American approached and asked piercingly if I spoke the English language.

'Sometimes,' I admitted

'I'd sure like to speak English with you,' he said.

'We'll go and have a coffee,' I told him.

'I don't drink much coffee,' he said.

'Well, I'll have a coffee and you can have a glass of water.'

'I don't drink much water.'

We entered a large cafeteria. Tall, thin, bearded and ponytailed, Denis' appearance arrested every movement in the restaurant. Forks stopped on their mouths. Jaws dropped open. Silence fell like a curtain.

'Are they looking at me or are they looking at you?' Denis asked.

'I'm afraid they're looking at you.'

'I thought so.'

It turned out that Denis ate only fruit: preferably windfall fruit. Anything else was destroying life; to eat a carrot was destroying a life form, whereas to eat an apple was not (he threw the pips away in a promising spot). He had set out from the US 'to found a fruit culture' in Australia (I did not point out that he had headed the wrong way from the US to Australia). Previously he had helped to found a fruit culture in Florida and now he was going to do it somewhere else. A fruit culture, it transpired, consisted of eating fruit. Only fruit.

Since leaving the US a week earlier, however, life had not gone well for Denis. For hundreds of miles he had been given a lift by two young French women, but they had gone off to the islands. He was convinced that (a) they could have spoken English if they had wanted and (b) they could have taken him further. He himself spoke no word of anything but English. He said that nobody was speaking English to him. And he couldn't get enough fruit. He was thinking of going home.

After the cafeteria we went to a shop. He bought some nuts and tried to pay with dollars. I lent him some money and ventured the opinion that dollars were the currency in the US rather than in Europe and that he might not expect European money to be proffered in a supermarket in New York. 'You're right,' he said humbly. 'I can see that.'

He had not eaten nuts for nine months previously, having eschewed everything but fruit in that time. Now he gobbled down half a bagful of nuts, suffered instant and chronic indigestion and had to give me the rest. This was the last straw for him. He decided to head for home. I tried to persuade him at least to go to Athens or Istanbul to see some more, but no. Where was I going? Well, I was catching a bus to Trieste actually. In that case, he would go there too.

In Trieste I was doing nothing for a couple of days, just poking about. He caught the first train back to London, then the first flight home. He had told everyone at home that he would be gone for eighteen months. Unfortunately he would be home in eleven days.

Since then, I have been wary of people who ask if I speak English.

Back in Dinant, the route followed the Meuse to Givet. In Hastière I thought I would post a letter back to England: quite a harmless undertaking, I thought, not likely to give offence to anyone. Not so. On stepping into the post office, I was given an instant bollocking by the postmaster for not wiping my feet on the mat. Then he indicated his contempt for my purchase. One stamp? Only one stamp for England? He asked three times if that was all. Then he refused to take the money out of my hand. He told me to place it on the counter. Actually, I wanted to say, my germs are quite capable of leaping from my hand to yours even without contact. I wonder how many customers he gets in his post office. Only very clean big spenders who do not try to touch him.

The Meuse was lovely. Sometimes the valley was shallow and bordered by sloping meadows, sometimes steep and fringed with rock faces. A renaissance chateau, a big bridge, a zone of industry and into the old town of Givet. We're in France. Another bloody great fort but no border post, of course.

According to my map of the waterways of France, a canal ought to stretch from here to Switzerland, hundreds of kilometres. The normal map says nothing about any canal; they ought to get together and sort out their differences. The road signs say we're going on a *route touristique* and keep talking about Verlaine and Rimbaud. All I know about Verlaine and Rimbaud is the namecheck given to them by Bob Dylan in *You're Gonna Make Me Lonesome When You Go* (rhymes with Rimbaud.)

Speaking of namechecks, Dylan took his name from Dylan Thomas, who was married to my mother's cousin Caitlin. Oh, shut up.

In the paper a number of people had been asked to name their books of the decade. I expected the usual pretentious rubbish, books no-one would read written by friends of the critics. However, this time they had asked (mostly) reasonable people with a bit of common sense and they had recommended Zadie Smith's *White Teeth*, Andrea Levy's *Small Island*,

W. G. Sebald's *Austerlitz*, Khaled Hosseini's *The Kite Runner*, Sarah Waters' *Fingersmith* and the book I have just read, Chimamanda Adichie's *Half of a Yellow Sun*. They also recommended some dross and left out some goodies but I wouldn't argue with any of the above. Nice to see them in touch with the mainstream, i.e. me.

Today was the shortest day so far, just under fifteen miles. That will be my rest day. The bad knee has been playing up in the afternoons, that's the excuse.

DAY 11
GIVET TO REVIN

That canal never materialised. Instead, they gave an explanation about what they had been doing with the Meuse.

Some time in the nineteenth century, frustrated by all their barges being swept away once a year, the people decided to tame the Meuse so that it was navigable all the time. To do this they introduced a series of weirs and locks covering a part of the river. I have no idea how this does the trick but they seem happy with it. Anyway, I can only think that the waterway map-makers think this means that the Meuse is a canal and mark it as such. It may be a canal to the boat people but it isn't a canal to the walker. Where is the towpath?

A cycle path led down one side of the river but the road was a great deal shorter. It passed a big chateau with attached mediaeval village. In Fumay I bought a cup of tea from a publican who so closely resembled the publican in the village at home, Paul Figura, that I was convinced it was him. From Fumay a cycle path led swiftly to Revin. The scenery along the road was probably great: wooded hills, mountain streams, the lot. Unfortunately I had to guess at it. Like most of the scenery for the last ten days, it was invisible.

I know I moan a lot and I know it's December, but really this is ridiculous. So far on this trip there has been one dry day. This morning it rained. This afternoon it piddled down. That's been about the pattern so far. My waterproofs are good enough for almost anything but today I did get wet. My boots too have never let me down but the water has got through them and they can't get dry enough to put some more waterproofing cream on them. Fortunately the clothes inside the pack are dry; like anyone who has walked the accursed Pennine Way, I keep them in bin liners. But I could do with some general respite.

Walkers, of course, are like farmers in that nothing is ever perfect. If it's wet enough for the sugar beet it's too wet for the barley. For the walker, it's either too hot or too cold or too wet or too dry. Given the choice, though, hot is better than cold, just as dry is better than wet.

Admittedly, it doesn't always seem like it at the time. The hottest place I have ever been was Khartoum but fortunately I wasn't walking there. Nevada was pretty hot for walking and I got sunstroke but it wasn't as hot as southern Honduras. The south of Honduras was once forested. Now, because they have cut all the trees down, the rain doesn't fall any more and instead a semi-desert has taken over. At six in the morning I used to buy a litre of cold orange juice from a vendor in a town square. By eleven I had to drink it hot because it had started to ferment.

The wettest single place I have walked was the rain forest in Grenada. In the rain forest it rains. It's easy to forget that.

The coldest place? Well, I have been in a few reasonably cold places but I was never allowed to set out on The Big Cold One. For years I wanted to walk from Moscow to Paris in winter. The idea (a very, very stupid idea as I now realise) was to do it faster than Napoleon.

The Soviet Union was still in its pomp when I first made enquiries at their tourist office in London. Like any other tourist I went politely to the counter and told the woman that I wanted to ask about walking in the USSR.

'No,' she said.

We stood and looked at each other for a while.

Then she sought to justify her position. 'How can you walk in the USSR?' she demanded. 'It is hundreds of miles.'

'Well, that's what I wanted to ask about,' I suggested.

'No,' she said again. That was that. End of story.

Some years later, following a thaw in East-West relations, I tried again. This time I prepared the ground. I wrote to the tourist office and I also wrote to the consulate, explaining that I was serious, and asking about walking from Moscow to the Polish border. I omitted the bits about Paris, Napoleon and invasions, which seemed undiplomatic.

Eventually I got a letter back which indicated that the two agencies had liaised and emphasised that they were extremely reasonable people. The letter was polite, logical and courteous in the new spirit of co-operation between nations. There was, they said, absolutely no reason why I couldn't walk in Russia (as it now was). Russia was a free country and I could go anywhere I liked.

There might, however, be one small problem which I would need to address. Tourists were only permitted to stay for the night in certain registered lodgings. I could, of course, choose any of these to stay in. However, they tended to be about three hundred miles apart. As long as I could walk three hundred miles in a day there was no problem, naturally, but…

I got the message and gave up.

The cycle path brought Revin quietly closer. No cyclist appeared all day but runners began to emerge from their lairs. Runners are a bit like seagulls: when you see them you know you're approaching civilisation and want to shout 'Land ahoy!' They slunk around Revin. They never talk.

Revin was closed. At the weekend very little sentient life could be found above ground. Only one hotel was not irrevocably shut and this one didn't want to admit it. I rang the bell, knocked on the window and finally attracted a woman's attention. She explained that the bar and restaurant were closed for the weekend but she said I could stay at the back. Thank God. I was wet. I tried to find a cup of tea.

Finding a nominal cup of tea is not the same, of course, as finding a proper cup of tea. That's the main trouble with abroad: they just don't know about tea. In Belgium the process is quite ceremonial, with a tray and a little biscuit, but it doesn't mean it's any good. In France you may get a whole pot but the same applies. I always remember my horror the first time I ever bought a cup of tea in a French bar. At first I thought I had got someone else's order. Then I thought perhaps I had gone colour blind. A glass of what appeared to be (and indeed was) warm water was placed on my table. Some time later a tea bag made its way in my direction, with the suggestion that I should introduce the one to the other. Oh God. Nice as they are, the foreigners (usually), they just don't get it. The water has to be boiling. If it's not, there is no point. You might just as well suck on a warm bandage.

There is one other reason why the continentals can't make a decent cup of tea. They use Lipton's tea bags. Nothing good ever came out of a Lipton's tea bag. Where is the Typhoo? Where are the PG Tips? How has Lipton's been allowed to get away with it for so long?

DAY 12
REVIN TO LUMES

What a day.

It was good to leave Revin, a decrepit little place.

The scenic route was said to be forty kilometres to Charleville-Mezières, the road twenty-five. No contest. The road climbed up a hill instead of following the river and disappeared into shrouds of cloud, the breath billowing in steam. Up here too it is probably pretty when you can see it. From the top I took the back roads through the forests. The river came back to the road in the twin city.

Nearly forty years ago I walked through Charleville. I can remember nothing of it from forty years ago; I will probably remember nothing in forty years' time too. In the imposing main square I was given information about somewhere to stay in Lumes, a village on the way to Sedan. The woman in the tourist office was so helpful, in fact, that I asked if she would like to accompany me for the walk. She pleaded pressure of work. I bet she would have come otherwise.

But my boots started to fall apart.

I looked down and they were flapping. I assume that it only happened today; it would be embarrassing to think that I had been walking about for days with flapping boots. These boots have lasted me for hundreds of years and thousands of miles.

Every now and then the cobbler in Swaffham puts new soles and heels on them. Then they last for another thousand miles. Not this time though.

My first reaction was to think, 'Oh God, disaster, got to go home', but that's just looking for an excuse to give up. The second was to think, 'Oh God, got to buy new boots, that means fresh blisters'. The third was to think I ought to buy some glue. I didn't know the word for glue so I had to ask the woman in the tourist office. *La Colle.* Then I had to find some.

First, discovering the way out of Charleville was not the easiest of tasks (again). The initial bit was clear enough, through Mezières, the working-class half of town and very much the poor relation. Then I found myself in an industrial estate. Extricating myself, I got out of town eventually. But where was Lumes?

It had disappeared. Getting there on the motorway was easy but getting there by any other means seemed impossible. It was really peculiar. A host of helpful people gave me directions at different times, all of them adding an apologetic shrug at the impossibility of it all. Several big circles, a few backtracks and then a single lane track under the motorway suggested that the authorities really do not want you going to Lumes. But I got there finally, in the dark.

In general, the French are very helpful at giving directions, much more so than the British. There is always the odd jerk, of course, like the woman in the shoe shop tonight who pointed me in totally the wrong direction just to get rid of me, but most seem only too glad to be of service. They also don't even seem to be terrified of the lone, wet stranger in town. I must admit that my first reaction at home when approached is to think 'Hello, it's the raving loony with a knife come to get me, run for it.' Fortunately for me, the French aren't like that at all. If they were, I would still be out in the fields tonight.

Speaking of which, a man stopped his car ahead of me today and came back with a gun in his hand. (Raymond Chandler always maintained that, when in doubt about how to proceed with a plot, have a man walk through a door with a gun in his hand.) However, the man was hoping to murder small furry creatures rather than me.

Curiously, following my discussion (or rather his discussion) about phenomenology with Derek in Leuven, the subject comes up again in the book I'm reading about de Beauvoir and Sartre. Isn't that just the way? You spend a whole lifetime waiting for one phenomenologist and then two come along at once.

I shan't be sorry if it's the last two, though. Phenomenology will be complete rubbish in the same way that all philosophy is complete rubbish. The only philosopher who ever made any sense was Karl Marx and look what happened to him. Climbing a mountain makes more sense. Or eating an ice cream. Or having sex. They can all tell you what is important in life. They're easier to understand too.

DAY 13
LUMES TO SEDAN

My efforts at gluing the boots together were laughable. Why am I no good at anything at all? Why am I so pathetic?

For a mile or two the soles still stuck to the rest of the boots in the way they were intended. Then they began to drift apart again. The rain continued as usual, negating any chance of the boots drying out. I dawdled. In a café the women came in for a coffee after the school run; it was nice to be greeted in a café by a bunch of women for a change instead of a bunch of men. I couldn't dawdle all day though. The rain grew heavier. Sedan was not much more than ten miles away but I stopped there to take suitable advice.

There was a cobbler in Sedan: a traditional cobbler, advertised as such. He was a bit of a character too, brooking no argument or insubordination. He showed me the problem. Yes, he could mend the boots, he said, but the problem was that they were saturated. Before he could attend to them they had to be dried out. Put them on a heater for the night, he said: not under the heater or near the heater but on the heater. Then we'll see how they are in the morning. Be here at 9.15.

I found somewhere to stay and switched the heater on. Unfortunately it works on a thermostat. If the room temperature rises to the set level, the heater goes off. The only solution is to open the window so that the room is freezing, then get into bed to keep warm and let the heater work its magic. It's a boring way to spend an evening but it works.

Sedan is a picturesque town which has played a central part in every war dreamed up over the past few centuries. The colossal castle was built in the fifteenth century. The Franco-Prussian War, the First World War and the Second World War have all left their indelible marks. Terrible battles have been fought and atrocities committed.

Not far from here, in August 1944 ten members of the Resistance were shot by the Germans in a cave. It reminded me of a memorial I saw a couple of years ago, also from August 1944, of ten members of a little village 'murdered by Nazi barbarism'. Presumably it was a reprisal. The village could not have had more than a hundred inhabitants. The youngest murdered was a girl of eighteen. There must still be people living in the village today who remember the victims.

My mother's cousin Pierre was in the Resistance. Two or three times he escaped from France during the war, made his way to Britain and was parachuted back in. His mother and sister would receive a cryptic postcard and know where to meet him. The first time he escaped, however, he made his way to Portugal, officially neutral, and was interned, not knowing whether he would ever get out again. He said he was British and asked to see the British ambassador or consul.

Pierre's name was Marojer but he gave his name as Majolier, his British uncle's name. The ambassador, seeing the name Majolier, came hotfoot to the prison to see him.

'Your name Majolier, old boy?' he asked.

'Yes, it is,' Pierre said.

'Any relation to Paddy Majolier, by any chance?'

'Well, yes, sir, he's my uncle.'

'Your uncle, by Jove! Soon have you out of here, old boy. I was at Eton with Paddy Majolier!'

Memories run long. Paddy Majolier, my grandfather, invalided in the trenches, died in the flu epidemic of 1918, more than twenty years before. But if you have been to Eton with a chap…

So Pierre came to Britain and performed his duty. Sadly, it didn't do him much good. He was shot during the liberation of Paris in 1944. When the main German army withdrew from the city they left snipers behind, and before the liberating armies arrived a running battle ensued between the snipers and the Resistance. Pierre was shot on a street corner. Many years later his sister Christine showed me the spot. From time to time she went to look at it: just to look.

Christine's husband, incidentally, was a doctor working in Paris during the war. Sometimes he helped the Resistance, going out to treat injured airmen, French or British, who had parachuted in. He told me that one morning he was coming down the staircase of his apartment building, on his way to work, when two Gestapo walked up it.

He went to the concierge's office. 'Who have they come for?' he asked.

'You,' she said.

He left and never came back.

One could go on. Christine herself harboured two Jewish women for two years in the family home in Congénies, in the south, while the German army were quartered in her garden. She made light of it. It wasn't the army you needed to worry about, she said. It was the Gestapo.

Sedan is full of museums recording many of these events. If I'm stuck here waiting for my boots I may go round some of them. I hate museums but I make an exception for World Wars. Otherwise I'll be off.

Sedan has been, in fact, one of my targets: looking at the map (when I have got a map) it is well situated as a milestone. It may indeed have arrived faster than I expected. Each day is an appalling trudge, endlessly boring and psychologically destructive, but that misses the point: I'm getting there. I never actually set a pace for myself; I never say 'I must go faster', let alone 'Slow down for God's sake'. I just set off. Sometimes I seem to go faster, sometimes more slowly. In any case, it makes very little difference how fast you go; what matters is how long you stop for. It's the same as people speeding along the motorway at eighty rather than seventy (or fifty-five in my case). They don't get there any earlier; see how long they stop for a cup of tea and then see who gets there first.

Life is like that.

Day 14
Sedan to Inor

He mended my boots!

I took them in at 9.15 as instructed and he said they were dry enough. He would do the business. It would take an hour and a half.

'That's fine,' I told him. 'I'll just sit here and read my book if that's Ok with you.'

'Haven't you got any other shoes?' he asked.

'No, but I'm fine.'

In that case, he said, he would do them in twenty minutes. Twenty minutes later they were indeed done. I asked politely if they would really stand up to anything now, since he had said it would take an hour and a half but it had only taken twenty minutes. Ah, he said, I used some very strong glue. He gave the impression that it was like hooch, not available to the public or police, brought out only in secret. Now you can go where you like, he said, walk as far as you want, do anything.

Then he charged me six euros. I said that was ridiculous and he had to charge more. He refused. All I could do was to thank him profusely and march off. I could only wish that I had as profound an impact on his life as he had on mine.

For the rest of the day I kept looking down at the boots, expecting them every minute to come apart. Nothing at all. No movement. I was ecstatic.

Then I got heart problems instead.

Since they sorted it out I have had very few problems with the heart. Today it went irregular a couple of times and didn't right itself. It may have been the stress of wondering what was going to happen in the near future and where I was going to get to tonight, since the day was pretty unclear. Calm down, for God's sake. You'll be all right. Something will turn up.

Wrong directions outside Sedan sent me half an hour on a wild goose chase. Returning to the valley, the Meuse ran through gentler hills, smaller and more undulating, studded with farms and villages, very pretty indeed. Cattle observed me placidly as I plodded by. A couple of deer grazed on someone's winter wheat. The Meuse itself did not have a path but the roads were not busy.

Mouzon was shut. The hotel was shut, the tourist office was shut, the main square was shut. A plaque commemorated a man who fell defending the bridge in 1914. At two o'clock the shop opened and I bought raisins and chocolate. A few kilometres before Stenay I stopped at Inor, probably about twenty miles for the day. From the look of the map, the Canal de l'Est might begin here. I've been looking for it for a hundred miles so it's about time.

I might need a canal to follow because there's a bit of a map problem. I've got a map of Belgium which finishes here. I've got a map of Switzerland which covers Alsace and Lorraine. In between, though, there's a gap. There's still the Inland Waterways of France map, which appears to be full of lies but has a great big red line where this canal is alleged to be. Let's hope so. If I can't walk along the canals I may have to navigate by the sun.

Which, of course, I haven't seen for about a fortnight. Today we had drizzle - but drizzle feels like a holiday, I had never realised how attractive drizzle could be. I ought to stop moaning.

The mind does run on, of course, when there is no-one to talk to and in fact no-one takes any notice of you at all. I was invisible today. Forty years ago this would have been unthinkable. Apart from anything else, it was impossible to walk through this part of France without getting stopped by the police. In every large village I used to be arrested. No, that's poetic licence. In every large village I was stopped, my passport inspected and my lineage examined. They didn't like me but for want of any outstanding crime they had to let me proceed after a while. One day I inadvertently found the answer to this police problem.

'Where are you going?' they asked as always. A stupid and irrelevant question but they had to say something.

'Switzerland,' I said.

Hmm. Very dubious.

'But,' I added, 'I like France so much that I might change my mind and stay here.'

'Ah oui?'

'Oui. Bien sûr. Pas de problème.' Or something like that.

'Ah, monsieur,' said the first one.

'Ah, monsieur,' said the second.

We're very happy to have you here, they told me, have a nice day, enjoy our village, vive la France, would you like to sleep with my sister, etc., etc.

Those were the days. Nowadays the bloody police don't take any notice of you at all.

Tonight marks two weeks of the journey so far. I suppose that's not bad; I didn't know if I'd manage two days. The absolute deadline for reaching Switzerland is another two weeks. I've no idea whether I'll make it or not.

DAY 15
INOR TO LINY (NOWHERE TO NOWHERE)

It's always been the same with me and existentialism. Just when I think I've got it, pinned it down, oops, there it goes again. In the past I have tried, many times, to give it a fair hearing. The truth is that, however hard I try, I just can't work out what it means.

Another question, of course, is why I bother. I would much rather read the newspaper. Or the football scores. Or a bus timetable.

Anyway, I am doing my best to understand the existentialist bits in the book about de Beauvoir and Sartre. The sex bits, however, are a good deal more interesting.

On a more mundane level, after Inor there really is the canal that I have been aiming for. What there really isn't, however, is a bloody footpath. This is very, very frustrating. The whole route has been planned (though that is a grandiose word for what took place) on the premise that there would be a footpath after Inor. In the past I have walked for many miles along canals not far from here that boasted beautiful footpaths. What has happened to this one? How would a horse have pulled a boat along here without a towpath? This is going to be a problem.

Apart from its beer museum, Stenay is dead; the supermarkets are outside town so the centre has been destroyed. But the tourist office employed a Scottish woman who was suffering from such a bad cold that she could barely stand up and I could not recognise whether her voice was French, Scottish or American. She told me I could walk along the canal for a while and this was true. It didn't mean that there was a footpath. After a while of trudging along the bank I gave up and went back to the road. It was more dangerous but faster.

Walking on roads is generally not too dangerous on the continent and I have only ever been hit twice. The first time, years ago, was in Germany near Donaueschingen. A car came from behind, overtaking on a stretch where overtaking was illegal, and clipped my arm with its wing mirror. As the arm flew up in the air the driver saw my horrified expression as I assumed it was broken. He tried to pull up. Unfortunately he didn't manage to do so while on the road and ended in the ditch. He jumped out of the car and ran back to see how I was.

'Your arm?' he said. 'What has happened to your arm?'

Somewhat embarrassingly, nothing seemed to be the matter with my arm. I felt it all over: perfectly sound.

'My arm is good, my arm is good,' I told him in what was alleged to be German. 'But your car?'

'Your arm is good?'

'My arm is good. But your car?'

'Don't worry about my car. You go now.' He was aware that driving into pedestrians was considered to be against the law, and he wanted to be hastily rid of me. As it happened, a breakdown truck came past at that moment and towed him out. What a fine scam that would be, the pedestrian and the breakdown truck in league! Unfortunately I hadn't thought of it beforehand or I might have been walking into cars all over Europe.

I was also hit once on the Adriatic Highway, the coast road in Croatia. Hugging the rock, tighter and tighter, I watched a huge transport lorry coming closer and closer. There was little doubt that he was doing it deliberately. He just nicked my rucksack: just a little clip as he went past. No doubt he was satisfied. I was terrified.

Dun-sur-Meuse housed a memorial and cemetery for the American soldiers (the doughboys) who died here in October and November 1918; it seems even more pitifully unnecessary than ever to die when the war had almost ended. Everyone must have known, for God's sake, that it was nearly over (it ended on 11 November) but still they kept killing each other up to the last minute.

The first time I went round First World War graveyards, forty years ago, the museums were staffed by old men who must themselves have been in the war. What could you say to them except for the barest platitudes? All those old men have long gone, of course, but it is good to see that there seems more interest now than there has ever been. All the cemeteries are, as always, beautifully kept and unremittingly tragic.

It would be good to know that politicians went round graveyards from previous wars before sending boys off to get killed.

After all this I walked barely fifteen miles for the day before stopping for the night with an elderly lady whose name was given me by the Scottish woman with the cold. She gave me a cup of tea and slice of cake before going off to the gym. Later we haggled over the price of accommodation: she wanted to charge me less, I wanted to pay more. Finally we compromised on a ridiculously small amount. We had a very nice chat too. A very nice lady.

When I'm walking, it's noticeable that my nails and hair don't grow; there's no energy left for growing. Plenty of toenails fall off but none grow. As for facial growth, it's well known that men's beards grow faster in periods of sexual activity. Ha! Mine must be positively shrinking.

Overnight it piddled down. During the day it also piddled down but only while I was, by great good fortune, in the toilet at Lidl. Apart from that, it didn't rain all day which is something new. They say it's going to get colder. It can get as cold as it likes, just as long as it stops raining.

Day 16
Liny to Verdun

The German First World War cemeteries are always very moving. Very plain but still immaculately kept, they are a reminder that two collections of young men were getting massacred. Today I walked round a German graveyard where each cross carried at least two names. A couple of fresh wreaths had been laid. One small headstone had been substituted for a cross. On it was a Jewish name; above the name was the Star of David and below it was written something in Yiddish. This young man was good enough to die for his country in the First World War, but if he had survived it his country would have murdered him anyway, twenty years later.

In the middle of a French cemetery I stood with tears in my eyes. The sheer scale is hard to comprehend. A hundred thousand Germans attacked on one day at Verdun. Over a period, two hundred and seventy five thousand Frenchmen were killed, wounded or taken prisoner. I was standing in one graveyard. Perhaps a thousand graves lay in it. Multiply that by a hundred.

That's just the battle of Verdun.

Marshal Pétain was the hero of Verdun. In the Second World War he became the betrayer of France.

Verdun is a lovely city surrounded by beautiful countryside, much of which must have been destroyed between 1914 and 1918. The city itself straddles the Meuse, a comforting town with a stunning war memorial in its centre. The whole area is indelibly imbued with war and death and it would be hard to pass by without paying observance to it. I went for a walk round.

It's snowing in Germany, Austria and Switzerland. Everywhere the stall holders are selling *vin chaud*, or *Gluhwein*; very nice it is too. Winter is here.

I bought a map. It's not a map of where I am now but of where I hope to be in a few days. So, if I can get through the next few days of not knowing where I am, perhaps I will be OK! Follow the river…

A sign says Neufchâteau 105 kilometres. Can I do that in three days?

DAY 17
VERDUN TO ST. MIHIEL

Each morning before setting off I try to put plasters on the various blisters that have not yet disappeared from my feet. This is difficult in the mornings when I can't reach my feet. My father, in middle age, used to have his bath in the morning to loosen him up for the day. At the time I thought it was rather quaint. Now I can see that we all become our parents. And there isn't a bath here.

It was 22 miles from Verdun to St. Mihiel. There was not much to be said about that. My longest conversation was with a horse. However, there were quite a lot of conversations to be had in St. Mihiel, largely on the subject of accommodation. There wasn't any.

One hotel was shut for the weekend. One didn't seem to exist at all. One had nobody, absolutely no-one, on duty. I went there, couldn't rouse anyone, walked for miles round town looking for alternatives and came back again. The *patronne* arrived. Sorry, we're full. Apparently a lot of men arrive at weekends to go out with guns and kill things. Things were looking grim. It was dark and there was nowhere to go.

Then she said there was one hotel, four kilometres away on the road to Commercy. Would I like her to ring up and find out if there was a vacancy?

Yes please.

There was a vacancy. Would I like her husband to take me out there and drop me off?

Yes please. Yes please very much. I was embarrassingly effusive in my thanks, which continued all the way there until I even embarrassed myself with my thankfulness.

Then I had to consider a moral dilemma. In the morning, am I going to walk back the four kilometres to St. Mihiel and then walk back again? No, I'm bloody well not. I walked at least four kilometres round St. Mihiel today looking for somewhere to stay. That will have to do.

While I was agonising about spending a cold night outside I consoled myself, or tortured myself, with listing the five most uncomfortable nights of my life. (This is the problem with being a man: you have to make lists.)

(i)   I once spent a night in a phone box on King's Cross station. You don't know whether to stand up or lie down.

(ii)   On a train in India I was last to board the sleeping carriage and so got the berth that was two feet too short. The consolation in this was that I met a man in the bunk below who travelled six nights per week for his work and read exclusively educational literature. He knew more than anyone I have ever met.

(iii)   There was a night in Greece. In a village café I unwisely bought a cognac late in the afternoon. The hospitable landlord then insisted on buying me a second and had one himself. I was left with no option but to buy him one back and have a third myself. Now, these measures of cognac were not inconsiderable, as John Major would have said. After three of them I could barely walk. The plan had been to walk another five or ten miles and find somewhere to camp. Instead I staggered out of the village in search of somewhere flat to lie down. There was nowhere flat (or, at least, that was how it seemed). Finally I propped my body against an olive tree to avoid rolling down the hill. In the morning I was sore but still there.

(iv)   One night in Honduras I found a nice spot by a stream. Fifty yards from the road I was comfortable and invisible so I had something to eat and settled for the night. Then a truck drove up... The driver did not get out immediately. He appeared to be waiting for me to make a move. He waited. I waited... In the morning, after a sleepless night on my part, he drove off! He had not been waiting to rob me or murder me, he had just stopped for the night. He didn't even know I was there.

(v)   But the worst night of all was spent in a sink. I was walking alongside a river in Nevada. I had sunstroke so was not in a very sweet frame of mind. I wondered if the river would lead me anywhere nice. Instead it disappeared completely. I hadn't known that a river could do this. It just led into a kind of swamp and never came out again. It was a nasty, soggy mess. I had to spend the night in this sink. My companions were fifty million mosquitoes. I had some fairly good anti-mosquito spray but it was wasted here. They simply ignored it. I had the choice of curling into the sleeping bag and being roasted in the heat or sleeping outside and being eaten alive. At about four in the morning I started walking again.

There have also been some very comfortable nights, one of them not far from here in a place called St. Blin. On a day of pouring rain I arrived in St. Blin expecting it to have a hotel, which it didn't. In a café I had something to eat and got talking to the mother of the *patron*, an interesting woman who in her youth had lived all over the Mediterranean while her father was in the army. We talked about life and St. Blin. Eventually I prepared, with obvious reluctance, to go out into the rain and find somewhere to sleep. But they asked me if I would like to sleep in the barn.

Yes!

Dossing down in the loose straw under a warm, cosy roof, it was one of the most comfortable nights of my life. Picking the straw out of my clothes for a few days afterwards was a small price to pay. Next morning I shared breakfast with the family, thanked them profusely (again—I'm a real crawler) and set off renewed. And dry.

This business about walking south doesn't seem to be doing the trick yet. Here I am, walking due south, day after day, but the days are still getting shorter and shorter. If I walk to the equator there will be twelve hours of daylight and twelve hours of dark at any time of year. There must be quite a long way to go, that's all I can say.

DAY 18

ST. MIHIEL TO PAGNY-SUR-MEUSE

On the subject of mosquitoes, I once met a man who eradicated malaria in Asia. He was probably the most fulfilled man I have ever met.

Egyptian by birth, he had been a tennis star in the 1950s, travelling the world with Hoad and Rosewall and all the rest of them at a time when they knew how to play the circuit. (Hoad once won the French championships after not going to bed at all the night before.) Then his tennis career came to an end and he returned to his original medical training.

For many years he was then employed by one of the United Nations health organisations and they set him to eradicate malaria in Asia. This he succeeded in doing and malaria has never returned.

Later, by now married to a Swiss woman, he retired to Geneva. A tennis court stood beside his block of flats and one day someone asked him if he played. 'I used to,' he said. He was invited for a game. When I met him he was world over-75 champion and a happy man.

I met him, incidentally, at a veterans' tennis tournament in Lenk, Switzerland. I had been on a glacier for two days beforehand with Andreas, who unfortunately decided that he wanted to descend two thousand metres (nearly seven thousand feet) in three hours or something ridiculous. Not wanting to appear a British wimp, I kept up, more or less, and then staggered off to the station and made my way to Lenk. I booked into a hotel and went upstairs for a lie down. Then I found, a couple of hours later, that I couldn't walk downstairs again; I could walk upstairs but not down. Fortunately I didn't have to play tennis the first day. Nor the second. By the third day I could make a pretence at playing. I lost to a Lithuanian dentist.

Just for a change, today it snowed. It snowed for most of the morning and it snowed for most of the afternoon.

At Commercy urgent thinking was required. To the south, on my planned route, all enquiries about accommodation drew blanks. Yes, there are many hotels in France, but they are never open. If you want to stay in a hotel, don't try at weekends. Or on a Monday. Or on a Tuesday. It's best to stick to Wednesdays and Thursdays if you want a bed, preferably between June and September. Suffice it to say that I would not be continuing south.

What's the matter with me? Why am I so disheartened? Why am I so grumpy about trivialities? This is France, for God's sake. It's easy here. If you get grumpy here, what happens when you get somewhere difficult?

Commercy has a startling main square with a massive town hall. In front of it, a large banner told the President of France to remember who elected him. There are evidently political disturbances, though not today. On a Sunday morning the town was lively, the food shops open, the cafés humming. On Sunday afternoon it was like a morgue.

I would go east to Nancy and try those canals. I dumped my bag in Commercy, walked to Pagny and caught the train back. In the morning I will return to Pagny and carry on. It was eighteen miles today, which will have to do.

DAY 19
PAGNY-SUR-MEUSE TO LIVERDUN

In the night I dreamed that I went back home for a couple of days to sort out a piece of outstanding work. However, this is nothing in the dream stakes. The previous night I dreamed that Al-Qaida mended my watch.

I wish they would.

Around lunchtime I wandered into Toul, a fairly unattractive town with a very unattractive cathedral. From time to time one crests the brow of a hill and sees, in the distance, a major edifice which might be a grain silo, a cement works or a cathedral. Usually the nature of the edifice becomes fairly clear fairly soon. Sometimes it doesn't; and sometimes, as on this occasion, a grain silo or cement works would have been more attractive.

The route out of Toul could not have been murkier. The tourist office was, of course, shut. In fact it was doubly shut: it was shut because it was lunchtime and shut because it was Monday. I followed a road out, probably in the wrong direction, until suddenly a cycle path materialised: Liverdun nineteen kilometres. Where had I seen that name before? It wasn't on any of my inadequate maps. Ah, it was on the train timetable. It was on the way to Nancy.

At last the Meuse had gone off on its own. To be honest, I was glad to see the back of it; it was pretty at times but all the way from Charleville it had not had a path and there appeared to be no working boats at all on it. The new cycle path followed the Moselle. Where did the Moselle spring from? What I was really after was the Marne-Rhine canal. This would do for the time being, though. It was water and it had a path.

It was freezing. In fact it was below freezing; the temperature never reached freezing all day. It wasn't a good day for fannying about enjoying the ambience. I pushed on.

For a while it all went well.

Then I lost that cycle path. I saw no sign of it branching off but suddenly there was only a small track. Then there was no track at all. Five intrepid ladies of a certain age, not to be put off their afternoon constitutional by the howling temperatures, agreed with me that the path had disappeared. The canal, or Moselle, that I had been following had suddenly turned into a very big river with nowhere to walk. I had to double back and take to the roads.

Later the cycle path reappeared for the last few kilometres to Liverdun, where I got cocky and made a stupid error. Shortly before the town, the cyclists crossed the river. Convinced that I knew better, I continued on the same side, undeterred by various signs telling me that it was private, that I was a no good son of a whore etc. By now it was dark. There had to be a bridge. Yes, there was a bridge, a big bold railway bridge with no access for pedestrians. Shit. Again I had to double back for a mile or more, cross the river where I should have crossed it before and walk in the pitch dark towards the town. If there was nowhere to stay in Liverdun, I had to catch the last train into Nancy and come back in the morning. The last train was at 6.25. It was touch and go. Would I make it?

I scurried, flat out, into the suburbs of town. It was even tighter. I will never know whether I would have made it or not. A kilometre from the town centre a taxi was standing in a lay-by, the driver feeding his accounts into a laptop. I gave him a hell of a shock knocking on his window. Would he like to take me to the station? He would be delighted: so delighted, in fact, that he cut his normal price. I like to think that Patrick Leigh Fermor would have taken a taxi too.

Later I almost passed out in a restaurant. Have I been doing too much?

Day 20
Liverdun-Nancy-Ludres

Many years ago I answered an advertisement in the Munich youth hostel for someone to share petrol expenses to Paris. It was an advertisement that brought Chantal and Monique-Paule into my life and changed it a great deal.

First we drove across Europe, rather embarrassedly playing the erotic Serge Gainsbourg and Jane Birkin record on the portable record player in Monique-Paule's car. At the end of the journey I was plied with whisky, with deleterious effects, by Monique-Paule's father. Meanwhile we spent a night in Nancy at some sort of youth house. On that occasion I saw nothing of the city and I have never been back.

Since then we have been in continual contact and Chantal became a regular Christmas guest in my parents' home. I went to both their weddings. Both were memorable but Monique-Paule's was the more amusing.

The wedding was in the mid-'70s. Monique-Paule had met Richard in what I always thought was a supremely romantic location: the queue for *Hair* in San Francisco. Richard had just been drafted into the US Navy. He chose the Navy because he was assured that in the Navy he would not be sent to the war in Vietnam. So guess what happened?

Richard was from Tennessee. His family had never left Tennessee except to go to Kentucky and once for an adventure in California (where, they said, 'folks was real nice. Folks were just like us'). They came to Paris for the wedding, wearing pink hats.

The wedding needed to have a political dimension. Monique-Paule had a French, Catholic, English-speaking, left-wing priest. Richard had an American, Presbyterian, French-speaking, left-wing pastor. The priest in his homily talked of the events of '68 in Paris. The pastor talked about the Vietnam War. The bourgeois French family sat in an appalled stupor, clapping their hands to their brows and crying 'c'est pas vrai, c'est pas vrai'. The American family were absolutely unperturbed by everything.

After the service, the guests divided into three. At one end of the reception were Monique-Paule's left-wing friends. At the other end were her family. There was no communication between the two parties. In the middle were Richard's family, being universally friendly to everyone they met. They were imperishably nice.

Unfortunately, however, it was very hard to understand them. Their Tennessee accents were not so much strong as heroic. French people who spoke fluent English were asking me to translate words like 'yes' and 'no'. Also, they were entertained by some of the names. One sister was called Agatha. 'Agathe? Elle s'appelle Agathe?' Then the family name, for better or worse, is Tubb. 'Tube? Il est Monsieur Tube?'

Among her other accomplishments, Monique-Paule once spent a cross channel ferry journey with Graham Greene. They fell into talking together and then, when they were about to disembark, he told her who he was. His French was so good that she hadn't realised he was English.

My other Graham Greene story concerned a pub I used to work in, the Blue Posts in St. James'. Upstairs was a small and discreet dining room, to which my duties included taking up bottles of wine from the cellar. One day one of the waitresses came up to me.

'A customer has just told me,' she said, 'that we've got Graham Greene eating in the restaurant.'

'That's nice,' I said.

'By the way,' she added, 'who is Graham Greene?'

He had been coming for years, just booking himself in as Mr. Greene. Presumably it gave him the anonymity he wanted. I never met him, unfortunately, though I probably took him a bottle of wine from time to time.

Pausing only to give the mediaeval town of Liverdun a miss, I followed the road through continuous built-up area for the fourteen kilometres to Nancy. Then it led past the arch of the Porte Desilles and into the spacious swathe of the Cours Léopold. I had to take a look at the famous Place Stanislas which is simply stunning, worth a trip to Nancy on its own. It was too cold to hang about, though, and I pushed on.

No-one in Nancy seemed very positive about walking on either the canal to Strasbourg or the Moselle to Épinal. 'You should have brought a guide,' the woman said. I thought this seemed a very good idea until I realised she meant a book rather than a person. As if I hadn't tried. My guess is that this is a canal you can walk along, but I'm not going all the way out there to find out. Another plan blown.

As I stood in the tourist office I got a message from Scott in Basle. He was going to join me for a couple of days but now is not. I can therefore make my own decision about the route—or, at least, I can make three different decisions as usual. Now I have made a real one. I am going to Épinal.

This is not the first time, as he well knows, that Scott has been going to walk with me and then hasn't done so. Inevitably I will discuss his pusillanimity with him, but not too often because he is going to give me a great deal of hospitality in the very near future.

From Nancy to Épinal lies a walking route of sixty-five kilometres; once a year (quite often enough) an event is held to walk the route. The tourist office can therefore give you an itinerary and a printout and, furthermore, tell you that it is exactly 9.5 kilometres to Ludres. Outside Nancy, a cycle path led through the blanket of industrial estates and shopping plazas and an extraordinary panoply of motorways. The printout says that tomorrow's journey is 36 kilometres.

A few years ago, Belinda and I went to Moscow in December. When the temperature there stood at zero, the locals described it as picnic weather. Well, it was picnic weather today, exactly zero in temperature. Pack up your picnics though, hang on to your hampers. It is forecast to go down to minus ten.

DAY 21
LUDRES TO CHARMES

What a nice name, Charmes.

On leaving Ludres I got very excited by a cycle path. That lasted about a kilometre; then paths went off in every direction except mine. Later in the day, however, when I was completely reconciled to walking along the road, two men in a café told me that if I went back to the canal I would find a footpath for the next few kilometres. That's always the way. When you're looking for a towpath there's nothing around. Then, just when you're quite happy and not looking for anything, one comes along as easy as anything. A bit like partners.

The men also asked, as people do, what I did for a living. This is always a difficult one. I didn't say: 'Well, I used to be a probation officer but I gave up in disgust at government policy and now work for the trade union.' A bit complicated. I just said I worked with people in trouble with the law. 'Ah,' said the landlady (who also became involved), 'a social worker'.

Well, exactly. Or, at least, exactly until successive governments decided to dismantle the social worker ethos. I and thousands of others used the social work approach very successfully to help our clients change their lives. Then the governments decided that we should be punishment officers instead. Most people left. Re-offending soared. Who cares about crime, though? What matters is what sounds good to the *Daily Mail*: and that's punishment.

It was indeed 36 kilometres, 22 or 23 miles, to Charmes. It's always the last two or three that are hard, whether it's 15 miles or 23. I used to average 25 miles per day but I can't now. A few times I have walked forty. Once when

I was seventeen I walked fifty miles in a day. That is a long way.

The route to Charmes leads up the wide, shallow valley of the Moselle, very pleasant without startling the senses. A couple of paragliders floated off the hills but that was the extent of the excitement. Signposts kept inviting me to branch off in all directions to get to Charmes but I ignored them and plodded slowly on. It was quiet.

In Charmes I didn't need the tourist office but it seemed disrespectful to walk past when it was actually open. The only occupant was a trainee; in fact I suspected she was on 'work experience', that odious euphemism for unpaid labour. She was very nice but I probably knew more about Charmes than she did. However, she confided after making a few calls that a cycle path led from here to Épinal. I didn't believe her but thanked her anyway. As it happens, I have now reached the area that I possess a map of. Now I shall certainly get lost.

I have known my friend Scott for 37 years now. We were both 37 years younger then. He has worked in Basle for all that time and longer. He is, of course, effortlessly cosmopolitan though he would deny it. We have done a good deal of walking together. Yet he is still racked with guilt (or at least I hope he is) about the times when, like this time, he has failed to walk with me. Above all, there was that time 29 years ago…

While I was walking across the US he happened to be there on holiday and promised to walk with me for a week. He asked for an easy first day but declared himself ready for anything after that. However, on the way out he bought a new pair of boots in New York which he proposed to wear immediately for long distances. The result was predictable.

By the time Scott joined me in Colorado I had walked nearly two thousand miles and, in all innocence, I thought an easy day was eighteen miles. Also we were at six thousand feet. At the end of the day he was appallingly blistered. On the second day he walked seven miles before he had to turn back. He resolutely refused all lifts and walked the seven miles back to the bus stop. Then he went off to San Francisco for the rest of the week to have a good time.

Ever since that fateful trip, Scott has been trying (perhaps not hard enough) to atone. A few years later he joined me in south-east Switzerland when I was walking from London to Split. On the last day we walked 48 kilometres, or 30 miles, from Davos to Klosters. Or, at least, we would have walked 48 kilometres if we had walked to the second station in Klosters as planned. I walked to the second station. He walked only to the first station. I told him that when I next passed through Basle I didn't want to hear from his friends that he had walked 48 kilometres when in reality he had walked only 47. But what happened? Yes, you guessed it.

I wouldn't know how many times I have been walking with Scott since then but I do know that I have been ill in his flat on numerous occasions, generally arriving *hors de combat* after some ill considered venture. I have stayed with him at least once a year over the last 35 years and often I have brought others with me. He is just about to give me a lot more hospitality so perhaps I'd better shut up about his failures.

Charmes is still in Lorraine but we have entered the department of the Vosges. That always gives me a little thrill.

DAY 22
CHARMES TO ÉPINAL

It was true! A great big, blue, beautiful cycle path led all the way from Charmes to Épinal. I take it all back.

(At least I think it was blue. When typing this out I can't read my own handwriting in the notebook.)

Conditions were perfect for walking. The temperature never rose above freezing all day but it was not cold. For half an hour the sun even shone, the first time in three weeks. Eighteen miles disappeared like clockwork.

The future may be murkier. Due to some meteorological quirk, heavy snow has fallen to the east, the north and the west. In the Channel areas children have not been able to get to school. In Paris the planes have not taken off (good). The forecast for the night is ferocious.

The wide, shallow valley of the Moselle is still wide and shallow. It was not, however, very scenic today. Old gravel workings are full of water; new gravel workings border the river. Mile after mile of factories and industrial outlets line the roads into Épinal. Nevertheless the town itself is a pleasant place, with an old centre, historic sites and open spaces leading down to the river. The canal came to a halt at a marina. So did I. Another five kilometres would have been good but all enquiries suggested it would be better to stay in the town. Common sense and sloth combined on this one.

To the west of Épinal are the mineral water towns of Vittel and Contrexéville, famous for a million bottles of water shipped all over the continent. To the south are the spa towns: Plombières-les-Bains, Luxeuil-les-Bains and, yes, Bains-les-Bains. This is the place to go to feel young. Why? Because everyone else will be older than you. It doesn't matter how old you are, everyone else will be older. In a restaurant, a park, a market place, the casino at Contrexéville, they have all come for the cure and they are all very, very old.

Épinal apparently has a history of image making and an annual festival at Easter. Now the Christmas markets dot the main square. Everybody has Christmas decorations on display: every town along the way, every roadside home is adorned with bits of fir and with those Father Christmases climbing up into windows and chimneys. Only eight days to go!

Over breakfast this morning a man of about my age began a conversation in halting English. He wanted to know the usual things: where I was from, where I had walked, where I was going today. (In India they want to know if you are married and, if not, why not.) He had trouble with the next question. I thought it was going to be about employment but he finally had to put it in French. 'Quel âge...?'

I told him.

He looked me up and down but said no more. It was clear that he had views about my age and the things I was doing. What was not clear, however, was whether he was envious of such freedom at my time of life or whether he thought I ought to grow up and behave.

A few weeks ago some sort of study was published in Britain which links to this question. Its thesis was that the best time ever to be born in Britain was 1948. Those of us who were born around that time benefited from the following:

1. The immediate introduction of the NHS;
2. Free education up to university level;
3. Not having to fight in a war;
4. Full employment;

5. The invention of the pill, which freed a whole generation;
6. Early retirement on a final year fixed salary pension.

At least three of these have now gone and two of the others are debatable. They should also have included the wonderful, wonderful music of the sixties when we were growing up and music changed the world. What cannot be emphasised enough is full employment. It gave the workforce the freedom and confidence to assert themselves—which is why governments put a stop to it as fast as they could.

The sixties also led to some of us being reluctant to settle down. Or, if we settled down at one time, we tried to unsettle ourselves again as soon as possible.

Now I'll shut up about the sixties and not mention them again.

DAY 23
ÉPINAL TO REMIREMONT TO ST. AMÉ

For breakfast I was given a coffee. Thick and black. No discussion, just given it. I haven't drunk a caffeinated coffee since my heart first went wrong, five years ago. Should I drink it? I was too mean to ignore it. Within minutes I had to lie down on the bed, heart thumping. Best to leave the coffee in future.

During the night an inch of snow had fallen on Épinal. Then snow fell in the morning and snow fell in the afternoon. We're still in a relatively untouched pocket of France, however, and no great problems arose.

Walking in the snow is a lot easier anyway than walking in the rain. Underfoot, ice is a problem rather than snow. You do have to work harder. The only other problem today is that my boots are starting to let in the wet. There must still be gaps which the magician of Sedan could not cover.

In Arches I was asked a question I have never been asked before. Stopping in a baker's for a mid-morning snack, I enquired as to whether any of the quiches were vegetarian.

A good deal of shrugging of shoulders and wagging of heads. General discussion among the staff.

'Do you eat snails, monsieur?'

I can quite definitively state that I have never, ever been asked before whether, as a vegetarian, I eat snails. Sometimes they annoy me quite a lot on the allotment but I have never, ever been driven to such a fury that I have wanted to eat them.

'Vegetarian, monsieur, it is a problem, n'est-ce pas?'

I had a very nice piece of custard pie instead. *Le flan*. No snails in that.

Remiremont is a lovely town. I have walked through it before, three or four years ago. It took me by surprise then and it took me by surprise today. The town centre is old, the historic quarter is even older and the cathedral is spectacular. I ate a pancake, got some information and passed on.

Now we're in the real hills. The blue line of the Vosges: this is where the real walking starts. I wanted to get through Remiremont if possible because I want to get over the pass tomorrow. There are three good reasons for this:

(a) It's going to snow;
(b) Last time I was here it was hard to find somewhere to stay in Ventron because it was out of the ski season. This time it will be hard because it's in the ski season;
(c) I want to get to Scott's nice flat in Basle.

Last time I was in Ventron I eventually stayed in a *chambre d'hote* half way up a mountain. The husband of the *patronne* spoke fluent English and indeed most other languages. A site manager on enormous building projects around the world, he would be in Brazil for months on end, come home for a bit and then go off to China. The family came from Normandy but had decided to settle in the Vosges; it made no difference to him where they lived so they thought they would head for the hills. No-one seemed to mind being uprooted, though two sets of grandparents were apparently not so happy about it. It's a long drive from Normandy to the Vosges.

From Remiremont a cycle path led into the hills along an old railway track. It is a wonderful idea with, at intervals along the route, the worst maps I have ever seen. I followed it for five miles or so to St. Amé.

DAY 24
ST. AMÉ TO KRUTH

Everyone has a snow plough. In St. Amé alone there must have been twenty. Every street, every backwater was cleared. Three or four inches of snow fell overnight but no-one's progress appeared to be hindered.

The Voie Verte was the Voie Blanche today. For several miles the old railway line ran through forests, cuttings and ravines. It must have been one of the world's most beautiful railways and there ought to be a campaign to re-open it. Like Buxton to Matlock. King's Lynn to Hunstanton. Don't get me started.

Up into the hills came the climb. The last time I came this way my heart was bad and I had chosen the easiest route over the Vosges and then the Alps (the Gotthard). Today was a little harder in the snow but the Vosges were beautiful. Every slope is covered in trees and every tree was hung with snow. In Ventron three busloads from the ski club of Thann were turning into the ski area. First they had to make an emergency stop. Why? A small boy was bursting and had to get out for a pee. Then they carried on.

Five kilometres further up the hill was the Col d'Oderen at 900 metres above sea level. In the Second World War ferocious fighting befell the area; Ventron was liberated by General Duval in November 1944 but it was weeks before the pass was taken. Today, at the top, three cars were parked. Where on earth had the occupants gone? I headed downhill for Kruth. It was 21 miles all told for the day but I could make it through the slush and snow.

On the downhill side of the mountain the sun never shone—but suddenly, on the other side of the valley, the entire mountains ahead were wreathed in sunlight. As I gazed around at the scenery, shrouded in snow or lit with sunlight, wandering down a mountain pass, I thought: not many people are lucky enough to do this.

The top of the pass brings us into Alsace. I once worked for a week on a farm in Alsace. At the start of the week I understood not one word of the Alsatian dialect. At the end of the week I understood exactly the same. Alsace and Lorraine were shunted from pillar to post over a century, through the Franco-Prussian War, the First World War and the Second World War, taken first by the Germans, then re-taken by the French, then taken again by the Germans and finally back to the French again. Each time they were taken by one side they were forbidden to speak the language of the other, sometimes on pain of death. They sought refuge in the dialect; they didn't want to be understood.

In the afternoon the temperature fell to minus five. From Kruth I took the train to stay with Scott in Basle, to have real conversations and not have to eat pizza. I'll come back in the morning to Kruth.

Day 25
Kruth to Thann

I left my sun glasses behind in Basle and spent the day worrying about snow blindness.

A few years ago I got snow blindness on the Haute Route from Chamonix to Zermatt. It was entirely my own fault, spending a cloudless day walking in the snow, high up, simply forgetting to put on the sun glasses. That night I was staying in a Swiss Alpine Club hut run by two elderly, stern but incredibly kind sisters. I was fine until I went to bed; then the eyes burned and watered and bulged throughout the night. Next day the sisters made me stay in bed with my eyes covered; and the same that night.

The morning after, one of the sisters led me by the hand from the hut through a tunnel to a cable car. One eye was completely covered and the other nearly so. From the cable car I was on my own. First I took the most obvious measure: rang Lilian and told her I was coming to stay for a few days. Then I made my way down the mountain and across the country via cable car and train. Then I lay down in the dark until I was better.

In fact my eyes have never completely recovered and a slight soreness remains permanently in the corner of the right eye. Nevertheless within a few days I could start to read again and normal life returned. I was very stupid and very lucky.

In Switzerland I normally get ill. This may sometimes be caused by the things I have been doing before I get here, but I generally get a fever of some sort and feel pathetically sorry for myself. If I am not ill when I arrive I then have an accident while I'm here. In Lilian and Andreas' house I walked into a glass door: I have the photo to prove it. A few years later I fell down a cattle grid that was invisible in the snow. Everyone found it very amusing; like piles or athlete's foot or getting hit in the crotch playing cricket, it's very funny to everyone else but bloody painful for the victim. That time I managed after a while to stagger back to Britain but was incapacitated for a month. Scott is used to my treating his flat as a hospital. I am the person who comes to Switzerland to get ill.

Fortunately the sun didn't shine today so my terrors diminished. Indeed this afternoon it snowed so hard that I eventually had to stop walking. The hills receded, the valley widened and eventually Thann arrived. What a lovely old town! Very much mid-European, Germanic rather than French, it is the personification of Alsace. Today, despite the weather, despite it being Sunday afternoon, Christmas shopping bustled in the town centre.

I wanted to get beyond Thann today but could progress no further. I walked to Vieux Thann, the next station, but there was no shelter and it was freezing. I turned back towards Thann itself but, nearly half way there, realised that I would not reach it before the next train. I turned back again to Vieux Thann. A later observer would have seen three sets of footprints in the snow: two heading one way, one the other. It would be a mystery. Or it would signify a very indecisive man.

Scott and I have now spent two evenings sipping red wine and talking of books, verbal usage, grammar and linguistics in the way that chaps do when they get together. One could get sucked into this lifestyle.

We do talk about football too.

More to the point, I have been able to get Marmite again, or at least the Swiss equivalent, Cenovis. Ah, cheese and Marmite sandwiches tomorrow. It's like being at home.

Day 26
Thann to Mulhouse to Habsheim

Alice, my not-stepdaughter, and Mimi (6) were due to arrive today by train. However, Eurostar has gone completely down the tube for several days now and no services are running at all. Last night Alice booked a flight instead, but London suffered a blizzard this afternoon and all flights were cancelled. Alice and Mimi have gone to stay with my sister Susan for the night and will have another go tomorrow.

Here, slush ruled the day. Mulhouse was 24 kilometres from Thann and I was sure I could get further. The last time I came this way I got lost after Cernay so this time I went south to avoid it. The route went well but the roads had been de-iced into slush and the pavements were not much better. Mulhouse was a city of slush.

Mulhouse used to be thought a provincial, parochial city but it has a fine old town centre and a batch of lively shops and it's very much the cultural capital of Alsace (though some would say that was an oxymoron). It was not at its best today, however, and I hustled unheedingly through it. This is not a cultural tour.

No-one but me is interested in this next nugget of information, but a train journey from London to Basle is much cheaper if you buy a ticket to Mulhouse, get off there and change to the local train. Make sure it really is the local train, though: get on another express by accident and the ticket collectors can be very, very nasty indeed. Extraordinary rendition might be preferable.

Today's minimum target was Habsheim, which I reached without much trouble. If possible, though, I was aiming for Sierentz. Should I press on? How far was it? For some reason the French sign posts have stopped giving distances and it was not marked on the map. Give it a go and see what happens.

I set off, through the long village of Habsheim, out the other side and into the country. It was bleak. It was growing dark. I plodded on, becoming the enemy of most of the cars on the road who clearly thought I shouldn't be out there. After some time a junction loomed, with signposts. It was four kilometres back to the train at Habsheim and six kilometres to Sierentz. The last reasonable train to Basle was due in Habsheim in fifty minutes; I could do that comfortably. It was due in Sierentz a few minutes later. Could I walk six kilometres and find the station in fifty minutes? I turned round and walked back to Habsheim.

Tomorrow I will come back to Sierentz. I will walk one kilometre out towards Habsheim and then one kilometre back again. Added to the four I have walked today back into Habsheim that will be six kilometres, the distance I have not walked today. Is anyone interested except me? No.

It was 25 miles of slush today. That's too much slush.

Day 27
Nowhere Much

As it happened I did not go back to Sierentz today. Alice and Mimi finally arrived, delayed a further few hours by snow, and I walked out to the airport to meet them; as it's on the route that's five miles I can skip later. I didn't make them walk back into the city.

I was ridiculously pleased to see them and we went to Scott's flat for tea and sympathy before they caught the train to Engelberg. They will actually arrive there at the appointed time, though without the planned stopover in Basle. I will see them later.

It is now 22 December and I confidently expect the days to be getting longer now: in fact I demand it. When I was a child, feeding the chickens was my afternoon duty and I used to think that by Christmas Day you could see the days growing longer. This was probably my imagination but by New Year the difference was clearly visible. It cheers you up through the dreary, desperate days of January and February. I hate winter. So does everyone else. I hope that by the time I return home the country will be bathed in the cheerful colours of springtime.

SWITZERLAND

Day 28
Sierentz to Basle to Liestal

23 December was my father's birthday. He died six years ago. Until your parents die, I don't think you can anticipate that it is something you will never get over.

After my father died, Belinda and I used to have a party on 23 December; by a remarkable coincidence it was her mother's birthday also. Two years ago we held a party in London followed on Christmas Eve by a party in Norfolk. The party in London began at half past six. People were still arriving at half past ten (particularly, as I pointed out to them, the black people). In Norfolk, the guests were invited for six o'clock. I told Belinda that at six o'clock the doorbell would be ringing. Indeed it was: four couples stood on the doorstep and the rest were not far behind. In Norfolk, it's quite simple. If someone invites you for six o'clock they're not inviting you for seven o'clock, they're inviting you for six o'clock. So that's when you come.

In the plain of Alsace the snow had gone. To the west, it still lay on the Vosges. To the east, across the Rhine, it lay on the Black Forest in Germany. To the south it lay on the early Swiss hills. On the plain, though, only a few lumps lay here and there. The transformation was total.

I caught the train to St. Louis, opposite the airport to which I walked yesterday. From St. Louis I walked out to Sierentz. Yes, I know I'm supposed to be walking to Istanbul not from Istanbul but who cares? At Sierentz I dutifully walked out that extra kilometre towards Habsheim then walked back again before catching the return train to Basle. I am now officially in Switzerland.

It has taken four weeks. From Calais I can do it in less but from Hook of Holland that seems reasonable. I had hoped to be a little further on by Christmas but I can't complain. Mustn't grumble.

Basle is a fine place. For the last forty years I have been here at least once a year and I never tire of it: the Marktplatz, the cathedral area, the old shopping streets, the winter fairs, the bridges, the Rhine, the cinemas and the bookshops. I like the cosmopolitan atmosphere, the sophistication and multilingualism of the inhabitants. I even like the capitalism and snobbery that imbues the city. I used to walk round the streets endlessly. Now I just come and do what I have to do (generally speaking, have a nice time). I will continue to come back as long as I am welcome.

It does have its downside, of course. From the French side the road leads through the mass of pharmaceutical factories that form the basis of the modern wealth of the city. The other end is none too beautiful either, and is certainly not designed to walk out of. There is no trouble finding the way (river-railway-road) but, unprecedentedly for Switzerland, footpaths and pavements disappear. Past the football stadium, past the major events hall, I risked life and limb on the road to Pratteln. Pratteln itself may contain something other than factories but if so I never saw it. I was more concerned with survival. Finally a cycle path led the way to Liestal.

Anywhere in the world, an allotment holder inspects other allotments, usually with envy and dismay. It is certainly a mistake to inspect Swiss allotments which are, needless to say, as clean as a toothbrush, immaculately laid out and nurturing vegetables so beautiful that they resemble still life paintings. For the Swiss allotment holder, however, the vegetables are secondary, a mere appendage, a necessary excuse for the real business in hand. What really matters is the hut.

Hut? These grandiloquent edifices are more like mansions than huts. They may have swimming pools and saunas in the back room. They may have bowling alleys.

Going down to the allotment in Switzerland is not a question of getting away from the wife (or husband) for the afternoon or the day. This is a serious trip. This is a well-now-it's-April-I'm-going-down-the-allotment-and-I'll-see-you-in-September type of situation. This is a second home (except that they have all got second homes as well).

I sated my jealous gaze. I never can grow Swiss chard like that.

Meanwhile Switzerland is in turmoil because of the minarets. The country's Muslim community had applied to build a modest number of minarets to supplement the few they already have. The Swiss right wing collected the necessary number of votes to hold a referendum on the subject. (Previous referendums have been held on such minor matters as whether the tip should be added to the bill and whether women should have the vote—there seems very little sense of proportion in their democracy.) Anyone with a sentient brain assumed the matter was a formality and no campaigning was done on behalf of the minarets. So what happened? The right wing won. Now no-one knows how to get out of the situation. When you compare the rather beautiful minarets that have already been built with the vulgar monstrosities of housing that have sprung up in even the most beautiful mountain towns… But of course it has little to do with aesthetics.

DAY 29
LIESTAL TO OLTEN

Christmas Eve. What a day.

In Switzerland, this is the big day at Christmas. The shops were bulging: the baker, the butcher, the Christmas tree person. Until the afternoon the towns were throbbing, then everyone hustled home to have the meal and celebrations.

Liestal and Sissach are pleasant, rather sleepy places to live, with picturesque town centres and trains full of commuters to the city. From Sissach the road branched off into the long, loping valley of the Unterer Hauenstein pass. It was lovely: hills, fields, rocks, farms, the lot. It would be good to say that the top of the pass was equally lovely but it would not be true. Well, it may be true on another day but today it was shrouded in cloud. In the morning I dawdled and in the afternoon I had to pick my heels up to get to Olten. It was only sixteen miles for the day, not really enough at this stage. It was good to have a little climb though.

There were distractions in the form of disaster. During the day I had a message from my sister Susan saying that on 20 January there will be a funeral service for my mother.

My mother died two years ago and had donated her body to medical science. Partly, of course, she just wanted to do something good. Partly, however, she did this because she really did not want a funeral. Now it seems she is going to have one. Can anything be done to stop it? Apparently not. Perhaps they are obliged to hold one, sooner or later. We had absolutely no idea that this would happen. Obviously I have to go; what kind of man doesn't go to his mother's funeral? It will curtail my ambitions, though, having to go home by 20 January. In fact it is a bloody disaster.

I might go like hell until the 19th but I have no idea how far that will take me. Just when I was starting to go well, too. Shit.

So there was my father's birthday yesterday, the message about my mother today, and then there is the reason why I chose to be away for Christmas.

This time last year, Belinda died in Whipps Cross hospital. She died at three o'clock on Boxing Day morning; I think she fought to stay alive past Christmas Day. Emily, Alice and I spent Christmas Day at her bedside.

Now Alice and Mimi are back in Engelberg for Christmas and tonight I have joined them: not myself to ski but to spend Christmas in the mountains in Switzerland. I will take two days' holiday from walking and return to Olten on the 27th.

Then I have to go like hell until 19 January.

DAY 30
HAPPY CHRISTMAS!

We had wonderful Christmases when I was a child. They were pretty good too when I was an adult. In later years I was always given the latest Elmore Leonard for Christmas. After the meal I would retreat with my book and read it from beginning to end. By then it was time for another meal. What could be better than that?

Perhaps today will match it. I write now at eight in the morning. We shall see what Switzerland can bring for Christmas.

I do have the book, although it is not a present. I have borrowed Colm Toibin's *Brooklyn* from Scott. Old Toibin has really given it some wellie on this one. Beautifully written, easy to read, irresistible and unputdownable. I have been wanting train journeys to last longer so that I don't have to put it down. But it's so sad. Why do these people have to write sad books? It made me cry on the train.

We came down the mountain, left the train and made our way to the jetty on the lake. With perfect synchronicity (naturally) a boat came towards us as we reached the shore. I could recognise young Mark on the prow (or whatever it is). Steering the boat—and later letting Mimi steer—was Andreas. They took us back to the house they have built by the lake.

It was a fine Christmas Day. Lilian and the other children, Thomas and Denise, were waiting. They gave us Christmas presents. We ate raclette, drank excellent Swiss wine and talked. Mimi played with Lord, the dog. Alice played with the Lego: they have a room devoted to Lego. It was a fine Christmas. When we returned to Engelberg it snowed, making conditions good for them tomorrow.

I first met Lilian 28 years ago in Norwich, where we lodged in the same house. She was over for the summer improving her (perfect) English. What impressed me more than anything was that she had a Swiss friend in the city but that they resolutely spoke English together for the extent of their stay. Anyway, a couple of years later I was walking across Europe and wrote to ask if I could stay the night at her parents' home when I passed through. She wrote back to say that she now lived with her boyfriend Andreas in Bern but that I must of course stay with them instead.

I have been doing so ever since.

I stayed with them for their wedding, for big family occasions, for small family occasions, for friends' reunions, for treks into the mountains and often with no good excuse at all. Oh, and when I get ill.

Earlier this year they had a joint fiftieth birthday party. As a birthday present from him to her, Andreas said that he would give her three weeks off from looking after the children. She said right, I'm going to England for a week! I took her to Norfolk, she visited Norwich for the first time in 28 years and she found that the Waffle House was still there.

Lilian used to work for a mushroom company in Switzerland. The company sold tons of mushrooms of all shapes and sizes, millions and millions of mushrooms.

What they really wanted though, their heart's desire, was to grow morel mushrooms in commercial quantities. Anyone who could do this would make unimaginable fortunes in the mushroom-crazy world of central Europe. Morels sell for six times the price of any other mushroom. No-one, however, can grow them in captivity in anything like commercial numbers.

Many have tried, including Lilian. She grew quite a lot. She liaised with mushroom growers in India and Michigan. (In Michigan, incidentally, they liaised when news was good but went awol when news was bad—bad news is not American.) She ate a lot of morels. Even I ate a lot of morels. They still refused to grow in commercial numbers.

In case anyone succeeds in growing them, however, Lilian has some morel spores in a bank vault. Should a breakthrough materialise, she will be poised.

Andreas is a businessman: a very good, successful businessman. He claims that he is not a socialist. However, on numerous walks up and down mountain passes and glaciers and everything in between, when we have been busy sorting out the world, I have unearthed many signs that he is not what he claims. He wants to know about trade unionism. He treats his staff very well, consults them and keeps them informed about the finances of the business. They clearly like and respect him—I have seen them at work and elsewhere. He helps them make money. They help him make money. Maybe, on reflection, that's not socialism. Maybe that's just capitalism as it should be.

When I first knew Andreas he was going to retire at forty. Then 45. Then fifty. Now it's 55.

Day 31
Sursee to Sempach

Mimi is unrecognisable from the skier she was a year ago. Then, five years old, she was unconfident and inexpert. Now, at six, she has total aplomb. I watched her zoom gracefully down the slopes, time after time, troubled by nothing, absolutely in control. It was great.

By this time it was impossible to make any real progress today on the walking. Look on it as part of the holidays. Olten was where I had discontinued but it was too far to go for just the afternoon. I took the train to Sursee and walked the seven or eight miles to Sempach: familiar territory since Lilian and Andreas used to live there. It's a stunning walk facing the mountains, through pleasant countryside along the shores of Lake Sempach with sweeping snow-topped views ahead. The Pilatus looms over Luzern, sometimes benevolent, sometimes sinister. An easy couple of hours slipped past.

In the evening I stayed with the family and we reminisced. Another time, another glacier. One time Andreas took me with a guide to climb the Todi, 3,600 metres, about as high as you can get in Europe without being a mountaineer. We slept the night in a hut, started very early in the morning and climbed for seven hours through knee deep snow. By then I knew I wasn't going to reach the top. The guide knew it too. It was only half an hour away so I would stay there until they came back.

I looked around for a spot. 'There's a dip in the snow over there,' I said. 'I'll sit there and wait for you.'

'Don't sit there,' the guide said. 'That's a crevasse.'

That's why you have a guide.

It has always pissed me off that I am fitter for almost anything you could name than Andreas. I exercise every day, I walk, I play tennis, cricket, squash, all the rest, yet he is better than me in the mountains. Always has been, always will be. Bloody Swiss.

Off they went, the two of them, to the presumably wonderful summit of the Todi, then duly came back smirking quietly and we went down the mountain.

Andreas told the children tonight the story of his getting on a plane to go from Mumbai to Delhi. It was early evening. The plane sat on the runway, full of passengers, ready for departure, but nothing happened. And still nothing happened.

Eventually the co-pilot emerged from the cockpit and walked to the back of the aircraft. He found a blanket, lay down on some spare seats and went to sleep.

Some time later, the pilot followed suit. He emerged from the cockpit, walked to the back of the aircraft, found a blanket and lay down on some spare seats to go to sleep.

By this time the passengers were beginning to get the message. They all found blankets, lay down on the seats and went to sleep. In the morning the pilot woke up and the journey proceeded. No explanation was ever given for the delay.

DAY 32
OLTEN TO SURSEE

For days I have known that there was something wrong with the prices I was being charged on the railway ticket machines. They were ridiculously high whenever I went through the procedure. I just assumed that it was due to my usual incompetence and stupidity and tried to get tickets from a ticket office instead.

This morning, however, we found out the reason. Andreas and I went through the whole business with the machines. In the German, French and Italian versions of the procedure they charged one rate. In the English version they charged double!

Apparently all the prices and systems were changed a few weeks ago. They must have made a mistake on the computer with the English version. Meanwhile they have made fortunes out of all the English-speaking passengers. As if the pound hasn't gone down far enough!

Andreas will send them an email.

This was the day for catching up with myself, for filling in the gap between Olten and Sursee which I had not yet walked. It's about twenty miles, pretty straightforward but long enough.

Olten is the fulcrum of the Swiss railway system, the Clapham Junction of the mountains. It lies in a canyon. To the north stands the range of hills I came over via the Hauenstein, in the middle is the River Aare and to the south is another, lower range of hills. I got off the train, passed the covered bridge leading to the old city and set off up the valleys. Olten need not detain anyone.

Aarburg, on the other hand, is home to a colossal castle on a hill. I ought to go round it but never have and probably never will. Zofingen has an ethereal old town centre matched only by Solothurn for beauty; I walked round it and carried on. From here, the valley leading eventually to Luzern is wide, flat and not unattractive. Towns and villages passed by. A man standing outside his house persuaded me to come in for a drink. Sixty-five years old, a farmer and agronomist now semi-retired, he has lived all his life in this house. His wife made a cup of tea and their son talked of student life in Basle. It's the sort of pleasant interlude that can lead to complete inertia. I made my excuses, exchanged addresses and carried on.

From here, on a clear day it is sometimes possible to gain a glimpse of the greatest view in the world. To the south, through a gap in the hills, the great mountain trio of the Eiger, the Mönch and the Jungfrau, subjects of a thousand posters (I used to have one above my bed), stand silhouetted against the skyline. An irresistible sight.

Not today, though. Cloud enveloped the southern area. Compensation came only through the huge range of mountains beyond Luzern, looming like a massive wall in the sky. From a hill above Sursee I stood and gaped. Then I hurried down into the town as the snow started falling.

DAY 33
SEMPACH TO ZUG

I'm on my own again now. All the people I was looking forward to seeing are behind me. I rang Scott tonight. Alice stayed with him on her way home and apparently they had a high old time. That made it worse. Apparently they talked about me. Can't imagine what they found to say.

On advice from Andreas, I skipped Luzern and went across country from Sempach to Zug. The trouble with Andreas is that, whereas I think a good walk merely means covering as much ground as possible, he thinks it involves fine scenery and as many ups and downs as a chap can find. I think fine scenery is all right in the right place but it's a bonus rather than a need. Ups and downs, though, are best avoided.

Luzern is a wonderful, classical city of central Europe but I have been there many times before. I have never, however, seen Sins….

The road to Hochdorf brought the first climb. Then a descent. Then a series of footpaths which really suffer from the Swiss disease—if there's a hill, climb it. All over the country are those little yellow signposts; almost all of them will take you the longest possible way, up a mountain, round a lake, anywhere but straight where you want to go. The ascent of the big hill to Hohenrain was quite gratuitous; once there, you simply had to come down again. Admittedly it was spectacular, with a big church and some sort of institution on top, but the path went to the highest point and then all the bloody way round it. The third climb of the day led over another hill to Sins. This is rural Switzerland. Hills, farms, villages. They even had a wild boar and some llamas!

To the south, in the middle of a range of mountains in the distance, was a flat-topped summit, higher than all those around it. Could it be the Todi?

Sins, Rain, Charm, Zug (meaning train). They like short peculiar place names round here. I wish I lived in Sins. It might excuse a lot.

Charm is pronounced 'Harm', with a soft H. Nothing there seemed worth delaying for and I pressed on to Zug.

Zug represents everything that is bad about Switzerland: financial malpractices that have been eradicated elsewhere in the country are still practised with gay abandon here. Specifically, tax evasion is nurtured. Rich people who don't think they should pay tax like anyone else can find themselves a haven in Zug. And they do, in large numbers.

It was over twenty miles and I was ready for a lie down. Hah. Only two hotels were open in Zug. One was very expensive and the other was even more expensive. I had a walk round the town, down by the lake, along an extraordinary old street with overhanging houses. I caught a bus to Baar for somewhere (marginally) cheaper to stay.

In Britain, incidentally, if you ask politely in a hotel whether they could recommend anywhere cheaper, they start to negotiate on the price. In Switzerland they take you more literally; they ring another hotel, book you in and write down exact directions. It is hard to know which is better.

All the same, do I think I've got problems? I had a message from Simon at home. He had gone all the way from Norfolk to Walsall to see Norwich City play—only for the match to be postponed an hour before kickoff.

However, Norwich won on Boxing Day. I have never seen a decent match on Boxing Day. All that chat about abstemiousness on Christmas Day, some monk-like existence that footballers suddenly adopt, is so much bollocks. Most footballers can hardly walk on Boxing Day, let alone play football. Three points for us is good, though, whatever the match was like.

Two large dogs pursued me across a field today, unrestrained by their owner, the local farmer. Since I was walking along a public footpath at the time I could only assume that he didn't agree with having a footpath on his land.

Day 34
Zug to Biberbrugg

Following the route of the number 2 bus I climbed out of the ugly suburbs of Zug and into the clouds. The clouds cleared to reveal, well, nothing very much, or nothing I can still remember at five in the afternoon. Then we reached Unterageri and Oberageri, tourist villages on a pretty lake. This is where you drive out on a Sunday afternoon to have lunch and a wander round the shore. Today the hills are covered in snow and the cloud falls nearly to the lakeside. It is a relaxed, timeless spot, unknown to international tourists, consistent with a gentler way of life.

Whatever induced me, though, to do the next bit? The fear of being called a wimp, I suppose. I had climbed steadily along the road for nearly ten miles in the morning. Now I had a shorter distance up to the Raten Pass but a climb of three hundred metres in altitude or over a thousand feet. By Alpine standards this is a minnow of a pass—1,077 metres high or about 3,500 feet—and it's all very nice when you reach the top; but God it's hard work on the way. It was steep to Alosen; then it was steep again after Alosen.

The restaurant at the top was doing good business and children were tobogganing; I ate some cheese and made haste down the hill to beat the gathering rain. This side of the pass was much colder and deep snow lay all around. By the time I reached the valley floor the rain was hammering down. I went in a hotel, unsure whether to have a cup of tea or stop for the night.

I should have gone further. It was only fifteen miles for the day and it was only two thirty in the afternoon! Unfortunately this was just the sort of Swiss *gasthaus* that is impossible to resist. Locals come in to read the papers. Occasional trippers look in for a coffee. Upstairs, everything is adequate, without fuss. In the evening, some combination of cheese and potatoes will be available for the vegetarian to eat: it all boils down to cheese and potatoes in the end. And it's raining… I decided to stop. I am definitely a wimp, no doubt about that. To prove it, I washed my hair for the second time in a week.

Tomorrow (always tomorrow) I will try to make up for it. The scenic route takes in another lake and a bloody great climb via Einsiedeln. No thank you. I shall try to make up time by descending all the way with the traffic to the shores of Lake Zurich. Not very scenic at all. First, though, I must try to patch up the bit of boot that is coming apart down there.

Due south from here are big mountains. Eventually this valley leads to Altdorf, Andermatt and the Gotthard Pass. Is that the Oberalp I can see? I once spent a night in the *gasthaus* at the Oberalp Pass. It was memorable for the friendly drunk soldiers who didn't in the least want to be doing their annual military service but did want to drink beer in the warmth of the bar. It was more memorable for the thunder snowstorm that hit the pass as soon as I got indoors.

I have only ever seen two or three thunder snowstorms. They are best seen from well inside a very safe building. I have never liked lightning since the day we were playing cricket at Castle Rising and all the fielders on one side of the wicket suddenly put their hands to their heads as if a rough comb had just been passed over them. We got off that pitch faster than we went on it.

Andreas, Nigel and I once sheltered in a mountain hut while thunder rattled round all the mountains outside, scaring the shit out of me if not them. It was a Swiss Alpine Club hut, protecting us against the wrath of God or anyone else. We intended to go much further that afternoon but my views on the matter became very clear and we never moved till the morning.

One day at Griesalp, in the Berner Oberland, an early autumn snowstorm brought all the farmers to herd up the cattle for the winter. They stayed in the guesthouse dormitory (*Matratzenlager*—mattress room) with me and a couple of other people. Spared from this cosiness, however, were the Dutch brother and sister whom I ate a meal with that evening. They laughed. They were sleeping in a private room. They looked across at the assorted farmers. 'You know which one you'll be sleeping next to?' they asked. 'That one!'

One enormous farmer, as broad as he was long, could only be described in the nicest possible way as a big fat slob. Would he be a snorer? They laughed…

Yes, he was sleeping next to me. Yes, he snored. He snored voluminously. He snored incessantly. He snored in my ear. I shoved him, I hit him, I kicked him. Each time I hit him he stopped for one moment. Then he started again. I went off to sleep in the showers.

In my guesthouse the radio has just played Paul Simon's *Homeward Bound*. It made me want to cry. It's one of the songs I sing as I go along the road. He wants to go home. 'I need someone to comfort me.' Oh dear. I wished they hadn't played it. The rest of the time, though, they played the lesser hits of Herman's Hermits. That's enough to make you want to stay abroad.

Day 35
Biberbrugg to Nafels

The heel of my boot fell off completely.

So much for my glue job last night. It was mid-afternoon and all was going well when suddenly, from below, a flapping, lapping noise came seeping up. Looking down, all I could see was something hanging off. I sat down and removed the boot. Oh dear. It was flapping. There was only one thing for it: to cut the flapping bit off. I now have one missing layer on the left heel. My foot will get wet. Also, with the balance altered, a blister is developing already on the left instep. It would be best not to write down what I said at the time.

If I wasn't so mean, of course, I would have bought new boots long ago. Now there may be no choice. Perhaps I should remind myself that, since I have to go home early, the budget will extend further. Or maybe I should just remind myself not to be so mean.

Overnight, the whole world had been soaked. For some reason Switzerland has been comparatively lucky. Spain is covered in snow. Britain is covered in snow and rain. Eastern Europe is frozen. Switzerland has got off lightly. Nevertheless everywhere was sodden when I set out. Rain fell for only a few hours in the afternoon (long enough to wreck my boot) but it was a good day to avoid the mountains. That has now become my rationale for walking all day along main roads.

From Biberbrugg a ten-kilometre downhill stretch led to Pfaffikon. (There's an accent in there somewhere but it's hard enough just spelling the word without worrying about accents.) Here lies the shore of Lake Zurich, long and sinewy, more like a wide river than a lake. The heart of overpopulated Switzerland lives on this lakeshore; every spot is built on. It wouldn't be a beautiful lake at the best of times and these certainly aren't the best of times.

Everyone wants to live in Switzerland and most of them want to live by a lake. It is a small and heavily populated country. Nevertheless they don't help themselves with their lax building controls. The mountains are full of second homes. And third homes. Most of them are empty for most of the year. Many of the mountain villages, spreading in their wonderful surroundings, are five times bigger than they need to be. Why is it allowed? Why, when the country is so conscious of conservation in so many ways, do they allow all this building? Money, presumably.

With or without a whole boot, today was the day for making progress. The big traffic went on the motorway. Cycle routes and footpaths ran along the other roads. Eventually I must have done about 25 miles. The daylight hours are definitely getting longer now, but still it was dark when I arrived at Nafels.

What a nice place this is! Surrounded by pretty mountains, in the summer it must be the jumping off point for a thousand family holidays. Today I have moved from one canton, Zug, clean through another one, Schwyz, and into a third, Glarus. We have come from thick snow to greenery and back towards the snow again. Much of the day was mundane but tonight is what the mountains are for.

This is my first time in any of these places but a sign in Nafels points to Elm and another to Sargans, which I am aiming for. The indomitable Kev Reynolds invented a cross-Switzerland walk, beginning in Sargans and ending near Geneva, and wrote the guidebook to it. I like Kev. He writes things like 'Two yards past the bush, turn left. Avoid the puddle.' Even I can follow a guidebook like that. A few years ago I followed Kev's walk and, particularly in the early stages, discovered beautiful places that are largely unknown. Sargans, Elm and then Linthal were a part of this.

I finished reading a book by David Sedaris which Scott gave me and which I left, at his instructions, in a book exchange. It brought my total for the year to a round fifty and, since today is 30 December, there is no danger of exceeding the target. I am now reading a crappy British thriller by someone who can't write (but who, according to the blurb, teaches creative writing!). Why do the Americans do this genre so much better? No, actually, they don't always. Think of James Patterson and Robert Ludlum, then shudder. They do crime novels much better.

Now here is some juvenile humour. *Gute Fahrt!* they wish you every day when you set out. Regrettably, there is no getting away from the British inclination to giggle whenever you are wished a *gute Fahrt*. 'Thank you very much,' I want to say. 'I'll do my best!'

Last night I had a distressing dream. I dreamed that I wanted to telephone my mother but couldn't remember her new number. I could remember the old number but not the new. She didn't, of course, have a new number. She died. It must be something to do with this funeral ceremony in January. It depressed me all day. It rather puts the boot problem into perspective.

Now, where shall I spend New Year's Eve tomorrow?

Day 36
Nafels to Flums

A long, steep climb led out of Nafels; I really will have to start looking at those contour things on the map before setting out. It was worth it, though, for the views. The road behind looked back to the Glarus valley and the mountains flanking it. This region is known to the Swiss as the Glarnerland, a hidden area of green valleys and sudden, sharp mountains, almost unknown to the outside world and probably, a hundred years ago, totally cut off from it too.

On the other side of the hill lay the beautiful Walensee. What an absolute poppet of a lake this is. Blue-green even under a grey sky, it lies under enormous rock faces, hundreds or even thousands of feet high. People live under some of these rock faces. It must be terrifying.

Cloud settled over the lake far below. Then it rolled upwards and a church clock disappeared, the village lost in a sea of mist. Then it rolled off again and the afternoon was set fair.

It had rained all morning. I debated buying a new pair of boots somewhere before the start of the day. I changed my mind and ploughed on. The boots got wet again. I walked into a sporting equipment shop in a tourist village. It was hard to say which was more frightening, the prospect of walking in new boots or the price. I convinced myself that the boots had been all right all morning so would be all right for the rest of the journey. I pressed on down the hill.

One way to assess the quality of a ski resort is to check out the number of Dutch number plates in the car park. Unterterzen turned out to be an odd place, situated at lake level but carrying by cable car an army of skiers and snowboarders up to the mountains at two thousand metres high. A complex of apartments had been built to house all the Dutch. The afternoon was incredibly mild. The holiday makers take the cable car to a world of snow and ice and then descend to a land where even a jacket is superfluous. It's a rather drab, confused spot.

I had the strongest, and worst, cup of decaf coffee of my life there. The café proprietor asked me questions I didn't understand and put forward two alternatives for my decaf coffee. I chose one at random. I clearly made the wrong choice.

In the same café a very old man, probably the boss's father, engaged me in a long conversation. After a while I told him, perhaps unkindly, that I didn't speak German. It made no difference as he carried on regardless. He wanted an audience not a respondent.

Once I worked in a factory in southern Germany for three weeks, demolishing its interior. My orders were translated for me into French so I learned very little German but I did become fluent in the names of power tools and the numbers of spanners (VIER UND ZWANZIG—it was a very noisy place). We were also instructed to shout 'ACHTUNG! ACHTUNG!' whenever we threw a solid metal beam from the third floor down to the bottom.

Now, to those brought up on 1950s war comics, the word *Achtung* is followed automatically by 'Spitfire', as in 'ACHTUNG SPITFIRE!' which the Germans were allegedly always crying out—followed generally by 'DONNER UND BLITZEN!' and then 'AAAARGHHHH!' Now I had to shout out 'ACHTUNG! ACHTUNG!' many times in the factory each day. It was all I could do, every time I slung one of these beams over the edge and threatened the life of anyone below, not to shout out 'ACHTUNG SPITFIRE!' and wait for the response 'DONNER UND BLITZEN!'

But I didn't.

To get back to the point, whenever we had a break in that job I used to stand outside the building or get a coffee, and a man from another department often used to engage me in conversation. I understood not a word he said but, as nothing seemed to be required in response except for an occasional *Ja, ja* I let him carry on with his conversation. This went on for about a fortnight. Then someone in our building got hurt and needed medical attention. I ran out of the building and came across my coffee companion. 'Doctor doctor,' I shouted fluently. He pointed to the medical centre. 'But I don't speak German,' I added.

He gave me an old fashioned look and went and fetched the doctor. We had no more conversations after that. He clearly thought I had been making a monkey of him for a fortnight.

There are worse ways to spend an afternoon than wandering along the shore of the Walensee, gazing across at the mountains. It was hard to say exactly how long the day was, probably seventeen or eighteen miles, by the time Flums arrived. By this time I could prevaricate no longer over the state of my boots. The left boot, which had lost part of its heel, was giving no trouble; but the right boot was now losing its sole. (We've all done that...) Flums had an Intersport and I went straight in, committed to buying the best boots available, no longer stingy. Unfortunately the best boots were not available in my size. In fact none of the boots were available in my size. Are the people very small round here? I had to buy a pair of walking shoes instead. It is hard to say whether they will withstand the rigours of this sort of walk. I will carry the crumbling boots in the rucksack, just in case.

It's New Year's Eve! Where's the party? In fact I'm a killjoy on New Year's Eve. (Some would say on every other day as well.) At home I always tried to work on New Year's Eve, in a pub or a hostel. I don't like it. On the night of the millennium I was in the village at home and went to bed at ten o'clock—only to be woken by the vicar, who had got a bit tipsy and started ringing the church bell. Needless to say, he has never lived it down. Whenever his name is mentioned, someone (probably me) will say 'Oh, isn't that the chap who…?'

Anyway, there's a party in the pub where I'm staying but it looks like being fairly staid. I wouldn't mind being woken up if it involved scenes of helpless debauchery but otherwise I think I'll sleep.

DAY 37
FLUMS TO BUCHS

Happy New Year!

It would have been nice to have wished it to someone. Switzerland was closed today. It was like a morgue, with nothing open and no-one on the streets. In Sargans I heard a British voice and called out a cheery 'Morning!' He showed no interest. So much for fraternal patriotism.

What's the matter with me? I have only been gone just over a month and I'm desperate to strike up conversations with strangers, just to hear familiar speech patterns. What about people who are away for years?

My sister Sarah told me recently that, when she came back from a year in Colombia, it was a huge relief to go to the supermarket and understand everyone there and everything that was going on. That's what it is: I want to be understood.

The question today was how the new shoes would be. It was a gentle uphill followed by a gentle downhill, about fifteen miles and as easy as you could get. To be honest, the shoes are too small. It was all I could get and I did manage the day but they're not right. I may try the boots again tomorrow until they fall apart.

To reach Buchs, first you have to go round a mountain. At Sargans, a flock of birds continually circled the little castle. Ravens? Round the mountain and heading up a fresh valley, it all looks insignificant round here. In fact it is momentous.

Completely invisible today, but over there somewhere in the valley, is the Rhine. Like the Nile, no-one is quite sure where the Rhine starts, but by the time it gets here it's a big river. At the end of the valley it enters Lake Constance. When it goes in, it's dirty. When it comes out, it's beautifully clean. It tumbles through Schaffhausen and riots over the monstrous, massive and spellbinding Rhinefalls.

No-one outside Switzerland and southern Germany seems to know about the Rhinefalls. The first time I came across them it was a complete accident: someone at the Schaffhausen youth hostel asked if I was going to see the falls. What falls? Next day I took a look and was simply stunned.

At the Schaffhausen youth hostel I also discovered my uncle's nickname.

My uncle Jim was a climbing instructor in the Lake District fifty years ago and was a figure on climbing programmes on Granada TV. He also made a commercial for Wrigley's Spearmint chewing gum. This much I knew. In the youth hostel were two young climbers from the Lake District and I asked them if they knew my uncle.

'What's his name?'

'Jim. Jim Cameron.'

'What! Not Wriggly Jim!'

I didn't know whether Jim himself knew that he had acquired this soubriquet and I thought it best not to ask.

Jim used to go on carrot juice fasts for a fortnight. He stopped when the palms of his hands started turning orange.

The Rhine constitutes the border here between Switzerland and Liechtenstein. I thought of crossing the border early to see Vaduz, capital of Liechtenstein, but it was out of the way and they say it's nothing special. Buchs is quite a large town, an important junction on old trade routes. To the north lie the Alps of the Appenzell, vast hunks of rock. To the north-east lies a gap which will lead to Austria tomorrow. When the shops open I really must buy a map of Austria. More decisions will have to be made and it would be useful to know where the hell I was going.

I may, incidentally, be the only person in the world to have Liechtenstein stamped on their passport.

Many years ago, I was walking down a little country lane frequented entirely by farm traffic. Liechtenstein had a border crossing with Austria but none with Switzerland and I was not too sure I had entered the country. Then I came across a little hut with one young border guard in it. He exchanged greetings with all the people passing to and fro but it was a long time since he had seen anyone new and he was keen to talk. He asked if he could look at my passport.

We had a little chat and he asked what I was doing and where I was going. He examined my paperwork which said I was a farm worker. 'What is farm worker?' he asked. 'Ah, *Feldarbeiter?*' We talked about cows and tractors and all the rest of it, or at least he did and I said *Ja, ja* from time to time. Then he asked: would I like Liechtenstein stamped on my passport?

'Ooh, yes please,' I said.

He beckoned me into his hut and found his stamp, pristine and probably never used. He took enormous care with the stamp, lining up the passport just right, making sure he got a firm, clear image, properly aligned with the page, nice and central. It looks lovely.

I have never met anyone who has had Liechtenstein stamped on their passport. Many have been there but none has the stamp to show for it.

LIECHTENSTEIN AND AUSTRIA

DAY 38
BUCHS TO BLUDENZ

Three countries in one day; or almost in one hour.

So it was under the railway line and over the motorway and the Rhine, not an attractive river here, and into Liechtenstein. Everything was closed. A couple of hours brought Feldkirch in Austria. What a very pretty town. It even had a book-and-wine shop, a very good idea indeed. I lingered over an apple strudel. In Austria, apple strudels may figure large.

Switzerland always makes me reluctant to leave. Yes, they do some very silly things, such as the embarrassment over the minarets, and after many years they are only just beginning to clean up on tax evasion and their secret bank accounts. However, they are ultra democratic in many ways and almost anyone can take part in local government. They keep the place clean, the mountains are unbelievable, the valleys and farms are picturesque—and, of course, the trains run on time.

Austria, however, is going to be a lot cheaper.

It will also be beautiful. Leaving Feldkirch, mountains appeared on all sides. Well, they appeared and then they disappeared; snow fell for much of the day. To the north, a sharp peak rose in a gap between other mountains. It was all lovely and all very exciting.

I had dawdled for the nine or ten miles in the morning and some sightseeing (and apple strudel) in Feldkirch and it was one o'clock before I set out on the twelve or thirteen miles for the afternoon. How far was it? The sign outside Feldkirch said 21 kilometres to Bludenz. I walked two kilometres towards Bludenz and it said 22. I walked another half kilometre and it said 22.6. At one time this would have made me angry enough to hit someone. Now I am more relaxed. Sod the bastards. Just let me get my hands…

In Feldkirch I finally bought a map of Austria. My God, is it really that far across? Surely Austria is a small country. I had been aiming for at least Vienna, maybe Budapest, by 18 January when I will have to go home. That is clearly impossible. If I am not going to make either of those targets, perhaps I should go off in a different direction which provides a straighter route towards Istanbul. Innsbruck (166 kilometres) would provide the first possible diversion, leading over the Brenner Pass to the South Tyrol. Hard decisions will have to be made in the next few days.

Tonight it was dark before reaching Bludenz: it should provide a lesson over time zones. Without a doubt the days are growing longer now, but as you approach the eastern boundary of a time zone it gets light earlier in the morning and dark earlier at night: compare London and Dublin, for example. For some time I have been walking due east. I got caught out in the dark.

Eventually, of course, you reach so far east that another time zone is necessary. Eastern Europe is a further hour in time from Britain. This was a feature unknown to the doctors who treated me a couple of years ago.

I was due to have a heart procedure in the excellent cardiology unit at Bart's in London. The procedure, known as an ablation, was minor but nevertheless it was new, only recently invented, and the unit at Bart's had been world leaders in the field.

A few weeks before the date, therefore, the head honcho in the unit rang me and asked for permission to televise my ablation live to a medical conference in Athens.

I agreed, of course, though not without requesting that I should be sent to Athens for publicity purposes. 'Yeah,' he said, 'you and me both.' Anyway, I went in to hospital the night before, had a few unpleasant things done to me and was all ready for the starting line scheduled for eight o'clock next morning.

In fact I was in the shower at six thirty next day when the doctor suddenly arrived, knocking urgently on the door. My presence was required instantly in the operating theatre.

They had thought there was a one hour time difference between London and Athens. In fact it was two.

Out of the shower I leaped and into a gown. 'Come with me,' said the doctor and strode off down the corridor.

I asked if I had to be wheeled down there. No matter how fit you are, you are never allowed to walk into an operating theatre; entry for the patient is only by trolley.

'You can forget about that,' he said. 'Come on.'

Inside the theatre it was bedlam. Doctors and nurses were flinging on gowns and scrubbing up or whatever they do. A German film crew were interviewing participants, uncoiling wires, calling out instructions and generally taking charge.

Everyone was barking important information to someone else, who wasn't listening. It was like a scene from *Casualty*.

Under my gown I was wearing only socks and underpants. It didn't seem a lot. Nevertheless it was too much. 'They've got to go,' someone informed me succinctly.

I took them off.

'No-one's going to see your face,' he added.

No, I thought, but they weren't covering my face. Another part of my anatomy will be very well known in Athens.

They did the procedure and the broadcast and through the haze of sedation I heard the whole thing being pronounced a success. Unfortunately a week later it all went wrong again though I doubt whether they broadcast that. However, next time it worked and they are all in fact rather wonderful.

Today I crossed yet another border without anyone taking any notice of me. It does seem odd that, as countries become more and more obsessed with illegal immigration, so they have fewer and fewer people on the spot dealing with it. In the same way, forty years ago there was far less crime but, on a walk across Europe, you could expect routinely to be stopped on the road. Now, crime figures have increased but the police have disappeared.

It was in the US, when I was walking from New York to California, that I was stopped most often. Sometimes it was a benevolent stop: one Saturday afternoon a patrolman suggested I got indoors hastily since, on Saturdays and holidays, good ol' boys tended to have themselves a few beers and start shootin'. (I took his advice.) Generally, however, it was the hands-on-the-car routine, the pat down, the usual hustling of anyone behaving differently.

It was in Washington County, Kansas, on another Saturday afternoon that I came upon a fateful deputy sheriff; or rather, to his consternation he came upon me. I was walking on the left hand side of the road, clearly minding my own business, taking no notice of anyone, when he pulled up on the other side.

'Hi, how ya doin'?' he declared, climbing out of his pickup. I could have spoken the next words for him as they were always the same.

'You got identification?'

I showed my British passport. He hadn't seen one of them before.

'Ah'll give ya a ride into town,' he informed me.

I explained that I was grateful but I didn't accept any rides. I was walking.

'Ah'll give ya a ride into town.'

It was a statement, not an offer. We went through the pat down and I got into his pickup. Then he explained that it was the sheriff's policy not to allow anyone to walk across Washington County, Kansas.

This was obviously total nonsense. No-one had walked across Washington County, Kansas, since 1840. In reality he had made up the policy on the spur of the moment when I told him I was walking. Later I was told that I could have fought his decision in court and I would have won. Unfortunately it would have cost me about six hundred dollars and involved a few nights in jail but I would have won.

I was not very pleased with my deputy and, having established that he was not going to pistol whip me, I told him so. I had walked fifteen hundred miles from New York by that time and he was proposing to break up my little journey because of some invented sheriff's policy.

He ignored all that totally. At the police station he gave me a cup of coffee and ran me through the computer. Yes, I was clean.

'Ah'll drop ya on the county line,' he announced.

'What?'

In the old days, if they didn't like you they dragged you to the county line behind the heels of a horse. Now it was a ride in the deputy's pickup. It amounted to the same thing: he didn't want me in his county. First, however, he rang the next county to tell them the situation. Then, if they felt the same way as he did about me, it would be their privilege to pick me up at the mutual county line and take me to their line on the other side. (I never heard anything from the police in the next county. They probably thought he was a lunatic.)

We proceeded westward to some nondescript dot in the middle of nowhere, the county line. First, though, about a mile from the line he suddenly spotted something extraordinary. Someone else was walking across

Washington County! The second since 1840!

In fact, as I discovered later, he was hitching most of the way but at that moment he felt like a walk. The deputy was incensed and astounded. How could this have happened to him? Two walkers in his county on one day? Furthermore, it was Saturday afternoon and he wanted to do his shopping and go home. He could not have us both in the car at the same time but he was damned if this fellow was going to walk the last mile across the county to the county line. He dropped me on the line, therefore, went back for the other geezer and brought him to the line too. And, being in a hurry, didn't search him.

By this time I was furious and marched on without wanting to talk to anyone. Not only had my trek been interrupted but it was eighteen miles to the next town instead of the seven I had been planning. However, the other walker came flying after me, shouting and yelling for me to stop. He walked with me to the next town and we shared a motel room that night. He showed me all the drugs he was carrying, many of them things I had never even heard of. They could have blown Washington County so high it would still be up there.

Back in Bludenz, I realise that this is another town I will not do justice to. Old town, castle, cable car, skiing…

Day 39
Bludenz to Stuben

Reliable information asserts that it is three hundred and eighty miles from Bludenz to Vienna. That's one hell of a long way and I can't possibly make it in time. It confirms the suspicion that I had better go another way.

In the valley it was cold; in winter these deep lower valleys never get any sunshine and never warm up. Living here must be depressing. Nevertheless it was very beautiful. Snow and frost lay on all the trees and it was easy just to gape upwards in delight. Into the mountains a big new road has been built, so for much of the day the old road had no-one on it. Then the big new road went into a tunnel under the Arlberg Pass and anyone wanting to reach the

ski resorts had to leave it. They did in numbers.

Even this road goes through tunnels. I have walked through tunnels before, mostly in Italy, and I'm not keen. They're very polluted and very noisy. The longest tunnel today was about a mile: perfectly safe but very unpleasant. With a sigh of relief I emerged at the other end. Then I looked back and saw that there was an alternative, a footpath that led all the way beside the tunnel through the snow.

For lunch I had the most wonderful apple strudel and custard of my life.

At the end of the last tunnel stood Stuben, a tiny hamlet of a ski village: every house, every building dedicated to the tourist trade. I wanted to carry on over the Arlberg Pass tonight but was intimidated by the volume of traffic on this, a Sunday afternoon. Also, how far was it and would I find somewhere to stay?

The man in the tourist office was clear. St. Anton is twelve kilometres away, over the other side of the pass. However, St. Anton is fully booked. So is the hotel at the top of the pass. So, for that matter, was Stuben. It is the height of the ski season; I had thought that the schools would be going back this week but in Austria they are a week later. You can ask from door to door, the man said, but the official information is that everywhere is booked. Don't carry on over the pass.

There is little doubt that this is the height of the ski season; they're at it in all directions and you can't step outside the door without being skied on. Streams of them come hurtling down from a ravine up above to the right. Nursery slopes lie to the left. Stuben is the family centre for skiing. St. Anton is the place for a good time. (There is also a village above St. Anton, of which I forget the name, where you go for an even better time. Alcohol and sex are alleged to be involved.) Stuben, however, seems to be the place where the kids read a book after the evening meal and everyone is in bed by nine o'clock. In the hotels are book exchanges with terrible books by James Patterson (again).

As the man suggested, I asked around the houses. Every one was full. I asked in the last hotel before the bus stop; if this wasn't successful I would have to take the bus back down the valley I had just walked up. Yes, they said, they did have one room. It was a very simple room, though.

I'm a very simple person, I told them.

It was the ski instructor's room and the ski instructor was just leaving after the weekend. I would have to wait for an hour while he cleared out and they cleaned the room. That was very fine with me.

By a quirk of fate, I have stayed in Stuben once before. Almost forty years ago I stayed a night here, not in the tourist season, before going over Arlberg next day. Then too I had walked here from England, though by a different route.

Thirty-nine years ago, when I was 23, I could never have imagined that I should have walked here again at the age of 62. For that matter, could I have imagined being 62? At the time, my father was only 54. The previous year I had been abroad for the first time, when Howard and I had driven in his minivan to Romania. (He wanted to swim in the Black Sea. His ambition at the time was to swim in every sea in the world. For some reason he has since given up the idea.) Arlberg was my first Alpine pass. God knows how I managed to get here. God knows how everything else has happened since. Could I ever have imagined how life would turn out? Never. It's all been a mystery to me.

Today I haven't felt very well. It may just be the altitude; even at this altitude I'm hopeless. We shall see what tomorrow brings, after sleeping up here. It may just be moral turpitude as usual.

Day 40
Stuben to Landeck

The early day skiers start in the dark. By nine o'clock in the morning the slopes were thick, the lifts were full and a continual procession of skiers and snowboarders was teeming down the long, long runs that start over the top of some mountain somewhere. I have never been in the least tempted by skiing but it's very pretty to watch.

It's a good haul up to the Arlberg Pass, which stands at 1,800 metres or just over 6,000 feet. The last time I was here, 39 years ago, there was not, as far as I remember, a single building up here; I had it to myself. Now, though, signposts had pointed to a place called St. Christoph that I had never heard of. Where was it? When I got up to the pass I found out; they have built a small town!

Ski lifts led in all directions. Lashings of snow stood high on either side of the road. National ski squads train here. Several thousand people must have slept here last night. No doubt they are all having a good or at least a useful time, but you can't help wishing they had left the place alone.

It is a little known, and quite extraordinary, fact that the British invented downhill skiing. They did it in Wengen, in Switzerland, as recently as the 1920s. The two founding British clubs are still there. I was a guest in one once. Very little in it had changed since the 1920s.

Half a dozen kilometres down the hill from Arlberg lies St. Anton. Further astonishing changes had taken place here since forty years ago. Then it was a ski village. Now it is a major industry with a budget to rival the GDP of a small country. It promotes very serious fun and it is enormous.

I bought plasters and a British newspaper; more British than Austrian papers are on sale here. The plasters came just in time, as I ran out last night, but yet not in time enough. The steep downhill from the pass brought blisters in places where I had never had them before. Why? Running repairs were needed en route. Then, when I finally took off the boot tonight, blood seeped through the sock.

The long, slow downhill from St. Anton wove through villages, over the motorway and beside the railway to the valley floor. Ahead stands a triangular mountain peak. Over the pass the morning was slow; the afternoon was an enjoyable slog despite the blisters. It was probably about 25 miles to Landeck and dark long before I arrived.

Down here in the valley there is no snow at all, just a bit of ice here and there. It seems extraordinary that in five or six kilometres one can walk from the top of the world, where the snow is several feet deep, to a bare, simply frozen land where the snow is just a memory. It must be amazing for the bus drivers who ply continually back and forth to the ski areas. It's like the trip the tube drivers take on the Central Line in London. They start in Epping, out in the Essex countryside, very nice, very leafy. They travel through the East End, grim. Then the City, unbelievably affluent. Oxford Circus, all the shoppers. Notting Hill: speaks for itself. Then it's out to the ultimate suburbia of West Ruislip. A lifetime's experience in a couple of hours.

Local knowledge says that all trips from here to Vienna, whether by car or train, go north into Germany, then via Salzburg and Linz. What's it like on foot, though?

Serious decisions will have to be made in Innsbruck but it's looking more and more like going south.

Day 41
Landeck to Otztal Bahnof (Where?)

Landeck was full of Russians setting off for the day's skiing. A young local woman, herself just back from California, suggested I took the cycle route to Innsbruck. What cycle route? I knew nothing of this. She showed me on the map and I was off, past the sewage farm and the recycling centre. Slowly.

The new blister hurt so much that at times I wanted to cry. Having a blister is a bit like having a cold. It's not glamorous. It's not serious. You will get better. Meanwhile, however, you feel dreadful. Somehow I covered about twenty miles.

Despite going downhill it grew colder; for some reason there was more snow and ice at a lower altitude. Ice flowed down the river. Ice also formed in the water bottle inside my rucksack; by mid-afternoon I couldn't get at the water. Yes, it was cold. The sun shone on the tops of the mountains. Down here, it didn't.

The cycle path was a success until I lost it late in the day. (How do you lose a cycle path?) Sometimes it went close to the motorway or the old road. At other times it went through a ravine: just the railway line, the river and me. Across the river stood a superb cycle bridge. For hours I saw no-one, then suddenly we adjoined a busier world. Lunch was the apple strudel in a motorway service station. In their toilets stood a resplendent Dyson hand drier. I was at school with James Dyson. He was a nice boy and a good lad. No-one in those days ever imagined that he would invent something quite as spectacularly useless as this hand drier.

Tonight the children are all dressing up as, I would guess, the Three Kings. They are wearing costumes and crowns, calling door to door and being invited in. Did the Three Kings play trick or treat? Tomorrow is Epiphany. Let's hope there is one.

I did some more looking at the map and agonising about my route after Innsbruck. It's time I stopped agonising and just did it. All the routes after Austria are intimidating; it's just a question of which intimidating route to take.

DAY 42
OTZTAL BAHNHOF TO FLAURLING (WHAT?)

Over breakfast I fell into conversation with Friederun, who then accompanied me for fifteen kilometres. Both of us were probably a bit surprised at spending the day together.

Friederun is German, married with four children under eight (imagine the hell of it), a teacher, religious but nice and a ballroom dancer who likes to try out her steps on the ice as she goes along. She has been given a couple of days off from looking after the children and has chosen to come here, a region which she has enjoyed before, to do some exam marking, go walking and possibly visit the cinema in Innsbruck. She had a great deal more energy than I have and was constantly two paces ahead of me, pressing on. It made me tired just looking at her, practising her dance steps, leaving me behind.

For a few hours we had a good time as casual acquaintances do on walking together. By the end of the day there were not many things I didn't know about Friederun's life and she might easily say the same about mine. (But she'd be wrong. I might be too, of course.) Then she caught the train back to do her marking and I plodded on. It had been a great interlude and it seemed unlikely I would find anyone else to talk to for a while. I was wrong there too.

Today, 6 January, is a public holiday for Epiphany. It is why the schools have not gone back yet. Nice for them but a bloody nuisance for the rest of us. All the shops were shut and only the apple strudel at lunchtime provided a lifeline for the lonely walker.

For a few more kilometres I plugged on. It was a short day but I had to stop for blisters and darkness. In the village of Flaurling I found the perfect pub to stay in, small and friendly and cheap and warm, with a landlady who has lived all her life in the same building. I could hardly expect good company as well.

As I sat down later for something to eat, the waitress said 'you're from England, aren't you?' I admitted it. 'Then you must sit with the lady over there,' she said. 'She lives in England.' She transported my cutlery to the other table and I did as I was told.

Maria is eighty-six. Born and brought up in this area of Austria, she remembers the events of 1938 when her father was sent to prison for opposing the German takeover of Austria, the *Anschluss*. She remembers also, of course, the hardships of wartime. She says it wasn't actually as bad on the farms as in the cities but I'd guess it was pretty difficult. She remembers too the American and French occupations after the war; the American was better, she said.

Maria's mother grew up in the south Tyrol when it was still part of the Austrian empire. This is living history!

Then, a few years after the war, Maria married a British builder who was on holiday in her country. Where did they go back to live in Britain? Loughton, Essex. Her son went to school in my street. Her daughter lives within walking distance of our house in Snaresbrook. Until last year, Maria played tennis locally at clubs that I know well. She visits Austria several times each year to see family and friends; her son is married to the landlady's sister. We had a long, long talk and exchanged addresses.

Local people are lamenting the lack of snow in the valleys. In previous times snow covered the ground throughout the winter but global warming has put paid to that and there has been less each year. It is ironic that Britain is apparently covered in snow at the moment and schools and businesses are shut down all over the country, but here, where it is supposed to fall, there is none. Climate change for all.

Nevertheless the views today were sensational: back to Arlberg, left to the Lechtaler Alps and ahead to, well, something beyond Innsbruck I suppose. Everything up there is magical and covered in snow. The peaks and the ridges swirl and sway and disappear and re-appear again. You could stand and gape for minutes on end. It's just the valleys that are frozen but barren.

Day 43
Flaurling to Innsbruck

Continuing my theme of last night, an inch of snow fell overnight, the first snow in Innsbruck this year. Britain has ground to a halt and they are comparing it with the winters of 1962-63 (the coldest, and didn't we know it) and 1946-47, which had the most snow.

In 1962-63 our farm, like every other farm, lost the bulk of its sugar beet crop. The ground froze on 10 December and remained frozen until the middle of March, by which time the beet had rotted; in subsequent years my father and everyone else got the beet up early. In 1947 my parents lived in Buxton, Derbyshire; they moved to Norfolk at the beginning of April. In Buxton during that winter my father had to dig his way out every morning to get to work—then dig his way back in again in the afternoon.

Incidentally, one day many years later I was working on the farm with Cally Shackcloth; we spent so much time together on a trailer that we knew each other better than our own families. 'Of course,' Cally told me, 'you'll never be a Norfolk man.'

'Excuse me,' I said. 'I've lived here all my life. How can I not be a Norfolk man?'

'Your parents weren't Norfolk people,' he said. 'So you can never be a Norfolk man. Your children could be Norfolk people but you could never be a Norfolk man.'

I suppose it's true. And I have never had children.

I shuffled down the road to Zirg and re-joined the cycle path which led all the way to the middle of Innsbruck. This seemed such a good wheeze that I asked later in the tourist office if there was a cycle route up the Brenner Pass. They had absolutely no idea.

All along today's route, just above the villages, a roll of cloud obscured the lower hills. Above the cloud, however, on all sides the tops of huge mountains glistened in the sunlight. It was an extraordinarily beautiful sight, the sort that leaves you spellbound and stationary in awe. Innsbruck is almost completely surrounded by mountains which, because of their proximity and the low point of the city, simply tower above it. The postcards do not do justice to it.

The city itself is no disappointment either. For a couple of hours I wandered round looking at the sights. (Actually I was trying to buy a copy of the *Guardian*, which I knew must be there somewhere, but I saw the sights at the same time.) The old town itself is everything it's cracked up to be. If you want shopping, that's there as well. Street after street of ancient buildings, museums (I never go in them), towers, churches, whatever you want is there. Even at this time of year the town is full of foreign tourists like me and plenty of Austrian tourists as well. It's a nice place.

(If I was Patrick Leigh Fermor I would now recount a history of Innsbruck in the tenth century and a detailed breakdown of architectural trends over the years. But I'm not.)

During the day I had a message to say that my mother's last surviving sister, Barbara, had died suddenly. Barbara was not only the last surviving sister of that family. She was also the last survivor of that generation, including husbands and wives, on either side of the family. As Sarah and I agreed, there's only us now. We have been orphaned again.

I have never seen as many bookshops in all my life as in Innsbruck. Every second shop seems to be a bookshop. English-language books proliferate. I bought a couple and will need to give away a couple that I have finished. There shouldn't be any shortage of recipients.

DAY 44
INNSBRUCK TO MATREI

Once you have decided to stop, the willpower sags. Mine does, anyway. Or maybe it's that moral fibre again. I'm pathetic. I hate myself. Rather than go on until the last minute I decided to stop in a couple of days. I had already arranged to go to Vienna and stay with my friend Irene next week before travelling home. I have now asked her if I can go on the 11th instead. Today is the 8th.

It's not even as if the foot hurts that much. Yes, it hurts, but when I have been going for an hour I barely notice it—as long as I'm going uphill not downhill. What's more, it hurts a little bit less each day, although it can be hard to remember that at the time. When I'm asleep it doesn't hurt at all.

Weather conditions aren't impossible either. Finally, the boots are still holding together, just. It's simply pathetic. I never ever reach my full destination. It's always best to aim for somewhere a very long way off because I tend to cover the same percentage of the trip, usually about fifty, however far it is. Have I ever reached the end? Maybe once or twice. I walked from Managua in Nicaragua to Guatemala City once; as far as I can remember that was as far as I meant to go. In India I walked from Agra via Delhi to Chandigarh, watching cricket matches en route, but that's less than five hundred miles so it doesn't really count. All the others I have failed on. Walking across Canada? Failed. London to Athens? Failed. Twice. Athens to Paris? Failed. New York to San Francisco? Only got as far as the Californian border and even then had to take a bus across the Salt Lake desert. It's a catalogue of failures really.

Another couple of inches of snow fell in the morning. Much heavier snow has fallen further east and in northern Italy. (That's where I would have been going. An excuse thereby presents itself. If only it had happened before I decided to stop…) After a blotchy start, though, it wasn't too difficult today wandering up towards the Brenner Pass.

Outside Innsbruck stand two villages called Mutters and Natters. My parents came here in 1957 on their first foreign holiday and loved the two names. They bought postcards, some of which they brought home and never used. I found them in their papers after my mother died and acquired them for a later date. That turned out to be today; I sent them to my sisters.

Then it was all uphill on a winter wonderland of a day, the trees full of snow, the visibility steadily diminishing as the road climbed. Above my road, the motorway in the sky climbed a series of monstrous bridges: one, across a whole valley, was so high that it terrified me even from hundreds of feet below. Traffic could be seen crawling along it as the weather worsened. Down on our road, very little moved except for snow ploughs and the occasional bus. Of the cars on the road, four out of five were German. Today is Friday and the holidays end this weekend. In travel conditions like this, everyone wants to get home early.

Matrei was only thirteen miles but the snow made it hard work and by the end I was covered in slush. It seemed time to stop. Tomorrow, weather permitting, I shall get up to the pass. Then I shall consider my future. That's the official version anyway. In fact I have already decided to stop. Patrick Leigh Fermor would not have stopped. He would have whipped out his pen knife and dealt with the foot: cut it off, probably. Then he would have wrapped his greatcoat around him, made a snow hole and hibernated like a marmot. That's why he got to Istanbul and I won't.

Stop going on about it. That's enough flagellation.

Matrei is a picturesque little town, all the central buildings decorated in traditional Tyrolean style. It's a tourist town without, at the moment, any tourists. I kept warm for an hour in a travel agency, home to the two most helpful travel agents it has ever been my pleasure to meet; they're in the wrong job. They tried and failed to get me home but by God they did try.

Day 45
Matrei to The Brenner Pass

The Brenner Pass!

It might as well have been the Khyber Pass for all you could tell. The pass was cloaked in murk. Cloud rolled down to the road. Fearsome mountains must hang high above, but they're not visible today. Visibility extended to the lower slopes, covered in trees. And greyness. And snow.

More snow had fallen overnight, nothing unusual. At Steinach the temperature was minus five, also nothing unusual. Ten miles or so led to the top of the pass, most of it slushy but not difficult. Then, a kilometre from the summit, snow fell in earnest. By the time I reached the pass it was settling faster than it could be cleared. This looked like a serious snowfall.

It would have been easy to carry on into Italy. In fact I did so accidentally, as I discovered when having to show my passport on the train back into Austria. The pass itself has been totally disfigured by a shopping mall, a truly hideous concept. Extraordinarily, people will actually drive up here in this weather to spend their money on quick-buck, probably duty free crap.

In Italy, this region is the South Tyrol.

A few months ago in Spain I met a man called Walter who comes from the South Tyrol. I had been told that I must meet Walter. He's a bit of a character. I was also told that he talks a lot; an awful lot.

Walter would not admit to coming from anywhere but the South Tyrol. I asked what nationality of passport he held; he ignored my questions. Eventually, when I more or less held him down and tortured him, he admitted that he held an Italian passport. He does not admit to being Italian, though. He is from the South Tyrol.

As far as the inhabitants are concerned, the South Tyrol is not part of Italy. They speak German, as many a surprised tourist has discovered. They do not think of themselves as part of Austria either, although the South Tyrol was once part of the Austrian empire. Terrible battles were fought here in the First World War. Like Alsace and Lorraine, the South Tyrol is so tired of being fought over that it just wants to be itself and left alone. Neither Austrian nor Italian, it is South Tyrolean.

So where does Walter live? Swansea.

Walter's main claim to fame is, as he is not shy in revealing, that he has been to 147 countries. Well, that was then; he will have been to more by now. However, 'claim' is the appropriate word, as I soon pointed out to him…

On listening to his travelling tales, I heard him mention that he had been to Greenland. I therefore asked, in my smartarse way, if he was including Greenland as a country. Why yes, he said. But it's not a country, I pointed out; it is, as we all know, a dependency of Denmark. He was unabashed. He continued to claim it as a country. Look, I told him, if we're including dependencies I could claim Gibraltar, Montserrat, St. Martin, St. Eustatius, Saba, to name but a few…

He didn't care. He was still going to claim it.

147 is a lot, actually.

Speaking of Greenland, in Nicaragua I met a Danish man who had spent twenty years in Greenland. When he was twenty years old he decided that he wanted to spend his life travelling. He therefore went to Greenland and spent the next twenty years there, not travelling at all but working in two jobs for very high wages (no-one wants to go to Greenland) and not spending any money (nothing to spend it on). When he was forty he gave up work and spent the rest of his life travelling.

On a train in Germany once I met an elderly Australian woman who had no home of her own but spent her life travelling between friends.

As for Saba, a Dutch dependency in the North Antilles, it is the size of a pocket handkerchief and rises to a volcanic point, the quaintly named Mt. Scenery. There is not a flat point on the entire island. Everyone speaks English as well as Dutch. The standard of living is very high. For many years it was extra popular with young Dutch people because of its renown for 'driving test tourism'.

Since it is part of the Netherlands, it was perfectly legal for Dutch people to go there to take their driving test. This was not quite like taking a test in the Netherlands: the island held only one road, it was unusual to meet another car and there was not a flat yard anywhere to be found. Thousands of Dutch people went there for the test, contributing significantly to the local economy. Sadly, they have put a stop to it now. Meanies. Health and safety, I suppose.

Back on the Khyber (sorry, Brenner) Pass, I reflected on the journey so far; but not for long, otherwise I would get too disenchanted with my lack of something or other.

I have got to go home, that is indisputable and beyond my control. I could probably go on for another four days before I had to turn round, but there's a bloody lot of snow falling in northern Italy and southern Austria and it does look a bit difficult ahead. That's my story, anyway. The nub of it is that at this moment I am no more than half way between Hook of Holland and Istanbul.

I'll do the rest later.

I cheered up with a cup of tea served by the world's friendliest barmaid. Except for me, I think she kissed everyone in the bar. That's a good note to finish on.

PART TWO

ITALY

Day 46
Brenner Pass To Gossensass: 16 October

A very beautiful, very stern young woman accosted me on the train from Innsbruck to the Brenner Pass. Unfortunately she was the conductor and she thought I should have bought a ticket before boarding. Furthermore she proposed my paying a 65-euro penalty for not doing so.

I told her that in Switzerland I had tried to buy a ticket through to the Brenner but had not been allowed to. I showed her the printed schedule for my journey, giving me four minutes at Innsbruck to run from platform 3 to platform 41 with never a ticket machine in sight. For a while we argued. Then she relented. 'Compromised' would be too strong a word. I said I would get off and walk it. She said I would get off, but I could buy a ticket at Matrei and get on the next train. I complied. It put me behind on my plan but it was worth it to avoid her withering smile.

Welcome back to the Brenner Pass.

It was cold and wet at the top. Snow is forecast for tomorrow at nine hundred metres and above. Yet again the tops of the mountains were invisible, shrouded as ever in cloud. I walked down for a couple of hours until dark and found sanctuary in the village of Gossensass. We're in Italy. Actually, of course, we're not in Italy, we're in the South Tyrol.

I should have been back here months ago, continuing the walk from Hook of Holland to Istanbul. It was January when I had to go home for my mother's funeral, two and a half years after she died. The intention was to come back almost immediately and carry on. However, then my heart went wrong again. Physically, that is.

At my mother's funeral, incidentally, it transpired that three of those present had been at the same football match in 1968 (the European Cup Final, Manchester United v Benfica). One of them was me. The second, Jenny, was married to the football correspondent of *The Times* at the time. (She later married my uncle Charles.) The third, a cousin, had been to only two football matches in his life and that was one.

It was five o'clock in the morning, not long after the funeral, when I was

woken suddenly by my heart. 'Oh, shit,' I said. It was all over the place.
For years my heart used to go wrong intermittently (atrial fibrillation) but I
never worried about it and it used to correct itself after a few hours. When
it goes wrong permanently, however, you have a problem: walking upstairs
is difficult, let alone walking up a mountain. I have had one electric shock
(cardioversion) and two ablations to try to combat the thing. They hoped the
second ablation would last for ever but it clearly hadn't. Time to get mended
again.

In March I was back on the waiting list but managed to get a cancellation.
Mark Earley, the esteemed doctor at Bart's, said I could have another ablation
if I wanted, which would mean waiting a few months, or I could try another
cardioversion in which case I could come in during the following week. Put
like that there was no choice; I had the cardioversion in April. The next few
months were spent taking life very gently and then slowly trying to get fit
again. It was October before I felt ready to set off.

After all that, will I be able to do the walk at all? I don't know. Only time
will tell.

One or two other problems had arisen while I was having treatment
previously. For some reason my white blood cell count was ridiculously low
and no-one knew the cause of it. Tests went off and my GP asked me to ring
him when they came back. I did. I was aware, of course, that doctors don't
remember everyone they see and so was not perturbed when, having told
me that my white cell count remained very low, he asked his first question.

'Are you black?' he asked.

'No.'

'Oh.' There was a long pause. Low white cell counts are normally found
in black people. The pause continued. I knew exactly what he wanted to say.

'Are you sure you're not black?' He didn't say it but it was hanging there
waiting. Eventually the doctor, himself black, moved on to safer ground.

Various other problems arose at the time and on one terrible day I was
lying in an outpatients department while a doctor had her finger up my bum.
She was so uninterested in my bum that she was simultaneously talking to
someone else about her holidays. I thought: is this what the future holds,
lying in a hospital with someone's finger up your bum while she talks to
someone else about her holidays? The answer, of course, is yes.

Before coming away I normally do standard grooming: teeth, feet, hair. I
cut my hair. (In 1967 I was so shocked at a haircut going up to three shillings

and sixpence, or 17.5 new pence, that I said I would never return; since then I have cut my own.) I trimmed my toenails. I also trimmed my eyebrows, the curse of the older man. As far as possible I was prepared.

I used to know an American woman who never had a doctor, only a dentist and a gynaecologist; she said that was all she needed.

How far is it, anyway? I have absolutely no idea; this is one area in which I am not so well prepared. The first part of the trip, from Hook of Holland to the Brenner Pass, took 45 days. If the body stands up, can I do the rest, to Istanbul, in about eight weeks? A couple of deadlines loom. In my bag is a 69-day supply of heart pills, flecainide; it would be a problem if they ran out. Then I have a half price annual Swiss rail card which expires on 21 December, and I want to go home via Switzerland. Finally, do I want to be home by Christmas? Not really, but nor do I want to be anywhere else.

As always, I am ambivalent about the whole venture. When I'm at home I want to be away. When I'm away I want to be at home. I don't really want to be trudging down Italy in the snow and the rain. What's the point? On the other hand, what else would I be doing if I wasn't here?

Oh well. I'm here now so I'd better get on with it.

In my bag are two enormous books. It should be illegal to write a book of more than 250 pages. Some time ago I was given *The Corner*, a non-fiction book about low-life drug users. Apparently it is very good but it is massive. Also I have got *The Lacuna* by Barbara Kingsolver, one of four books I have read from this year's Orange Prize shortlist; that too will be great if it's as good as her other books but it is over four hundred pages. The bag is bursting. Tonight I finished a book by Susan Hill which I will leave here but I need to do some serious reading quickly.

Incidentally my uncle Charles, married to Jenny who went to the European Cup Final, wrote lots of books about psychoanalysis but also went to Moscow in 1936 with Anthony Blunt. In the 1950s Charles was always being interviewed by the secret services about Blunt. They knew all about him as the fourth man (or was it fifth?) in the Burgess and Maclean spy scandal. They could never do anything about him, however, because he was the keeper of the queen's pictures and, in the words of John Banville's novel about him, the untouchable.

My ex-schoolmaster Neville Blackburne was also mixed up with Guy

Burgess, whom he knew at Cambridge in the 1930s. When Burgess defected in, I think, 1951, MI5 (or is it MI6?) went through his papers and found an invitation from Neville to a party in 1935. They came to see Neville.

'Did you invite Guy Burgess to a party in Cambridge in 1935?' they asked.

'Yes, I did,' Neville said.

'Seen him since, have you?'

'Well, no, I haven't.'

'All right, thanks, old boy. That's all we wanted to know.'

End of interrogation. They took his word as a gentleman, naturally, that he had had no further contact.

DAY 47
GOSSENSASS TO FORTEZZA

Shortly after midnight I was woken from a dream about structuralism. Is there such a thing as structuralism or had my dream invented it? My friend Howard Davies was arguing vociferously on the subject. (I think he was against it.) I hope Howard knows more about it than I do.

It was not, however, structuralism that woke me.

'Oh, shit.'

The heart had gone crazy again. Seconds went past without a heartbeat and then five came at once. It was all over the place. It hasn't done this for months, since before the last procedure; in fact it has never been this bad. What caused it? Exercise? I haven't done a lot. Stress? Apart from the encounter with the Valkyrie on the train, there has been very little. More likely, it just went wrong because that's what it does.

The outcome would be total ignominy. Admittedly I told everyone that I might be home next week if things went badly, but I didn't mean it. I visualised catching the first train back to London.

The question at midnight was: would it correct itself? In the last five years it has never done so. Since the cardioversion in April it has been fine but no-one knows what will happen next.

I took an extra pill and went back to sleep.

At four o'clock it was steady.

At six o'clock it was firm and regular. It had rectified itself.
Bloody hell. Now we wait to see what happens today.

Overnight, a fresh coating of snow had settled on the hills. I headed further away from the Brenner. Fifteen miles turned out to be enough for the day. There's no getting away from it, these ventures are hard at the start. I followed road, footpath, pavement and cycle path; they all crammed into the valley with the river, railway, old road and motorway. By the time all this reached Fortezza I was totally stuffed.

My nice landlady from last night drove past and stopped her car. She was on her way to a farmers' festival forty kilometres away—food, clothing, drink and general good cheer. Would I like to come?

Oh, what a temptress. Furthermore, if I possessed an ounce of culture - or the capacity for pleasure - or even sociability - I could have gone with her and returned later. But I don't.

In new boots, the blisters are coming along nicely. On returning home from the first part of the walk in January I took the old boots to the cobbler in Swaffham who has sorted out my problems for the last twenty years. (Boot problems, that is. The rest remain unsorted.) He picked them up, turned them round, held them up to the light and gave them back to me.

'You'd best invest in a new pair,' he said.

So I did. I left the old pair in a litter bin in Swaffham.

The new boots are similar in style to the old pair. They're good boots which will, I hope, last for a hundred years. But new boots mean blisters.

A couple of weeks ago, to my consternation, I discovered that someone has followed Patrick Leigh Fermor's route from Hook of Holland to Istanbul. He has even written a book about it which came out this year, shortly after my return from the first part of the trip. In fact he hasn't walked most of it but instead has just followed Leigh Fermor's route via the Danube. But how can it be that, after all these years, two people have had the same idea at the same time? I haven't read his book yet and I'm sure he's a good guy. I bear no ill will towards him at all…

DAY 48
FORTEZZA TO ST. LORENZEN

St. Lorenzen boasts the world's angriest tourist officer. As I entered she was shouting wildly down the telephone at some recalcitrant she was negotiating with. For several minutes she harangued him or her. I quailed, expecting the same treatment - maybe she just didn't like tourists - but when she turned to me she was polite and helpful.

Forty years ago I walked along this road to Bruneck. I remember nothing at all about it. At that time I continued over the border into Austria, ending the journey at Villach in a tempest of snow and witnessing my first ever thunder snowstorm. It was all too much for me; I bought a huge tub of Austrian jam for my mother and turned for home.

Today, traffic on the road was heavy but fortunately a cycle path led to St. Lorenzen. The only problem with cycle paths is that they, like Swiss walking paths, tend to follow remorselessly the scenic route. Who said I want all these views? Views are a bonus. All I want is to get as far as possible as fast as possible with as little pain as possible.

I am reminded of the exchange between Learie Constantine, cavalier West Indian cricketer of the 1920s and 1930s and later representative of Trinidad in London, and an England cricketer of the time. The two teams were travelling on the same boat back to England between Test series. One night a breathtaking, burning sunset emblazoned the horizon. Leaning over the ship's handrail, mesmerised by the grandeur, Constantine turned to the Englishman standing beside him.

'That looks rather fine,' he declared.

'Yes, old boy,' replied his companion. 'But don't go on about it.'

A man after my own heart. A chap can appreciate the world, fair enough, but he doesn't want his emotions to let him down.

Just for the record, today brought magnificent views of Alpine scenery. Up the valley the road rose steadily. High, pine-covered hills lined each side of the valley, which opened out gently as the day went on. Behind the hills, mountains laden with snow rose on all sides.

On all sides? Suddenly I realised that the road I was going to take tomorrow rises to well over two thousand metres. Twice! Bloody hell. Not only am I nowhere near strong enough at the moment, but there's going to be a hunk of snow up there. Brrr. It would be a climb of four and a half thousand feet in the snow. There has to be another way.

Muhlbach was a pretty little town. St. Lorenzen is another. They speak a very funny language round here, a German like none I have ever heard. *Nacht* becomes *nicht*. Then half of it is in Italian. I am managing without a German phrasebook because I forgot it but tomorrow the Italian must come out of the bag.

One other problem with cycle paths is that they tend to attract cyclists, those misbegotten terrorists who drive relentlessly through red lights, over pavements and in between cars regardless. In addition they seldom wish you a good day. Today I hardly saw one. That was a good day.

DAY 49
ST. LORENZEN TO TOBLACH (DOBBIACO)

Forty years ago, as I remember, Bruneck was a quaint, autumnal sort of town, little disturbed by the outside world. Now I fought my way through factories, offices and wholesale outlets, none of which was built forty years ago. Even the town centre was largely new.

Allegedly a cycle path led out of Bruneck. Wherever it was, I couldn't find it. I spent a miserable couple of hours on the main road, flattened against barriers, walking on top of low walls or in ditches and through fields. Through the morning fog the headlights of heavy lorries threatened a nasty end.

Then two things happened at once. First, a sign indicated a new cycle path. It didn't say where it led to but I didn't care; I would take it anywhere. Then the fog suddenly lifted to reveal a whole range of three thousand-metre mountains on the right.

What are the happiest few notes in popular music? The guitar intro to the Beatles' *Here Comes the Sun*. Play it to anyone and see them smile: they know the words that follow.

The sun shone on stunning scenery, Alpine pastures leading to wooded hills with rocky mountains on all sides behind them. The cycle path took a few kilometres longer than the road, it was over twenty miles and it was much too far. However, if you've got to be knackered, fed up and bad tempered, this is the place to be it in. Behind Toblach are some very spiky mountains indeed.

The best part of the day led beside a reservoir. There is nothing much better than walking beside an autumnal reservoir. At the same time, reservoirs are sad because of what was once there. Take the Ladybower, for example: in times of drought I can remember seeing the church steeple of the flooded village. The Goyt Valley, Derbyshire's most beautiful spot where we played as children on holiday, now lies largely under water; my father remembered walking down the valley before even the lower reservoir was built in the 1930s. Sarah Hall delineates the whole sadness of it in her excellent novel *Haweswater*. There was a world which we have destroyed in our appetite for growth.

All the cycle paths round here are signposted in German. Someone has come along afterwards and handwritten the Italian translation. A patriot. A patriot with time on his or her hands.

I left the rucksack in St. Lorenzen and carried only a small bag to Toblach, hoping to make the three hundred-metre climb a little easier; then I caught the train back and will return in the morning. Could I make the ticket machine work? No. On the train, the conductor looked at me with what I can only describe as great sadness. He let me off at St. Lorenzen and told me to buy a ticket there. I couldn't even find the machines at St. Lorenzen. If they'd only staff the places properly I would happily buy a ticket.

In the evening I talked to a British couple who have moved here to live. Why? They like it. They were at pains to tell me that they paid their taxes properly in Britain. She is a translator, he a health scientist who in retirement is working all over the world. In winter she looks out of the window to see if the sun is shining. If it is, she goes skiing. If it isn't, she doesn't.

Day 50
Toblach to Cortina

At eight o'clock in the morning snow began to fall. By nine o'clock an inch or two lay everywhere on the ground and all those green Alpine pastures had disappeared completely. Grey clouds squatted lumpily over the valleys. What would the pass be like?

Then the clouds lifted and by eleven o'clock the sun shone. Cortina, at the end of the day, held no sign of any snow.

Up the valley went the road and the old Dolomite railway line. At least the snow kept the cyclists off the cycle path on this side of the pass. As the clouds lifted, huge rock faces emerged on either side of the narrowing valley. Further on, high pinnacles of mountain rose up into the sky. I'm never sure where Alps end and Dolomites begin but these are definitely Dolomites and they're devastating.

In the end it was nothing but a gradual climb. Past Lake Toblach. Past the First World War cemetery, housing over 1,250 bodies of 'diverse nationalities'. A couple of deer strayed on to the path. From behind came a strange noise, a combination of gasping, panting and whistling; then two dogs drew level - and another two - and another. Eight dogs were pulling a miniature tractor, a man sometimes running alongside and sometimes jumping on the tractor. They must be practising for the tourist season to come.

Twofold disappointment lay ahead. First, both the road signs and the cycle path had indicated twenty-eight kilometres from Toblach to Cortina; then, at a junction, another road sign said it was thirty-two. Really this is quite a big difference when you're walking. Second, the map seemed to show that the top of the pass was about 1,430 metres high. I climbed. And climbed. 1,430 went past. So did 1,500. Finally it was 1,530 metres, over 5,000 feet. At the top I sat and ate the last of the large piece of Gruyère given me by Scott in Basle as I passed through. Eating it must have reduced the weight load considerably; and, since it is now five days old and hasn't been refrigerated...

The old railway came down slowly, slowly from the top, hidden in a world of its own, far from the road. It emerged from the trees. Blimey. At the bottom of a vast canyon lay the river. A bridge led over a massive ravine; best not to look down. No-one was around until suddenly a cyclist emerged from a tunnel. If we had met in the middle of the tunnel we might both have got one hell of a shock. He was the first sign of civilisation on the other side.

Then a walker appeared without a rucksack. It's like the first seagull when lost at sea. Two women who were not, shall we say, svelte turned up with two dogs who were definitely not svelte. Then a runner; they're usually close to town. Down from the world of brutal rocky mountains the land around

Cortina opened up, the ski lifts stretching away from town, almost everything shut now, out of season. Apparently Cortina was the place to be seen in the 1970s but now it is thought to be rather tacky. To the approaching walker it looked pretty nice. I made the mistake of finding somewhere to sleep that was very close to the church clock.

The top of the pass marked the end of the South Tyrol and no more German will be spoken. My German is deplorable but it's a great deal better than my Italian.

A restaurant displayed the very best in Italian hospitality. Everyone knew everyone else, all the customers and staff. Familiar greetings were exchanged and meals discussed in detail. The two best meals of my life were in Italy. The first was years ago in Milan when Ian Boag was the British vice-consul in the city; everyone in the trattoria seemed to home in on the debate about what to cook a vegetarian. The second came a few years ago in Verona when the waiters became so excited that they actually ran between tables and kitchen, or just from one table to another. I don't remember what I ate on either occasion but that was not the point.

Verona lay on my route across northern Italy on my intermittent walk to Venice. The roads between cities were grim, but what cities: Bergamo, Brescia and Verona were extraordinary. Now I am back in the region where all signposts lead to Venice.

Day 51
Cortina to Valle Di Cadori

Here is a question. Throughout the world, how many old bath tubs are used as water troughs for cattle? Thousands, millions or billions?

It was a totally cloudless day. It might be invidious to talk of even more stupendous scenery. Leaving my bag in Cortina I padded downhill for a few hours then caught the bus back from Valle, a one horse town without a horse. I will return on the bus in the morning and continue.

In the sun I wore a rather tasteless yellow baseball cap which I bought in Guyana when my previous hat blew into the Essequibo river (five miles wide). It says Phat Farm. I have no idea what this means.

At the time I was trying to make my way up Guyana overland (not easy in itself - most of it is water) to visit Megan, daughter of Nigel and Bridget, who was teaching for a year in the far north. After a near disaster in a seaborne canoe I gave up, to my eternal shame, and went back to Georgetown. In Georgetown there is nothing to do except drink, so I went to the library one day and read a whole book (by Wilson Harris) from cover to cover, something I had not done since childhood.

Both my visits to Guyana have been linked to cricket. On my previous visit the rain had fallen so hard at the ground that it was impossible to leave. I got talking to another spectator who turned out to be a Nigerian, training Guyanese radio producers. He took me drinking in the public service club and asked if I would be his guest on a morning radio programme.

'What do you want me to talk about?' I asked, flattered.

'Africa. And cricket.'

'Africa?' I had told him about my insignificant travels in some very small parts of Africa but I was hardly an expert. On the other hand, the opportunity to talk about cricket on national radio...

We fixed a day and I arrived at the radio building. However, in the meantime I had contracted a stomach bug. When George (Chukuma) came to collect me, I explained that I was still very happy indeed to appear on his show but that he would have to leave the studio door open and point me to the closest lavatory for emergencies.

Which he did. Then he began his show with: 'And now we have as our guest today a Britisher...'

I got through the show delicately but without crisis.

Megan, incidentally, is pregnant as I write. Not long ago, as it seems, I was babysitting for her when she was one year old. *Tempus fugit.*

In the morning I sang a medley of Beatles songs. (*Come Together, A Day In The Life, I Saw Her Standing There.*) Then, as I entered the supermarket at San Vito, Beatles music came over the sound system. Serendipity. For much of the day the path led along another old railway line, completed by the Austrian army in the First World War and last used in 1984. I switched to singing railway songs of the 1950s - *Last Train to San Fernando* and *The Runaway Train Came Over the Hill.* Then, influenced by the 1950s, I found myself singing *How Much Is That Doggie in the Window?*, a dreadful song.

My insides are all over the place. Cough, sneeze, burp, hiccup, they're rebelling against something. Last night I thought I'd got constipation as well, a terrible fate. Now it seems I haven't.

Finally I finished the Kingsolver book and can give it away and lighten the pack. It's a very good book but would have been even better if it had been two hundred pages shorter. These people are obsessed with writing Epics. They ought to stick to writing Good Books.

It is good, however, to see an American writer sympathetic to organised labour. Even sympathetic to Trotsky! Mind you, if truth be told, she is a bit more sympathetic to him than he deserves.

Day 52
Valle to Longarone

I left the Kingsolver in a book exchange and for once didn't acquire anything else. I am steadily reducing. The pills are being swallowed slowly but surely. Every day I shave, reducing the shaving soap, clean my teeth, reducing toothpaste, and put powder on my feet. I can start sending the many postcards that I always carry from home. (Some people don't like getting pictures of Cornwall from someone in Cortina.) I can't think of many more reductions apart from that.

The route turned due south. According to the map the old road lasted only a few kilometres but in reality it covered most of the day. Where it didn't, I was hemmed against a crash barrier overlooking a precipice. At regular intervals, dents appeared in the crash barrier where vehicles had failed to make the turn. Not reassuring really.

Walking along the old road was much further but absolutely tranquil. Through steep hairpin bends it wound down to the floor of the huge valley. Old staging posts, now sleepy and sometimes decrepit villages, dotted the route. In Ospitale a very nice young person served a very nice cup of tea. Well, relatively nice. It comes in a very, very pale grey round here. Because of my heart I have cut down on stimulants. I don't know how to order a decaf coffee in Italy so have had no coffee since starting out. The tea theoretically has caffeine but I can't see how this tea has much of anything. I have one beer per night and haven't had any wine. No other stimulants have been present on this trip unfortunately.

Across the valley stands minor industry, mostly sand and gravel and water works. As the valley flattened out, so it became less attractive. Longarone is not as far as I should have gone today but the next few miles hold uncertainty so it seemed sensible (not just lazy) to stop for the night.

One of the toes looks hammered today. Minor surgery lies ahead tonight and then a large sticking plaster in the morning and we shall be right as rain.

My Italian phrasebook, written some time ago, perhaps at the time of the Grand Tour, tells me that: 'Immediately you arrive in Italy you become involved with the extrovert happiness of the native and a certain gay indifference.'

I hope this phrasebook isn't going to get me into trouble.

Later. So much for the good intentions over the wine...

DAY 53
LONGARONE TO VITTORIO VENETO

First, traffic thundered past. Second, I had minor chest pains, the sort that led me to call an ambulance the first time it happened in England; now I ignored them. Third, I dreamed of people I knew who had died, the houses they lived in, the dogs they had owned. Fourth, I was too hot and too cold. All in all, it wasn't a good night.

That was written at seven in the morning. I was counting on a good cup of tea to sort out all the problems. So what sort of tea did I get? Bloody Earl Grey, that's what. I detest Earl Grey.

And why do they put cereal on the table but never any milk?

The off-road route from Longarone led through an industrial estate, deserted on Saturday, and into an orchard trap: you could walk in one end but the other end was barred. When I eventually climbed through a gap, various old roads beside the railway led all the way down the valley. Like the buses in Westacre, the trains appear to run twice a week. I never saw one. Perhaps they are like the trains in the old westerns. Yup, come Wednesday sunup, that train be coming round the mountain.

Now the mountains lie behind. Near Belluno a town called Ponte something held a castle and a bridge that gave me vertigo. The road turned left. After the junction with the motorway it suddenly became the venue for Bikers' Saturday Afternoon Out.

It was a strange event to witness. I walked along Lake Santa Croce, drained at one end but then a fine sight under the barrier of mountains to the north. But what happened to Santa Croce itself? Bypassed now by the motorway, it was a ghost town. Then, however, near the top of a ridge, a café turned out to be the rendezvous of a thousand bikers, zooming up from Vittorio Veneto before zooming back to try and kill themselves on the way down.

Some of them succeeded. A bike shop was even called Death Road. A memorial to a young biker called Max stood nearby. Further down, two more youngsters were commemorated. Most bikers no doubt drive sensibly and well. Those you remember, however, are the maniacs overtaking round blind corners and then swerving back in, six inches before they are shredded.

A different sort of memorial contained a macabre curiosity. A plaque commemorated several partisans killed in 1944; after Italy left the war and hanged Mussolini the partisans fought against the Germans. Two of those remembered on the plaque had the same names: one was born in 1895, the other in 1912. Could they possibly have been father and son?

Cyril Goose, resident of Westacre, was an Italian prisoner of war - taken, I think, at Tobruk. While a prisoner, Cyril was sent out of the camp each day to work on a local farm; and, of course, he became friendly with the farmers. When Italy left the war, the camp gates were opened and the prisoners were told they had twenty-four hours before the Germans arrived. Cyril and a friend went to the farmers, who hid them.

The Germans came looking. Cyril and friend were hiding behind straw in the barn. The soldiers poked bayonets into the straw but didn't find them and went away. The British clearly had to leave because they were endangering the lives of the farmers. Borrowing clothes, they headed north, aiming for the border to neutral Switzerland, where they would be interned but not imprisoned.

They climbed on to a train, then alighted at a station but had no way of getting out without tickets. They were saved when a Gestapo officer saw them and ordered them to carry his bags out of the station! (Cyril told me this story in our kitchen; it seemed incredible.) They made their way to Milan, where someone in a café gave them the key to an apartment. Eventually they reached the Swiss border.

They waited and watched. It looked clear. They made a dash for it.

And were caught by the Germans.

They were taken to a German prisoner of war camp where Cyril was amazed to find Billy and Bob Thaxton, brothers from Westacre. One outcome of their ordeal turned out for the good. When they eventually returned home, Cyril, who then lived in the next village of Narford, spent a lot of time with Billy and Bob. Then he married their sister Peggy.

All three men are now dead, sadly missed. Their wives are very much alive, Peggy, Grace and Eileen.

Bob Thaxton first taught me to steer a tractor, aged about four, while the men topped sugar beet behind it.

Not that I was ever any good at driving a tractor later on. Among other mishaps, Cyril once had to pull me out when I got stuck in a bog. It was Frank Welham's fault. He suggested that I took a short cut back to the farm. Frank knew that we would get stuck in the bog but he also knew that I didn't know. It was years before I heard the end of it.

I have played cricket with four generations of Thaxtons. I would like to make it five but it is probably best for everyone (their youth, my age) if it never happens.

Sweeping above the old road stands the motorway, an airborne monster, hundreds of feet above, carving up the valley. It was scary even to look at. For want of any alternative I ploughed on to the outskirts of Vittorio Veneto, probably twenty-five miles in all. Apparently this road stands on the route of a famous walk from Austria. Well, now it stands on the route of two famous walks from Austria.

I feel better than I did this morning.

DAY 54
VITTORIO VENETO TO PORDENONE

Sometimes, along the straight flat roads of northern Italy, you just have to put your head down and go. It was just over twenty miles today and it was pretty boring.

The mediaeval city of Vittorio Veneto has, frankly, seen better days. However, the newer part of the city, maybe a hundred and fifty years old, was very fine: classical architecture, wide boulevards, lovely parks and wonderful trees. To make the experience even better, I managed to buy a copy of *The Independent* which I devoured throughout the day.

Sacile also had an old city but not much was happening there or anywhere else; a market in the town centre had more stallholders than customers. Sunday is a day of rest. In fact it appears to be a day of sleep and it is hard to know where all the cars were going. I pushed on. Fontanafredda is only a little place but it boasts both an Indian restaurant and a Sexy Shop; the one holds a great deal more attraction than the other. Pordanone took ages to arrive. It was spitting with rain and I was knackered so I chose the first hotel that I came across. Could I have found somewhere cheaper? Possibly, but I didn't bother. It was posh.

It does embarrass me sometimes to be staying in hotels instead of bumming it. On the other hand, sometimes it doesn't. I still nick a couple of rolls from breakfast to eat for my lunch and this embarrasses me also, though obviously not enough to stop me doing it. They speak English in the posh places which is handy. The landlady last night was once an au pair in Hampstead, spoke English, French and German and had a degree in Business Studies. The young man behind the desk tonight grew up in Las Vegas.

His family originate from here, however, and he has come to the area to live near his grandmother. He is trying to learn Italian. It is hard for him, though, because the local dialect is very close to Spanish and he gets them mixed up. He seems to be getting on fine, however. He also told me about Longarone, where I stayed the night before last. In the 1970s a dam burst in the valley above, villages were destroyed and thousands of people drowned: bodies were found many, many miles down the valley. Longarone now is new and rather soulless. I just hadn't realised why.

We talked about Puerto Rico, where his father is from. I had the most miserable holiday of my life in Puerto Rico, researching for my sister Sarah's handbook. The beach area, where the sun shone, was full of monumental hotels and fat tourists. In the hills, however, it rained all the time - all the time. It was nauseatingly humid. I walked all day in the rain, found somewhere to stay, took off my wet clothes, hung them up to dry - and found they were just as wet in the morning as the night before.

DAY 55
PORDENONE TO PORTOGRUARO

(I can't remember these names!)

I told the morning desk clerk that I would be grateful if he could give me some advice about routes after I had eaten breakfast.

'But you have no shoes,' he said.

It was self-evident that I had no shoes on, but it seemed unlikely that I would be walking like that.

He said it again.

'But you have no shoes.'

Then I realised. I had to wear shoes for breakfast.

So I went back upstairs and put on my walking boots, sleek with fresh waterproofing gel, and entered the dining room for breakfast. Actually the desk clerk was very helpful and gave good advice. He just liked standards to be maintained.

Furious thunderstorms were lashing Pordenone in the early morning. I wasn't going outside the door in this, let alone walking. Then there was a let up and I set off. After a few kilometres another thunderstorm sent me scurrying into an enormous wholesaler. (The alternative, across the road, was the Bunny Bar.) Because I had entered the wholesaler I felt obliged to buy something. Then it appeared that you had to be registered for the catering trade. An order of 1.78 euros for a chocolate bar, a piece of cheese and some almonds wasn't quite what they had in mind but, with a mass of paperwork, they let me have them. I am now registered for the catering trade. Perhaps.

After another let up came another downpour. In a cheery bar, everyone except me was drinking alcohol in mid-morning. After this it didn't seem worth stopping for every downpour so I persevered. Sometimes it rained hard, sometimes it rained very hard, sometimes it rained even harder than that. It was very, very, very wet.

But there was no more thunder.

Occasionally the rain relented but then it poured again, the wind rising, the temperature dropping. The forecasters had said this would happen; apparently it's even worse in the mountains. Storm after storm, they said, and they were right.

Walking into Portogruaro was a thoroughly miserable experience on narrow roads without pavements in the teeming rain. Then the town centre arrived and - it was lovely!

The centre is ancient and elegant, studded with cloisters and discreet, classy shops. It centres round an enormous, leaning clock tower. At busy times the town must be full of tourists. I had a quick gander then went to bed and watched BBC World and ate chocolate. It was that sort of day.

Accidentally I negotiated my hotel price to an acceptable level. I have done this before, always accidentally. Baulking at the asking price I asked if they could guide me to a cheaper hotel. They immediately offered a price that was twenty euros lower. Some people negotiate like this all the time but I haven't got the nerve.

As darkness fell, thunder rolled back again. Clothes are drying all over the room. I do hope tomorrow is different.

Day 56
Portogruaro to San Giorgio

It didn't rain.

Over to the left, the mountains ranged against the skyline, one long enormous barrier of rock. As the day went on, blue sky seeped through on the other side of these mountains; Austria stood in sunshine. Then, in the afternoon, the clouds slid back southwards and the tops of the mountains themselves, full of new snow, glowed in the sunlight: a beautiful sight. At the end of the day, clear skies reached everywhere. The night will be cold.

Water stands everywhere today. The rivers and dykes are bursting from the mountains to the sea. At some time this land must have been reclaimed and a series of conduits constructed, as in the fens or the Netherlands. That was about the only interesting thing to say about today.

To while away the boredom I spent a long time thinking about other boring places where I had walked. Unfortunately they are too boring to write about (except to say that Illinois will undoubtedly always be the tops).

Across the whole of the north of Italy, road signs have been written in two languages. At first it was Italian and German, now it is Italian and the local dialect, which looks Slavic. But which Slavic? I am embarrassed to say that I thought Italy had a border with Croatia; it came as a surprise to find that

Slovenia came in between. What language do they speak in Slovenia? Once, we just took a Serbo-Croat phrasebook and muddled along. Now, Serb and Croat are not to be mixed up on pain of death. And which is Slovenian closer to? It's all so difficult.

One language it doesn't seem worth learning now is Italian. Sorry, but I'm leaving in a couple of days and I intend never coming back here or anywhere else. It really has been that sort of day, or perhaps that sort of week. I want to go home. I'm never leaving the country again. I've had enough.

I did about twenty miles through Latisana to San Giorgio, then what seemed another twenty miles round San Giorgio looking for accommodation. There wasn't any. It was all full, as a super-cool jerk at the main hotel told me. I caught the train to Monfalcone and had almost as much trouble there. It's not even half term until next week so what's going on? I will go back to San Giorgio in the morning.

Two things in my life I have clearly and definitively been wrong about. The first is non-fiction. I used to think non-fiction was the last refuge of the scoundrel but I now find that I can enjoy a biography quite a lot, even when it's not about cricket. The second is white wine. I can enjoy that too and I reflected on it tonight.

DAY 57
SAN GIORGIO TO MONFALCONE

In desperation I bought a *Daily Telegraph*.

I don't think I've ever bought a *Telegraph* before, for obvious reasons. I do draw the line at a Murdoch paper or the Mail but I thought the *Telegraph* might be a sort of civilised conservatism, read by (possibly even written by) decent old chaps with a feeling for the people.

How wrong I was.

For entertainment value the letters page alone is worth the price of the paper. I had thought that the mock-*Telegraph* letters in *Private Eye* were a raw pastiche. In fact they are a faithful copy. Straight from the 1950s, they bring on an overwhelming nostalgia.

'Sir,

Pshaw! Disgusted! The youth of today! And the trade unions! And women!

Can nothing be done?
I remain, sir, your obedient servant,
    I. Disgusted (ret)
    Tunbridge Wells.'

I paraphrase very slightly.

The obituary page is a few weeks out of date. You can imagine the obits editor at work at his desk:

'I say, Radders! Old Johnno's pipped it, don't you know? Ask old Binkie to run up a column or two. Send him a bottle of port, that ought to do the trick.'

They run obituaries of obscure officials whom no other paper has heard of, officers who fought at the battle of Bull Run or Omdurman, Brigadier Aspic, Lord Valium of Valium, who later became our representative in Minsk and was inevitably a cousin of the queen mother. You can picture the scene on the grouse moors, opening the paper while seated on a shooting stick, muttering 'dear dear, old Aspic's bought it at last, must get Florrie to send Gertie a card or a dog or something.'

Mind you, the *Guardian* veers as far in the opposite direction. Favourite obituaries include the fourth backing singer of a free jazz bluegrass combo from Zanesville, Ohio, whom Richard Williams once saw perform a fifteen-minute set in Palooka, Tennessee in 1964.

(Incidentally there really is a place called Zanesville, Ohio. I spent a night there once. It's named after Zane Grey. Or he's named after it, one or the other…)

I'm really struggling with this dense six hundred-page book about drug users in Baltimore. I can list very briefly the big books that justify their bigness:

1. Leo Tolstoy, *War and Peace*;
2. Paul Scott, *The Raj Quartet*;
3. Harry Thompson, *This Thing of Darkness*.

Even Vikram Seth's *A Suitable Boy*, a very good book, is two hundred pages too long. The Bible would be a lot better if it was two hundred and fifty pages; there is a lot of repetition (four gospels, for example). Notice how all the big books are written by men? Women haven't got the time.

Trying to find a clever short cut into Cervignano, I fell into a ditch. Trying to find a clever short cut out of Cervignano, I walked a couple of extra kilometres. The town itself was pleasant enough. The road ran past Trieste airport. Oh, how tempting to escape from all this! On a cloudless day, with white clad mountains in the background, it was indeed a beautiful day for a flight.

Monfalcone is a historic place, mostly destroyed in the First World War. Its fortress at the top, nearly two thousand years old, was originally called Verruca Montis Falconis. Not to be confused with *verruca plantaris*.

DAY 58
MONFALCONE TO TRIESTE

The sea! The sea! I forget who said it first, some old Greek. Thalassa! Thalassa!

Trieste is a very nice place, curled around the bay, a natural harbour and stopping place for centuries of traders and travellers and full of fine old houses. Its acquisition by Italy has been relatively recent. Mind you, Italy itself hasn't been going all that long.

I have been here a couple of times before. The first time I was on the way back from somewhere or other and thought I ought to have a look round for a couple of days. The second time I was with Howard (the other one, not structuralist Howard) who had walked with me in the Dolomites and then rejoined me here. He was full of beans because someone had told him he looked like a Phoenician.

At the time Howard and I had a book crisis because we were down to the shared phrasebook, having both read everything else. Howard then found a copy of *The Island* by Aldous Huxley, a totally unreadable tome which I at least struggled to complete. I remember a time when, all round the Med, second-hand bookshops were filled with the legacy of pre-war British travellers, well heeled and comfortable and leisurely. In Egypt you could feed on Dornford Yates, Sapper and Captain Marryat, writers whom no one today has ever heard of.

Round here, they have an annoying habit of marking distances on the signposts to the edge of towns rather than the middle. Trieste was much further than the signs indicated and I was pooped on arrival. It didn't help that I followed a sign to Sistiana Mare, thinking that if it was Mare there was bound to be a coast road. Sistiana was very pretty but it was a long walk down and a long walk back up again.

After Sistiana, however, a coast road did indeed branch away, and very lovely it was. The sea was blue, so was the sky, villas sat along the coastline and ships stood out to sea… Following the mountain scenery in the Dolomites, it ought to be considered a privilege to walk this way.

Slowly, slowly the body is improving, which helps. The blisters have reduced. The joints are easing. In the right foot a couple of bones hurt. When I was about nineteen I sustained a march fracture; now it would probably be called a stress fracture. I broke it through over-training, skipping repetitively on the concrete outside our back door. For a time the doctors didn't diagnose it because at exactly the same time I got a carbuncle. (Don't ever get a carbuncle. Very, very painful. And when they lance it…) Occasionally I have wondered why I haven't had any more march fractures.

At different times two male motorists stopped their cars to make phone calls. For female motorists, however, it appears to be obligatory to drive and make phone calls at the same time. (Sexist comment of the day.)

My trousers are starting to itch, which I take to be a sign that they need a wash. Since I have only the one pair, I hope they can dry out overnight.

Slovenia tomorrow. New map, new phrasebook.

I needed to buy a spoon. The smallest number I could buy was twenty-five, but fortunately they're plastic so not very heavy.

SLOVENIA

DAY 59
TRIESTE TO KOZINA

Trieste is indeed beautiful; I didn't give it enough credit yesterday. Magnificent, stately buildings and elegant squares, backed by government institutions, fringe the waterside all along the bay. You could spend a holiday here. I stayed longer than intended, first searching for the tourist information office, never an easy task, and then meeting the rudest, most unhelpful tourist person in the whole of Italy.

No, she didn't have any of the information I wanted. 'I don't live here,' she said. Perhaps, I thought, they should find someone who did.

I took a big road in what seemed the right direction and, through good fortune rather than assistance from the tourist office, it turned out to be the right choice. From the city the road made a long climb, the hardest since I had my heart fixed. That was my excuse for finishing at three o'clock. By that time I was in Slovenia.

Slovenia had a big, bold border post. It did not, however, appear to have any border guards. Oh yes, there was one in the distance. No one took any notice of me or anyone else.

I have only been turned back from one border, Czechoslovakia in 1969. Howard and I were trying to get in there for the first anniversary of the revolution but the border officials took a dusty view of our trip. (Howard decided to speak Russian to them, which didn't help.) All the old Iron Curtain countries were grim to get into in those days, even Yugoslavia. The present state of affairs, however, is rather pathetic at the opposite end of the spectrum. Can't they be just a little bit hostile?

On the connected subject of *War and Peace,* mentioned above, I was reading it while travelling back from a weekend in Paris and had it in my hand at the customs post. In those days British customs officers tried to prevent smuggling and, like many others, I was stopped at the counter.

'Excuse me, sir,' said the man.

'Me?'

'Good book, isn't it?'

'Well, yes.' I was sweating slightly because I had exceeded, by a millilitre, the alcohol limit.

All it seemed he wanted to discuss was *War and Peace* so we talked about it for a couple of minutes. Then he said: 'Just have a look, shall we?'

I opened up. He wasn't in the least interested in my surplus of alcohol. We went back to discussing *War and Peace* until he went on to the next traveller.

Climbing up to the border was hot and sweaty. In an effort to look more respectable I took off my sunglasses and yellow hat; as I said to someone in a letter the other day, I looked like a gangster auditioning for a circus. The road rose into thickly wooded hills. All the traffic was running between Trieste in Italy and Rijeka in Croatia; Slovenia was merely the filling in the sandwich. Incidentally, I still don't know what language they speak here; perhaps I never will.

On the edge of Kozina stands a monstrosity, a vast new hotel and casino complex designed to bring gamblers to the province. I have never understood the appeal. The whole concept of Las Vegas is environmentally abhorrent, a city in the desert where no city should be. Reno, however, in northern Nevada, is a natural town that has always been there. Hotels and food are very cheap as they try to lure in the punters. I was lured, stayed in the hotels and ate the food but had to put a quarter in a slot machine, just to say I'd done it. I didn't win. The intriguing question, though, was why many, many people would drive two hundred miles from another state just to play the slot machines in Nevada. Something wrong with them?

A severe woman rented me a room in Kozina and assured me that nowhere in town could I buy a breakfast. Her room was spotlessly clean and, like her, very severe.

CROATIA

Day 60
Kozina to Sapjane

At last I was stopped by the police!

It was quite nostalgic. We didn't do the hands-on-the-car routine and in fact they never got out of their motor, but they did do the equivalent of the US Hi-How-Ya-Doin'-Ya-Got-Identification routine. In Slovenia it is *Dobar Dan* (Good Day) Can I See Your Documents? The main man spoke English, made a radio call to check that I was clean and then gave me the all clear. He asked what I was doing so I gave him the gist of it.

'Just for fun?' he asked.

Well, that was a good question.

At the border, the young woman official had more piercing questions; before she would let me into Croatia she wanted to see proof that I had money. This hasn't happened to me since I first contracted grey hair. I hope she was impressed with my Nationwide Building Society debit card.

Speaking of Nationwide…

For many years the Nationwide has been lucky enough to handle my money. I think the directors pay themselves ludicrous sums of money out of our savings and I think they rig the elections, but the society is still a mutual and it hasn't done most of the stupid things the other banks have done in the last few years. Furthermore, until now there has been one important perk for belonging to the Nationwide; they didn't charge you for using your bank card abroad.

Until now…

After the end of October, i.e. tomorrow, Nationwide will start charging its customers for use of the bank card abroad. This will cost me and everyone else quite a lot of money. In 'exchange', so they say, you can get free travel insurance if you have a certain amount of money entering your account each month. Well, this fair exchange is robbery. I don't have that much entering my account each month and I haven't got insurance anyway. Finally, I'm damn sure they wouldn't give me free insurance for the present venture.

For November, therefore, I have been trying to stockpile cash. First, though, I need to find out how much the Croatian currency is worth. Do I need to take out ten *kune* or a million?

Outside Kozina, a group of very cheery firefighters stood outside the fire station. They were preparing for a Saturday outing to the country or the seaside, which they quite clearly intended to enjoy. They were a fit looking bunch, men and women; nowadays everyone fancies firefighters, the modern equivalent of miners, active, physical and probably political into the bargain.

The mother of my friend Odile lived in old age in a supported flat in Paris. Round her neck she wore an alarm which unfortunately she was always setting off when she was asleep. In Paris these alarms are connected to the fire services; in this case the fire station was just across the street, so when the old lady's alarm went off they would pop over.

The firefighters would ring the doorbell but she never heard it so, using their key, they let themselves in. They called out but still she didn't hear them so they went upstairs and knocked on her bedroom door. Finally, gaining no answer, they would go in and Odile's mother would wake to find several hunky firefighters standing round her bed. Everyone seemed quite happy with this arrangement. Indeed a number of my female acquaintances have said that it would suit them quite well too.

I decided it was no use trying to do without caffeine altogether; in fact I would try to get as much tea as possible, regardless of caffeine. That was the idea, anyway. In reality, round here they give you fruit tea. That's what tea is, fruit tea of one sort or another. Yuck.

At one time I could order tea, two fried eggs and two chapattis please in Swahili. In fact I still can, although I don't have much call for it any more.

It turns out that there is indeed a Slovenian language, similar to Croat. Patrick Leigh Fermor would, of course, have mastered it by now; twenty-four hours ought to be enough for anyone. I did manage please and thank you before it was time to leave.

The road ran up and up through pastures and wooded hills towards the border with Croatia. In the morning the fields were blanketed by frost. Over to the right, rain shrouded the higher hills. From the border the road ran down more steeply into Croatia. Tomorrow it's back to sea level again.

Tonight the clocks go back. Until now I have remained on British time, one hour behind the continent. I like to think I do this to keep me in touch with home, but actually the reason is that I can't move the dial on my watch. Now it will be right. The change of time does mean, though, that it is going to get dark early and I will need to find accommodation by five o'clock.

I hate it when the clocks go back. It's dark, it's mean and winter is coming in. Roll on April, the happiest month of the year. Five months to go.

DAY 61
SAPJANE TO RIJEKA

At eight o'clock on Sunday morning, Radio Istra was playing what all radio stations play at this time of the week, when everyone is asleep: the stuff that no-one listens to but they've got to play. At home, Radio Norfolk does Christianity, lacing it with that insufferably jolly God Rock. Radio Istra plays traditional folk/country local stuff. The rest of the day they play western rock.

I detest country music. People always say 'oh, but you should listen to the real stuff' and cite Steve Earle, Hank Williams and Woody Guthrie. That may be all very well but that's not what they play on the radio. Walk into a diner in Kansas and hear about the boy who's got one leg and whose daddy (a trucker) got killed on the road and whose mom is an alcoholic with eighteen chill'n and a dog. One thing you learn on walking across the US is that there's a thin strip down the east coast and a thin strip down the west coast - and the rest listens to country music.

I wrote a country music song once:

> Muh pillows 're empty, muh sheets've gone gray,
> The bed ain't bin made since muh wife wen' away,
> The coyote's howlin', the river's run dry,
> The world's doggone mis'ble and so, Lord, 'm I
>
> Uh'm tryin' t' bring up muh six fav'rit sons,
> The rest 're fuh sale with muh six fav'rit guns,
> Uh'm spendin' muh life jus' t' get stuff fuh fryin'
> When most 'f the famly 're crippled or dyin'

There are another twenty-six verses.

Not to be outdone by their Slovenian colleagues, the Croatian police stopped me within a hundred metres of setting off in the morning. Same process.

It rained all morning. Nothing much else happened. The hills came down to the sea and the road slid into Rijeka: past the spectacular football stadium on the sea shore, past the docks, past the railway station where the destination boards read Ljubljana and Vienna and into the city centre. I had a quick cultural tour and bought a very good bag of chips. They were advertised as Belgian chips. Nothing could ever surpass the chips I had on the main square in Antwerp but these were a good effort.

For the next couple of weeks it should be hard to get lost. Keep the sea on the right. If the sea is on the left - or straight ahead - I'm going the wrong way.

DAY 62
RIJEKA TO CRIKVENICA

It was a day of three halves.

The first half was a grumpy one, due to lack of sleep. How does anyone sleep under these duvets? They swamp you, they don't stay in place, your feet stick out and get cold but the rest of you is just too damn hot. A chap needs sheets and blankets.

I ploughed out of Rijeka in the rain, past more docks and oil refineries and up the hill. Uphill? This was supposed to be a 350-mile promenade along the seashore. In reality it was up and down - and up and down - big long hills, up away from the sea and then back down to it again.

It's 350 miles to Dubrovnik. Who on earth would want to walk 350 miles along the coast to Dubrovnik? Why? Because it's there? Oh, for goodness' sake.

Oh, and there's another thing. The map showed the new motorway as being constructed or under construction all down the coast, taking all the traffic away from the old road along the sea. By this time, you might think, the whole road would have been constructed. Not a bit of it. Nothing more seemed to have been finished since the map was made. A couple of hours out of Rijeka the motorway ended and all the traffic came back down. I spent the afternoon flattening myself against a wall or a rock face.

Every village seemed to be a port, often very attractive. At the end of a huge inlet it transpired that tea is now called *chai* (*caj*); from here to India it is some variation or other of the word. Up the hill again, I ate a sandwich amongst the daytime drinkers, of whom there seem to be a number; in Rijeka some of them rooted for food in wheelie bins. Jobs are not available for everyone in Croatia.

The second half of the day was different. It was shirtsleeve weather in the sunshine and the country showed its colours. Peninsulas went this way, islands went that way and bridges ran in between. I found that I was quite enjoying myself. (Must put a stop to that.) This, I thought, was better than being in an office in London. Then I remembered that I left the office in London eight years ago. It must be better than something.

The afternoon brought good headway and Crikvenica arrived in comfortable time. There it was: sea front, cafés, restaurants and couples strolling arm in arm along the bay. This would be a restful place to spend the third half of the day. But then there was nowhere to stay.

Crikvenica is a big place but everything had closed for the season. I saw a good deal of Crikvenica as I walked round for an hour finding everything shut against me. Eventually I asked a waiter - an extremely well educated waiter - if he knew anywhere. He sent me to one hotel. Closed. He sent me to another. Closed. He said this was no good, he would drive me to one himself. Then he asked a friend to do it. On the way the friend, who had a degree in American Studies and a good job with a pipeline company, said they had just been discussing the dire financial situation in Crikvenica this winter. For the first time, all the hotels are closing, jobs have disappeared and there is nothing to do. The cause, they say, is a lack of investment over the last twenty years.

DAY 63
CRIKVENICA TO SENJ

Twenty-six years ago I walked into Senj, bought some food and was putting it in my bag when I was approached by a young German woman. I was the only other person in Senj with a rucksack and she wondered if we could have a chat.

We went for a coffee and I found out about the wondrous Dorothe.

She had no money. Well, not exactly no money; she had about a fiver with her. She didn't seem to need money, however, because people gave her things. She had hitched from Germany. Recently she had worked with a farmer for a few days picking grapes in exchange for meals. She stayed where she could. Sometimes people gave her accommodation, otherwise she slept in her tent. She said she was inconspicuous because her tent was green. I didn't point out that all the surrounding land was brown.

I asked her what items she had bought since leaving Germany but she struggled to think of anything at all. She had been given a cabbage and she was carrying some German army margarine that her brother had given her. She seemed to think that all the food she was subsequently given had fitted in with one or the other.

Concerned for her welfare (yes, it's true) I told her where I expected to be on each of the next four nights and told her she could share my room if she wanted. Then I recommended walking and she went off hitching. That night, she was waiting at the junction for the village where I intended to stay the night.

We climbed down from the main road to the seashore and it turned out to be lucky she was there. In those days many of the middle-aged people spoke German, for reasons they would rather forget. They explained that the licences for letting rooms in the summer had expired and that the government inspector might come at seven in the morning to check. If we could leave before then, we could stay.

We were gone before seven but neither the government inspector nor anyone else visited the village that day. The Bora struck.

It was extraordinary. The road back to the main thoroughfare was two kilometres long and it took an hour; it was all we could do to fight our way up at all. The Bora blows from land to sea and strikes only at this time of year. It howled down from the mountains and throughout the day I was blown from one side of the road to the other. No-one came out. I saw four cars all day and one of them picked up the windswept Dorothe.

Two or three days later she appeared again on a corner, having fixed accommodation for us in a camp ground. After that we parted but exchanged details; later I visited her in Germany and she came to England. Subsequently she married an Indonesian and had children. They would be grown up by now but I have lost touch with Dorothe.

According to tonight's weather forecast, something like the Bora might happen again tomorrow. Nothing like Dorothe will happen again, though.

The only other occasion that I can remember doing anything so importunate was at the airport in Delhi. Confirming my flight home the next day, I met an English woman also checking in but continually having to rush to the lavatory. She had been in India working for a few weeks, had been perfectly well for most of them but was considerably ill on departure.

I bought her a black tea to see if that would help. She tasted it and fled to the lavatory again with her hand clapped over her mouth.

Our flight left very early the next morning and I said I was off to get a hotel a short distance from the airport. Would she like to come too? She agreed.

We took a taxi to a hotel about a mile away but the hotel had only one room. She sat in the taxi and I came out and explained this to her. She wasn't bothered. I said I would go and look at the room and report back. I did so but returned rather embarrassed. The room had only one bed. She wasn't bothered about that either. She was far beyond caring.

We were there for only a few hours. Needless to say, absolutely nothing happened between us. Apart from any other considerations, the slightest move on my part would have made her instantly sick. (I have this effect on women.) Next day, her husband met her at Heathrow and I never saw her again.

At the end of all that, Senj is a pretty place where busloads of tourists disgorge and take pictures. It even has a castle.

Day 64
Senj to Stanica

Actually, Stanica to Senj rather than Senj to Stanica.

I still maintain that it doesn't matter which direction you do it in, as long as you do it. Since I had somewhere settled to stay in Senj but Stanica was uncertain, I caught the bus out there and walked back; tomorrow I will catch the bus back to Stanica and continue from there. It was nearly forty kilometres (plus detours), but without a full backpack it's easy.

Over breakfast I met a Swiss man, returning home from six weeks in Sudan. He said it was 47 degrees there and he couldn't get any alcohol. In Wadi Halfa it hadn't rained for forty years. I've been to Wadi Halfa, which stands at the end of Lake Nasser behind the Aswan dam. (The original Wadi Halfa was submerged by the lake.) Apparently the boat from Aswan to Wadi Halfa is more modern now. When I took it, three boats were strapped together; only the engine in the middle one worked. It was the dirtiest journey of my life, lasting two days which seemed like two decades.

From Senj the motorway begins again, which was just as well as the old road was often stuck between a rock face and a precipice: occasionally it was a precipice on both sides. The coastline here is not, it has to be said, very pretty. Rugged, perhaps, but not pretty. Most of it consists of tumbling rock and scrubby trees. The islands, not far away, appear to be just huge lumps of rock. Rab, which my bus was continuing to, has apparently been a tourist spot for 120 years but it is hard to see why. They must come for the sea. Actually, when the sun came out the blue green lapping sea looked rather charming. That's it then. Enough scenery.

In the morning I amused myself by picking an all time Norwich City first eleven. Only one recent player got in for sure: Darren Huckerby. Possibly Gary Holt. Dion Dublin? Past his best when he came back to us but still a great man. Number one, of course, *numero uno*, is the great Martin Peters. Phil Boyer, Ted Macdougall, Dave Watson, Steve Bruce, Ron Davies, Barry Butler, Craig Bellamy, Mark Bowen, Dave Stringer, Duncan Forbes, Justin Fashanu, Kevin Keelan in goal... The hardest man ever seen in Norwich, or anywhere else, was Trevor Hockey. He played a handful of games for us, saved our season and left most of us still shaking thirty years later.

Would there be a place for Terry Allcock? Now the grand old man of former Norwich players, Terry was a hero in his time and a very, very nice bloke. At one time he coached me at cricket. When he retired from football he became a funeral director. I wonder if he told his funeral customers the same filthy jokes he told us teenage cricketers.

The waitress last night originated in Bosnia. During the war her family went to Germany, where she learned German and English. When they returned after the war they found their home was not there any more. Nor was their previous life. They settled in Croatia where she said they were happy. Most of the people here have had such eventful, and tragic, lives: all of them much harder than mine or most other people's.

DAY 65
STANICA TO KARLOBAG

I finished that bloody book! Six hundred pages about drug users in Baltimore! Every page took ages to read. It was a good book but it would have been five times as good if it had been one fifth the length. I've got a nice little number by Alice Hoffman in my bag which I shall look forward to.

I left the book for whoever wanted it. I hate giving books away. Once I sold four hundred of my parents' paperbacks to make space but I regretted it ever afterward. Some people give books away with ease to charity shops; they've finished them so they don't want them. Books turn up in surprising places. The Red Lodge twenty-four hour transport café, near Newmarket, has a charity book exchange with remarkable stuff in it. Many lorry drivers obviously don't mind giving away their classics.

Some people, of course, have the opposite problem. We all know people who collect old telephone books, and indeed telephones, or newspapers or magazines. I can't throw away letters. One of my colleagues never gave back case files. We don't like to let go of the past, even if it's just contained in a telephone directory. The past was good and we want to hold on to it.

Today was hot. By eleven o'clock the chocolate in my pocket had melted. I happened upon a little café where a cheery woman ripped me off royally for a pint of Fanta. The roads were empty: except, of course, for the police. They checked me out once more, three of them this time. Presumably they keep a record centrally of all the times an officer rings to check someone out; in this case they must be plotting my progress along the coastline.

Karlobag is a terrible name but a pretty spot which turned up sooner than expected. I sat and ate an iced lolly and looked at the sea. Then I found a cheap place to stay where the TV doesn't work and the water is cold.

Incidentally, somewhere in my belongings I have a hard boiled egg. You wouldn't think a hard boiled egg would be hard to find but I have definitely misplaced it.

It turns out that under the Habsburgs the first language of Croatia was Latin. It also transpires that Croatia has applied to join the EU but that they will not be allowed in until they do something about the Mafia. Can this be true?

Thinking of books, and where I keep them, made me decide where I want to spend Christmas: assuming I'm home by then. I want to be alone in the village at home. Curmudgeonly? I don't think so. I might go down to The Stag at lunchtime and then go to sleep. (I'm hopeless if I drink at lunchtime.) I might make myself a nut roast in the evening. I can read a book. That doesn't sound like a sad way to spend Christmas. It sounds great.

DAY 66
KARLOBAG TO TRIBANJ (OR NOT)

It was too far, forty-three kilometres, to walk to the next accommodation. I was therefore intending to catch the bus to Tribanj, thirty kilometres away, then take the bus back to Karlobag and return by bus in the morning.

The 9.30 bus didn't come. Or perhaps it was the 9.45 bus, everybody and all the timetables had a different opinion. Either way, it didn't come.

The tourist office had various bits of information, most of it conflicting with other bits of information. What was now clear, however, was that it was impossible to complete any of my proposed plans in daylight.

So I did something so embarrassing that I can hardly write it down.

The map said that fourteen kilometres from Karlobag was a large hamlet called Lukovo Sugarje. I would therefore walk from Karlobag to one kilometre beyond the hamlet and then walk back again. This would be thirty kilometres and I would count it as having walked to Tribanj and skip the second fifteen kilometres.

How warped. It really means you haven't actually walked all the way. I did this for one kilometre in Alsace but this is fifteen kilometres. It's embarrassing and shameful.

In my defence (although I wouldn't defend myself), it could be said that it was impossible to tell the difference between one bit of coastline and another. I could walk it twenty times and not know the difference. Rocks, sea, inlets,

boats. More rocks. More sea. Lots more.

So I walked to Lukovo Sugarje and then resolutely walked one kilometre beyond it. Then I walked back to Karlobag. Thirty kilometres, which will count as having walked to Tribanj. On the way back I noticed the kilometre stones, which never lie. In fact I walked at least an extra kilometre in each direction. This will be my punishment.

I know I've walked the full distance but I also know that I haven't really walked every step of the route. Should I tell anyone?

It was dark when I got back to Karlobag and I was just as tired as if I had walked to Tribanj. It's tiring walking round here. Flat bit, then climb up, then climb down again. On the way back, up a climb, down a climb then flat bit.

Let's hope the bus comes tomorrow.

I met a young German man once waiting for a bus by the Dead Sea. I asked him what he thought his chances were. 'If it don't come, it don't come,' he said. 'If it come, it make me very happy.' It's a worthy philosophy but not one that is always easy to adopt.

Once in Canada I came across hitchhikers somewhere on Lake Superior: Sault Ste. Marie, I think. It was alleged to be the worst place in the whole of Canada for hitching. The hitchers all stayed in the youth hostel in town. In the morning they went out to the highway. In the evening, unsuccessful, they came back to the youth hostel. The record wait was said to be a fortnight.

But there were worse panic stations today than the non-appearance of the bus. I've run out of books! That nice little number by Alice Hoffman turns out to be something I've read before. Within half a page I remembered it. Shall I read it again? Not if I can help it. Apart from the Hoffman, though, I have only got the phrasebook and a pamphlet of excerpts from the work of Edith Durham, a traveller in Albania a hundred years ago. Unfortunately that won't last long. I might get something in Zadar in a couple of days but it will be Sunday. From the map, the airport at Split looks close to the road and I should get something there, at least a newspaper, but it's seven days away. Help!

By the side of the road, wire mesh prevents rocks from falling on me and others. I'm never sure whether to be reassured at this defence or alarmed that it's necessary. Anyway, as I sat down for a drink today I managed to tear my jacket on the end of the mesh. Damn. My trousers have already been torn by brambles so I'm looking a bit torn.

In the late autumn sunshine, plentiful bees are making the last honey of the year. By the road, big blue or black beetles and endless flying grasshoppers scurry. I haven't seen lizards for a few days but several small dead snakes lie around. Noisiest of all the animals, though, are the bloody dogs that bark at me everywhere I go.

Day 67
Tribanj to Starigrad (Hardly Worth Doing)

Well, the bus that didn't come yesterday didn't come again today. All official opinion was that it would come. When it didn't, I couldn't get to Tribanj in time to cover any sensible distance. The following bus dropped me at Tribanj at 12.30. Ten miles was all that was feasible to do, so I'll have to make up for it tomorrow.

In fact the bus driver had never heard of Tribanj but it turned out there were three of them! Each had a different suffix. I chose the first one and wandered along to Starigrad.

I found that boiled egg!

In a layby, minding their own business, I came across a couple from Herne Bay and their dog, Buster. In their 25-year-old camper van they had been travelling for four months, via the North Cape, St. Petersburg, Ukraine, Montenegro and all points east. In Finland the van needed new bearings. In Russia it was the starter motor. Recently a door fell off; it is currently wedged on. They are very slowly making their way home.

The couple's children, now adult, of course think they have lost their bearings in more way than one. I said they might have a point. These days it's a funny role reversal. We used to go away for months, the only means of communication the occasional postcard; it's hard to know how our parents could stand it. Now the parents go away and their solid, reliable children await their text, blog or email, convinced they are wild and irresponsible.

A short day has one benefit. I've got a bit of the bum trouble that is an occupational hazard for walkers. Piles would be too strong a word. Pillocks maybe. In any event, I bought some Nivea cream which I hope will do the trick. I will not be reporting further on the matter.

Tonight, in the absence of proper reading material, I made the mistake of turning to the tourist information. What I've been missing! Rijeka has one of the world's five biggest carnivals. Senj is world famous. Ahead, Sibenik's cathedral and Split's town centre are world heritage sites. Watch out for them!

DAY 68
STARIGRAD TO MURVICA

In the evening, a large party celebrated in a cavernous hotel. They had been celebrating for hours and the musicians were on their second set. Two accordions and a guitar, they were playing traditional Croatian folk. At least I hope it was traditional, I hope they don't still make it. It was good fun, anyway. All the guests knew all the words and sang along.

Apart from that, there was nothing worth writing about today.

Thinking I was still 35 years old and fit and strong, I aimed for Zadar which would have been well over 25 miles. Darkness put paid to that idea and I found a cold, depressing room. Fortunately the restaurant cheered me up.

A bridge lay across a gorge from the sea to an inland lake. It is sometimes the scene of bungee jumping. No thank you.

Moving temporarily away from the mountains and into the promontory that houses Zadar, the land becomes agricultural again. Lettuces and tomatoes are still growing, and of course the ubiquitous peppers. Then I saw something that really made me yearn for home. How are my broad beans coming on? Have they come up? Will they resist the frosts? Never mind about loved ones, home, work, football…

A boy racer nearly took my arm with him as he careered onwards. I was amazed he didn't crash. All along the road stood shrines to young men who didn't make it. One other memorial recorded avoidable deaths: a war memorial to the Croatians killed in 1992, a few of the many thousands killed in the 1990s as Yugoslavia fell apart.

Day 69
Murvica To Zadar To Biograd

The day began, or would have begun, with toast. My room contained a hot plate and it seemed a good idea to toast some bread on it. They toasted instantly and I began to eat them. After a couple of bites they began to taste funny.

I was eating the cleaning fluid they had used on the hot plate.

End of toast.

That set the tone for the day, which ended as badly as it had begun.

Nine kilometres brought Zadar. A very big detour led to the town centre; it seemed churlish not to visit the historic city so I followed it. This was the second bad decision of the day but not the last.

The old town was all right, though the Dutch do this sort of thing better. Built on moats and ramparts by the Venetians to keep off the Turks, it sticks into the sea and is full of little old streets and parks and fortifications. For breakfast I had a nice big *burek* and a cup of tea. (But not in the same establishment. Why can't their cafés sell food?) The old barracks now house the city grammar school, so at break time all the kids were eating from the same bakery as me. They looked reasonably happy about it all. I wanted to say to them: 'Make the most of it! These are the best days of your lives!' Actually I'm not sure that's true. The best days of my life were before I ever went to school.

Both the road and the countryside out of Zadar were very different from before and a lot more interesting. First came the industry: always something to look at. Then came foliage, definitely a new departure. Solid forest came right to the edge of the sea; it's not exactly Holkham, perhaps the best beach in the world, but definitely a good effort. Finally, lush gardens proliferated everywhere. The soil must be very fertile. Cabbages, lettuces, spinach and above all potatoes are still growing everywhere in November. How do they do that, without the potatoes getting the worm? Do they plant them late? Do they grow two crops in the year?

In the early afternoon I reached Sukosan. I went to the tourist office to ask about hotels between there and Biograd.

'What's the matter with our hotel?' they asked.

Nothing at all, I explained, I was sure it was excellent but I was walking through and wanted to get a bit further in the day. Biograd was too far for me but was there anything in between?

If only, if only I had taken up their suggestion and stayed in Sukosan, a lovely little place by the sea, a forest of sailing masts the first indication of the marina.

Ah, they said, Ok. There is one hotel at the first village after eight kilometres, nothing at the next one but another hotel at the third after 13 kilometres.

'Will they be open?'

'Of course they will.'

Hah! Of course they won't.

Rain fell intermittently in the morning, nothing too serious. The deluge began in the afternoon. For a fortnight, since that terrible Monday in Italy, no rain has fallen at all. To have two weeks in November without rain is extremely lucky. On the other hand, to have two Mondays like this in one year is pretty bloody unlucky.

The first hotel was shut. The second hotel was shut. Everything was shut. There was no option but to walk to Biograd. This was a big town, a tourist town, scene of a recent boat show as all the posters proclaimed. Accommodation in Biograd would be bounteous.

By the time I reached town darkness had fallen and I had walked about 25 miles, much of it in a downpour. Biograd turned out to be a lovely place and it had more hotels than you could shake a stick at. Unfortunately every single one of them was closed.

So too were most of the private rooms in town. To cut a long story short, after traipsing over most of the town several times I'm in a bungalow in a camp site. I wanted a hotel room where I could turn on the TV, dry my clothes on a heater and get into bed with a yoghourt. I didn't want a room where I had to dry the clothes in the oven, cook in the evening and make my own breakfast. The proprietor of the campsite says we are having an Italian cyclone. (Everyone always blames some other country for their bad weather.) She says there's more of the same tomorrow.

DAY 70
BIOGRAD TO VODICE

All night the wind blew. For most of the night the rain fell. Then, in the morning: no rain. In fact it didn't rain until the afternoon. At this stage it rained hard by most standards; by yesterday's standards, however, it was a gentle sprinkle. The young woman in the chemist's, seeing me dripping in front of her, told me I should carry an umbrella.

The scenery was nondescript. The road runs on a narrow strip of land between the sea and an inland lake but you can't see much of either. Outside Vodice, on top of a conical hill, stands an ugly modern building, miles from anywhere. It could be a church. It's a long climb up there to worship, but, once there, it's a short step to heaven. On the other hand it could be a quarry or a telephone station.

On advice from the young woman in the chemist's I went down to the sea. What a nice town! Old, narrow streets are broken up by wider, tree-lined avenues. The sea beats on the quayside. My hotel (yes, a hotel) welcomes bikers and offers a ten per cent discount for cash. The young man in charge went to London a few years ago to watch Hajduk Split play at Fulham. He showed me his album of photographs.

It is now eleven days since I bought a British newspaper. I'm really worried that I'm missing the obituaries and people may be dying without my knowing about it, particularly old cricketers. And what about Patrick Leigh Fermor? Is he still going? It's hard to cut oneself off from normal life.

Once on a plane I met a man who had put his entire previous life behind him at a stroke. Originally from the Caribbean, he had emigrated to Britain as a youngster around 1960. For a decade he led an active life in Britain before re-emigrating with his wife to New York in 1970 and Houston, Texas, some time after that. Professional people - a doctor and a lawyer, something like that - the couple caused a bit of a stir as black professionals in Texas in the early 1970s.

He had an encyclopaedic knowledge of West Indian cricket in the 1950s and 1960s. So have I, so we had plenty to talk about. He had also followed Arsenal during his time in Britain. However, from 1970, when he emigrated, he had neither read nor heard a single word about cricket or football; he had simply put them behind him. He had never heard of Viv Richards, Michael Holding, Brian Lara or Curtly Ambrose. When I mentioned their names he looked completely blank.

When I met him he was travelling back to London to visit a terminally ill friend. He was eager to know what had been happening at cricket and football over the last few decades. I wanted to take him to matches to show him what he had missed. It was one of those occasions when, at the end of a journey, you look at each other and wonder whether to exchange details. We did not and I subsequently regretted it. It was one of the best conversations of my life.

As well as newspapers I miss the cinema when I'm away. Like most people, I began the cinema habit with my parents. At university I knew a man who tried to see a hundred films in an eight-week term. (With double bills in those days you could see four films in a day.) It seemed a worthwhile aim for a university career but he gave up at about fifty. From time to time I have seen three or four films in a day but I have only once been to three separate performances. It was Easter Sunday 1969. I was working in a pub and we closed early at lunchtime for lack of customers. At two o'clock I went to the long lamented Academy One in Oxford Street, where I had my favourite seat (M26; it sat in a corner where I could put my feet in the aisle next to a radiator and fall asleep). At five o'clock I went to Academy Two. At eight o'clock, unable to resist the challenge, I went to Academy Three. Having spent the tube fare I had to walk home to Hammersmith.

Now I haven't been to the cinema in a month. The television often has an English-language film in the early evening, which helps; most of them have Sandra Bullock in them. Perhaps there will be something in Split or Dubrovnik.

DAY 71
VODICE-ŠIBENIK-PRIMORSKO VRPOLJE

At five in the morning the wind was blasting against the tree tops, the waves pounding the shore line. At lunchtime I was sitting in the sun sipping tea.

Funny old world.

The ancient town of Šibenik hove into view across a massive bridge. Fortunately the bridge was being resurfaced, with traffic restrictions, so I didn't have to walk close to the edge. After a few more bends and some unpromising suburbs, there was Šibenik: castle, cathedral and a lot of cool-looking people.

I didn't trouble with the castle but thought I should give a look to the World Heritage cathedral. The outside was lovely, the interior a gloomy let-down; to be honest, it could do with a bit of a clean. Around it stood a collection of old buildings with little streets and steps leading from one level to another. Below them was the sea frontage lined with cafés and lots of people all leading better lives than mine.

That's the way it seems, anyway. They sip their drinks, push back their shades and gaze along the promenade, all of them fitting into categories that seem to escape the rest of us: cool young things, suave young men about town or successful parent with happy partner and children. Oh well. Maybe they're very unhappy really.

On the map a train line led into the hills, perhaps on a short cut beside the old road to Split which would cut a day off the journey. The short cut is too far to do in a day but could I walk some of the way, take the train back and carry on from there tomorrow? I made enquiries. Yes, I could. In fact I could take the train out and walk back. So I did. Primorsko Vrpolje wasn't even on the map but it was on the train ticket. It worked out well.

At last I bought a book! I could have bought a hundred, though most of them would have been science fantasy which doesn't count. In the event I was tempted by a Harlan Coben but was finally split between Peter Carey and Anita Shreve. Both are very good writers but the Shreve was lighter (literally). I took it to a bar and read fifty pages, the best hour of the journey so far. Then I read another fifty pages. At this rate it will barely last until Split.

One of the characters in the book drank something called a rusty nail (Scotch and Drambuie). This is the first mention I have seen of a rusty nail since I used to serve them to Judy Garland's last husband in the pub opposite the Ritz in the late 1960s. Judy Garland used to book into the Ritz under a false name because the trouble she caused had led to her being banned. The last husband, whose name I forget, was brought to the pub by a bevy of journalists looking for a story. They bought him rusty nails but he didn't talk. They bought him more rusty nails but he still didn't talk.

All along the road today, elderly couples were gathering olives. Surely the world cannot consume all the olives it produces? What does a raw olive taste like, anyway? I picked one from a tree and tasted it. Yuck!

DAY 72
VRPOLJE TO TROGIR

Just a few notes and then I must get back to my book.

Walking through the hills was very pleasant; at times, the stone walls and rugged banks made it look like the north of England. A shepherdess (is one still allowed to say shepherdess?) exchanged cheery greetings; her sheep were so obedient to her that we both laughed. Four schoolgirls ran up to the school wall to call 'goodbye' and 'I speak English' as I went past. A shower caused me to sit in a bus shelter on a plastic chair with three legs.

At least, it looked like only a shower. (Famous last words - Noah probably said much the same.) I waited - and waited - for it to stop, then thought I'd better set out anyway. Then the thunder started.

Fine weather was forecast all day. That was probably down on the coast, not up in the hills. To the right, a big ridge held thunder clouds for hours, intermittently scaring the wits out of me. In a café I stopped for a cup of tea, but the future could not be postponed. Up and up went the road; it never seemed to go down. Surely we had to come down to sea level some time?

Over the crest of the last hill a spectacular view unfolded below.

Far, far down there lay Trogir, many hundreds of feet below. A flotilla of islands spread into the sea, which itself was calm and serene. The sun was sinking. Far away to the left lay Split, the destination for tomorrow. Round and round a long series of hairpin bends the road comes down to eventual sea level again. It was miles and miles and it was dark by the time I reached Trogir.

Now back to the book.

Later. Trogir in fact is a special place and ought to have a proper mention. A spread of alleys holds a variety of bijou shops and restaurants, very ancient and exclusive. The alleys lead down to the bay, fronted by battlements and more elderly buildings. A clutch of expensive four-star hotels suggest that this is the place to come for your holidays or at least a dirty weekend. There must be a history. I ought to know about it.

Tonight I counted the heart pills. I seem to have 32 days' supply left. Shouldn't I have about a week longer than that? Did I miscount in the first place or could there be more, hidden somewhere in my bag?

DAY 73
TROGIR TO SPLIT

Split is half way between the Brenner Pass and Istanbul, that's my assumption. There is no mathematical or geographical basis for this assumption and I can't even remember what the map of Europe looks like but it seems a good concept. Is it half way? Does it matter?

This afternoon my knee started to hurt for the first time. In addition, one of the middle toes is a nasty sight. (Blood in the sock never looks pretty.) I ache all over. The day after tomorrow, Sunday, is planned as a day off. Perhaps I'll take half a day off tomorrow as well and another half day on Monday. We'll see how the knee is. I don't really want to delay too much: winter is coming and I want to be ahead of it. On the other hand, I'm knackered. Sometimes this morning I seemed to be barely moving.

Walking into Split was frustrating. From the start, parts of the city could be seen in the distance; then suddenly they were there, just across the bay. They were there but they weren't there; it was miles to walk round the end of the water. After that it was a matter of finding the middle of the city, not as easy as it sounds. The endless suburbs are hideous; this must be the fastest growing city in Europe, a thronging density of high-rise blocks. The signs for the centre led one way. They expired. I kept walking the way they had pointed but walked much too far. A woman was swimming in the sea. Eventually I made my way back to the large semi-circle of the old city. I went into Diocletian's Palace. Very nice. Who was Diocletian?

I finished the Anita Shreve and, in a book exchange, picked up a copy of *The Reader*. I enjoyed the film (not just because Kate Winslet takes her clothes off) but haven't read the book. It's infuriating when you ask people if they have read a book and they say 'But I've seen the film!', so I need to rectify this.

Half the world is on holiday in Split, either for the weekend or for a late break. The hotels, bars, shops and restaurants are all busy. It's a handsome town which was established many centuries back. I'll leave out the tourist information. It's a nice place to sit beside the sea. Its promenade makes you wonder why you should move on.

DAY 74
SPLIT TO DUGI RAT

A man sitting at a bus stop asked me if I wanted a woman. I thanked him but declined. He asked if I wanted a man. I thanked him again but said I didn't want one of them either. He said: 'I want a woman every day!' I said I was too tired.

Walking out through the suburbs of Split was no more fun than walking in, but by the end of the day the scenery was lovely. The road wound up into the traffic then wound back again to the sea. The sun shone. Coves and inlets and harbours brought boats of all sizes. Beaches studded the afternoon. Houses spilled up into the hills and down to the shore: all of them new houses, built in the last twenty years and reflecting the changes in Croatia. It was a pleasure to be there.

But it was a short day. The knee hurt at the start, then didn't hurt, then it hurt again. As for the toe…

Reflecting on the kind offer of a woman, I wondered what people thought when they looked at me. I'm not very smart so don't appear rich. On the other hand I don't appear poor. My overwhelming characteristic, of course, is not immediately visible: I'm mean. This is not, I hasten to add, the reason for declining the woman (or man) but, if it was visible, it might prevent my being pestered by all manner of people anywhere.

In the supermarkets I generally buy one of everything: one banana, one apple, one biscuit. Then I am ashamed and try to buy two apples, which I don't really want. I generally fail, however, because of my other problem: I am completely unable to open those cellophane bags they have at the fruit counter. It's just the same at Sainsbury's; I am humiliated every time I have to ask the cashier to open the carrier bags for me. So now I carry one apple in my basket to the checkout with the price label stuck to the side, and one banana, and they think I'm even meaner than I actually am.

From Dugi Rat I caught the bus back to Split. In the warm November sunshine the sea front was a very pleasant place to be. Day off tomorrow. I hope to spend much of it lying down.

Day 75
A Day Off

Day 76
Dugi Rat to Pisak

Rather than Split, I spent the day off in Trogir, which seemed quieter and cheaper among the ancient scenery. Little did I know that this was the weekend of the patron saint of Trogir. Sunday morning brought a long ceremonial procession along the old city, an annual celebration that has been going on for hundreds of years. Everyone joined in the fun.

Indeed the celebrations lasted for much of the weekend. It was, no doubt, this religious fervour that caused the bikers under my window to shout and laugh and rev up their bikes all night long. Sometimes the adrenaline of worship, why, it just takes you that way.

My own enthusiasm for religion can be contained. In fact it can be contained in a thimble. Nevertheless I am well informed about clerical affairs through my French friend Jean, a religious journalist (that is, a journalist about religion) who comes to stay whenever something outrageous is happening in British churches; this is apparently most of the time. Jean keeps me informed on the pope, women priests, gay vicars and everything else you need to know.

At one time Jean was convinced that the Anglican Church was using a French aperitif as communion wine, and he asked me to buy a bottle so that we could test it. I duly went to the clerical suppliers, just north of Oxford

Circus. It has to be said that this was an intimidating experience. I tried to look clerical. I looked round the dog collars, the clothing (I can never remember the difference between a hassock and a cassock) and all the rest of the store. Then, as if by accident, I came across the communion wine and took a bottle to the counter. They batted not an eyelid. Perhaps everyone does it.

Later in France we compared the communion wine with the bottle of French fortified wine that Jean had in mind, an aperitif drunk like port or sherry before a meal. They were identical. The communion wine was also very good. So that's what packs 'em in.

Starting again at Dugi Rat, the road soon reached a dramatic surprise, the town of Omis. Standing under a large rock cliff face, straddling a river that emerges from a gorge, the town leads down to the harbour via a narrow shady main street with bustling shops. It was tempting to stay longer but I pushed on to finish the day at Pisak, described as being part of the local Riviera. It was a short day. Having two short days and a day off brings a danger of falling behind schedule. Fortunately I don't know what the schedule is.

In Pisak I congratulated myself on finding a room in a house close to the main road, so that I didn't have to walk down half a mountain to the sea shore. Then where was the shop? Half way down a mountain to the sea shore. To compound it, I got lost on the way back, not an easy thing to do when there's only the one road.

Years ago, signposts told you the distance to the next town or village. Now they don't. Why not? Don't they want you to know? All countries have followed this obscurantist policy. The only indicators of distance are on motorways or other major roads. In Croatia these are almost invariably incorrect. From here, for example, they say it's 180 kilometres to Dubrovnik. My map says it's 160 and I think my map is right.

The day off did my knee good. It also did my toe good. Unfortunately another toe has decided to give trouble today but there's always something; life is like that and you have to ignore it.

Tonight I bought a packet of cereal for my evening meal. For lack of anything else I had to buy a cereal with chocolate in it. It's absolutely disgusting. Why would anyone eat cereal with chocolate in it?

Day 77
Pisak to Makarska to Igrane

In the evening in Igrane it is absolutely piddling down. Thunder and lightning are crashing and flashing. For most of the day, rain clouds hung over Hvar, the long island lying opposite this coastline. Showers fell to the north and a storm passed to the south. I was very lucky today but the forecast is bad for tomorrow.

It was a day for covering ground. Nineteen kilometres brought Makarska, a bustling seaside town. The young woman in the tourist agency said that tourism had ruined local people. How? And are tourist officers supposed to say things like this? She said tourism had stopped people being polite.

Certainly tourism has transformed the region; twenty years ago, ninety per cent of the houses along the coast were not built but now whole villages have sprung up. No doubt things are different inland but here, along the coast, almost everyone understands some English, lets out a room or works in some other way with tourism. It may have made them less polite but it has certainly brought them more money.

The young woman was polite but it would have been better to be accurate; the information she gave me was totally duff. All the hotels before Ploče were closed, she said, but private rooms were open and plentiful and I would have no difficulty in finding accommodation. This was a complete fabrication. I climbed down from the main road to Igrane and knocked at all the front doors advertising rooms. Everyone had shut for the winter. I walked all over Igrane and eventually found myself at the harbour. A very helpful couple with a house on the sea front were closed themselves but made a phone call to the last woman in Igrane with a room open. She turned out to be a treasure.

She climbed down to the shore, not an easy proposition for her; elderly and not very fit, she declared that the steps would be the death of her. She took me to a cubby hole which passed as a room and which I was delighted to be in for the night. She told me all I needed to know about Igrane, gave me the keys and suggested I just left them there in the morning. She was going out.

The private rooms are all cheap but immaculate and have every necessary facility except a working TV. (They have all broken down.) There's not much to do, though, and it's a bit depressing gazing at the walls when you just don't want to read any more. Usually there is no heating except for the cooker. I can't be bothered to cook properly but have to get some nutrition so I buy a packet of soup and a tin of something healthy. Last night it was lentils and borlotti beans. Tonight it's chick peas. It doesn't look good, it doesn't smell good and it tastes pretty average. It might make most people sick but by God it's nutritious.

The helpful couple at the quay asked a few questions about what I'm doing and I gave the usual inane answers. Then the man asked something which I didn't quite catch. I asked him to repeat it but still didn't understand him. It was something about friends. Afterwards I thought I realised what he was saying. Was he asking if I was doing this walk because I didn't have any friends?

At last. Now we know.

Tonight is the night they make the olive oil in Igrane. Everyone from all around brings sacks of olives to a central building on the quayside; thousands of kilos of olives have to be unloaded by farmers, elderly couples and anyone in the region with an olive tree. It's a vital day in the local economy. Whatever they do takes place indoors where the machinery is, but they've got a terrible night for it and everyone will get soaked unloading the sacks.

During the day an absurd and embarrassing snatch of song floated into my mind, dredged up from childhood. Even when no-one was within a mile it was still toe-curling to be singing such a ghastly ditty.

> I love to go a-wandering along a mountain top
> I love to go a-wandering with my knapsack on my back
> Fol-de-ree-ee, fol-de-ra-ah, fol-de-ree-ee,
> Fol-de-ritta-titta-titta, fol-de-ree-ee.:.

It is extraordinary that within the last hundred years people could have been prancing round singing about knapsacks. Within a hundred years of Oasis, or the Kaiser Chiefs, not to mention 50 Cent or Dizzee Rascal…

And I remember it!

Day 78
Igrane to Ploče

A couple stopped their car in the middle of the road in the hills above Ploče. They wanted to give me a lift into town. The woman got out and placed a bin liner across the back seat in case I was worried about making it wet. They wouldn't take no for an answer. I explained as best I could about walking, thanked them profusely but still declined. They carried on driving but did not understand.

Thirty years ago, when I last walked in south-east Europe, it was the same everywhere. In those days a number of people walked but that was because they didn't have the bus fare. A number of people were vegetarian, also, because they couldn't afford meat. A walking vegetarian therefore was a very poor person indeed and I was always being offered rides and little presents. Out in the country, I'm not sure how much it has changed today.

Following my discussion about motivation yesterday with the man on the quayside, I wished I could have told him about the perfect walk as I envisaged it. Some years ago, the cricket World Cup was being played in the sub-continent. The ideal way to watch the matches, I thought, was to walk between them, beginning in Gwalior and then travelling vaguely northwards. A number of matches were scheduled in that area and it ought to be idyllic: walk, watch cricket, walk, watch cricket…

Unfortunately it did not work out quite like that. First, it was bandit country between Gwalior and Agra and I was assured that I would be killed if I was foolish enough to enter it on foot. I took the train. Then they hadn't scheduled the matches right. One match would be in the middle of the area; the next would be a hundred miles south-east; the next would be two hundred miles north-west; the next would be due south again. It appeared to be deliberately obtuse. Were they trying to stop walkers?

I did find a few matches in a straight line from Gwalior, omitting the first section. I walked from Agra to Delhi and saw a wonderful match between India and Sri Lanka (a story in itself), then walked on to Chandigarh for the semi-final. The final was not far away across the Pakistan border in Lahore, but there was not time to walk it and I had to catch train and bus. The border crossing was very enjoyable; I counted fourteen people who examined my passport on one side or the other. The idea in general, however, was fecund but not practical. It would be a lot easier to walk between all the teams in the West Norfolk cricket league.

Another impractical idea which I entertained at one time was walking between all the capitals of Europe in alphabetical order. I'm afraid there aren't enough years left, though.

Sometimes every corner on the Adriatic Highway seems to reveal a new seaside resort, clinging to a cove with a marina, a diving school and perhaps a small beach. Today, though, was different. The afternoon brought a ridge of hills, eventually overhanging a series of lakes. Then the evening brought Ploče. Now here is a surprise.

By no stretch of the imagination is Ploče pretty. It is an industrial port. Full of pre-tourism, communist-era blocks of workers' flats, most of which have seen better days, it is a monument to atrocious town planning. In recent years, efforts have been made to catch up: a marina, a few bars, a couple of pizzerias and a rather lovely new church and clock tower. This cannot conceal the fact, however, that this is one ugly town.

Rain fell in the afternoon, but not enough to frighten the horses. The evening brought more terrific storms. A pattern seems to be developing: fine in the morning, rain in the afternoon, terrible storms at night. Please get up earlier.

BOSNIA

DAY 79
PLOČE TO NEUM

The Bosnian border guard placed my passport under the machine. The machine didn't work, of course.

'Ah, technology,' he said. 'We were better off without it.'

He tried the machine several more times.

'This is what the European Union gives us,' he added. 'All the shit coming out of Europe.'

He spoke very good English.

We had a chat and he let me go. It wasn't clear whether the machine had worked or not but he had had enough of it.

Down to the coast runs a sliver of Bosnia-Herzegovina, giving the country access to the sea. Neum is the access. A few years ago it must have been just a village. Now it has grown exponentially. (No, I don't know what the word means either but it's the one they always use.) It is a duty free zone and trippers drive many miles to shop here. Not long ago, a hundred thousand people died in Bosnia in the most awful of circumstances. Now, Neum is a duty free zone resort. Who would have thought it would come to this?

It's hard to imagine the effect the slaughter must have had on people. Everyone lost family and friends and witnessed atrocities. Many homes were destroyed and ways of life annihilated. How do they function now? How can they ever lead a normal life?

The road from Ploče led in huge semi-circles away from the coast and then back again. Opuzen held the junction for Mostar and Sarajevo. Once in the 1970s I caught a bus to Sarajevo. In those days many of the roads were still unpaved and female passengers, dressed in black, brought paper bags to be sick into. In Sarajevo I caught a train. On the station a student came up, wanting to talk. We began a conversation but then he realised the secret police were watching and made himself very scarce.

The plains were full of tangerines, millions and millions of them. The road climbed over another ridge of hills and down to the border crossing for Bosnia. Apparently the Croats want to build a bridge out into the sea to circumvent Bosnia when travelling up Croatia. It's not a popular idea with Bosnia: all those duty free revenues going to waste.

Originally I planned to come back into Bosnia after Dubrovnik. However, I now realise that I'm not tough enough for the interior. There will be hills and mountains, it will be cold and there may not be accommodation. Going all the way down the coast may be further but I will skirt round Bosnia and spend more time in Montenegro; this way I hope to postpone any difficulties. At some time the mountains are inevitable but for the time being it's out of sight, out of mind.

CROATIA (AGAIN)

DAY 80
NEUM TO SLANO

In Manchester, they say that if you can see the hills it's going to rain. If you can't see the hills it's raining already.

It's much the same in Croatia. If the wind's blowing, rain is on the way. If it's not blowing…

Just as I was about to set out, the heavens opened. You couldn't cross the road, let alone go walking. On the edge of Neum is a bus halt, where all the long distance buses disgorge their passengers for half an hour of duty free shopping. I sheltered there for an hour. A bus was going to Dubrovnik. I could go there, hide for a day and then walk back. I admit it: I had the money in my hand. Then the rain eased up.

For an hour or so it eased. Then, abruptly, thunder arrived and enveloped the whole area. Four separate times the thunder struck within three seconds of the lightning. Once it was one second. I hugged the rock face. Was I frightened? Of course I bloody was. I was terrified. Sometimes I think I'm a hard man. That lasts a few seconds. Most of the time I think I'm a stupid man. I could be at home!

Apart from the rock face, the only shelter from rain and thunder was an advertising billboard. When a billboard is your only shelter, you've got problems.

In the US they have those triangular billboards that you can get inside. When I was walking across the country I said I wanted to sleep in those three symbols of North American history: a covered wagon, an advertising billboard and a jail. I did sleep one night in a billboard and I slept half a night in a covered wagon. One desperate cold night the chief of police in Newville, Pennsylvania, offered me the jail which I leaped at; but eventually he put me up in his own house instead.

Being struck by lightning is, presumably, like being shot; you don't know much about it at the time but waiting for it is tricky. I cringed and waited.

Then the next crack of thunder was further away. It had passed.

Thinking of home is a craven pursuit which I followed too much today and is bound to lead to emotional disaster. When I have these fantasies I find that I don't think of my home now, or indeed at any time in the last forty or fifty years. In fact I find that almost everything that passes through my brain happened more than fifty years ago. There's too much time to think!

The weather died down. The mileage was encouraging. Even this morning they said it was seventy kilometres to Dubrovnik, which it clearly wasn't. By this evening they had got it right. From Slano it is thirty kilometres, which is comfortable tomorrow if the weather holds.

What is this in Slano? It's a five-star hotel! The village is tiny and I had assumed I would have to catch the bus into Dubrovnik for accommodation and come back in the morning. The hotel was a monstrosity but I wandered towards it with a view to opening negotiations; I have never stayed in a five-star hotel and probably never will. Was it open? Before I could find out, the bus stop appeared with a bus just about to leave for Dubrovnik. I climbed on board.

Last night in Neum the room was passable but the meal was disgusting and the water almost cold. In Dubrovnik I found a room, very cheap, rather dirty and totally without hot water. What is it with these people, don't they like hot water? Then I went into the old city to re-acquaint myself with the English language: newspapers, books and tourists. As I walked round, I kept ducking into doorways. Was that lightning? I was like the traumatised soldier reacting to the bang of an exhaust. It wasn't lightning, it was the constant flashing of a hundred tourist cameras.

Day 81
Slano to Dubrovnik

A few weeks ago, I was talking to my friend Liz about our trade union history together. There was a time, I said, when we used to be somebody. As you get older, you cease to be the somebody you were. You lose your professional standing, you're not playing for your cricket club, you don't have a position as chair of this group or treasurer of that. People don't ask you to do things; basically they don't want you any more. At the same time, your powers are waning. You are, in fact, getting old.

No-one likes it. Some can be philosophical about it, some can't. We rage against the dying of the light. Personally, I don't want to be someone who used to do things. I want to be doing them. Soon, bits of me will be dropping off and I won't be able to do anything worthwhile. Meanwhile I'd better try to finish this bloody walk while I can.

Each day is hellish; it's just a question of less hellish or more hellish. Anyone who walks down the Adriatic Highway for fun is in need of serious counselling. (In the days when thugs worked in the Social Services, I heard one say that he had given a lad some 'heavy counselling', i.e. beaten him up.) Three times previously I have tried to walk across Europe. Forty years ago I tried to walk from London to Istanbul but gave up in southern Austria. Thirty-three years ago I headed from Athens to Paris but got ill somewhere or other. Twenty-six years ago I tried London to Athens but gave up in Split. It's time to get the thing done and stop bellyaching.

I didn't know where or when the buses went from Dubrovnik to Slano but I knew exactly where they left from Slano and at what time because I did it yesterday; so I walked out there and caught the bus back.

Outside Dubrovnik is a very, very high bridge. Half way across, a shrine recorded the death of a young man in a traffic accident. Christ. There? Did he go off the side? I concentrated hard on my feet in the pretence that vertigo did not exist.

Dubrovnik, as most of the world knows, is a very beautiful old city. How much of the present city is original I don't know, as the war twenty years ago did massive damage. Nevertheless after restoration it is a lovely place to walk round and eat and drink in and possibly visit a museum or two. Even now on 20 November, it is busy. When the cruise ships come in, like floating cities, it is busier. It is good to see that, for the rest of the time, the majority of people using the city are Croatian.

On the road, a man stopped his car and asked the way to Albania. Well, there is only one road. It goes south…

Day 82
Dubrovnik to Cilipi (Airport)

The supermarket was full of fathers and small children, doing their Sunday duties. I needed some toothpaste. Every tube, it seemed, had a special offer. More of this one, ten per cent extra on that one. I don't want more; it's too heavy. Don't give me more, I wanted to say. Give me less!

The road from Dubrovnik began with a steep climb, followed by various ups and downs and then another climb to the airport. It can't have been easy to find a flat bit of land round here and the airport was twenty kilometres from the city up a steep hill. This was not far enough for the day but I was worried about accommodation ahead. Was there an airport hotel or anything in the vicinity? I went in and asked.

Walking to an airport from the city, rather than taking transport, is generally a pleasant way of arriving. I've done it a number of times in the Caribbean - Tobago, Grenada, St. Kitts, Antigua and St. Vincent (where, as the plane landed, the cricket match I had come to watch was spread out below). In Europe, Basle-Mulhouse is the only airport that springs to mind for an easy walk. The trouble now is that entering an airport brings the serious possibility of using it. Was I tempted to take a flight home? Sleep in my own bed, have a bath, go to the allotment, eat Marmite on toast and come back again on Wednesday? Perish the thought.

Airports are stressful places, of course. Social workers are employed there to counsel staff and deal with traumatised passengers, as a cascade of human drama unfolds every day; it's an attractive job which I once nearly applied for. Most of the drama, however, never prompts official intervention: families and friends tear themselves apart without assistance. At Mexico City airport I once met two Canadian men, both casualties of relationship breakdowns, going on holiday together as a male bonding exercise (years before the wonderful film *Sideways*).

Unfortunately, while still travelling to their destination, they weren't getting on. 'I hate him!' one of them confided to me. Then the other one came and told me the same. It didn't bode well for the rest of their holiday. Has anyone written a study of relationship breakdown in airports?

I asked whether there was a hotel near the airport. There was nowhere near the airport, the woman said, but there are lots of hotels in Cavtat, five kilometres back the way I had just come. Might they not be closed at this time of year? This was something that had not occurred to her. She made a number of calls. Yes, they were all closed. Was there a hotel between here and Montenegro? No, there was only private accommodation (if it wasn't closed). Would I have to go back to Dubrovnik then? Well, there was a bus outside, meeting a flight, if I was very quick.

Twenty minutes later I was back in Dubrovnik. I didn't go back to the hideous room I had been in before but walked again across town to a hotel. It was warm! It had TV! I could wash my trousers, something that needed doing before they hopped in and washed themselves. I can postpone thinking about the morning and watch the BBC instead.

Generally it is getting too cold to sit about during the day so I eat on the road. Most days I buy a cheese *burek*, substantial and rather nice. (For eighteen years in the Walthamstow probation office I ate a toasted cheese sandwich for lunch every day except for the time when I broke the toaster, something I have never admitted until now.) It's very easy to forget about eating altogether but in fact it's necessary. I had a schoolteacher once who ate one potato for lunch every day; he was afraid of getting fat. We told him that the energy expended in eating the potato was greater than the energy gained from the content. It didn't change him.

For twenty years I have played tennis weekly with a man called Kelly. In the last few years he and I have both become increasingly preoccupied with his waistline. As an incentive for him to regain the contour of his youth, I have offered on 1 September to buy him and his partner an all-you-can-eat buffet at the Star of India if he can get down to twelve stone. (I won't say what he is now.) Each year, as he has failed to make the grade, the offer has been extended to the next year. It has now survived six or seven years and a change of partner. He didn't make it this year.

While I am away, my other weekly tennis partner, Gulam, has been supposed to monitor Kelly, playing him weekly and inspecting his waistline. I suspect it will not happen, though, as Kelly routinely avoids him. I may send Kelly a postcard soon to remind him of his obligations but I suspect that in my absence he will go to pot. So will the world.

DAY 83
ČILIPI TO GRUDA

There was no bus to Čilipi for a couple of hours so I had to take one going to Cavtat, get off at the junction and walk the same three kilometres I walked yesterday, a very aggravating process. A clap of thunder lifted everyone in the bus shelter from their seats. Then it seemed to die down and I set off. It was a false dawn. I sheltered in the post office from a major storm. It cleared and I set off again.

Then, two hundred metres from me, I actually saw lightning hit the ground. Christ Almighty.

I stood there, unable to believe my eyes. I had watched it strike, almost within throwing distance, certainly within striking distance. I was terrified.

The heavens opened. It lasted for hours. By enormous good fortune a building, a sort of workshop, had a door open and I went in and sheltered. It was hard to know what would have happened otherwise because I have never seen anything like it. The rain was solid.

After a few minutes a man came in and asked what I was doing. I explained and he gave me tea and the offer of food which I had to decline. (His cat was eating a plate of spaghetti but the food offered to me was not vegetarian.) The man was the owner of this small factory which designed and made items of machinery. He had told his four staff not to come in today because of the weather; indeed the road behind me was now closed by a landslide. All his three sons are at university, the eldest studying machinery design at Zagreb. He told me the weather round here is notoriously bad, flanked by mountains and getting very little sunshine. He pointed out a nearby range of mountains in Montenegro where they have a million litres of rainfall per year (or something).

We talked about the war and how it had affected the area. He said it was terrible. His parents and family had gone to Zagreb. When they returned, their house was destroyed. Yet again, I wondered how anyone can return to normal life after internal strife of this sort. He said he could get along with Montenegrins but he wasn't at all keen on people from Herzegovina.

Eventually the rain eased enough to go outside but by this time it was too late to make any more progress for the day. Through the weather I have lost a day, but it was bound to happen some time and there is not much I can do about it. The factory owner very kindly found me a room for the night

in Gruda with a very friendly old lady where I think I may freeze to death. Fortunately the village has a cosy bar where everyone stops for a coffee after work or a drink later, staffed by an excellent, very friendly barmaid. Next door is a pizza place which appears to be someone's front room; indeed it is someone's front room. The lady in question knows all her customers (except me) and shares their conversations.

MONTENEGRO

DAY 84
GRUDA TO HERCEG NOVI

Perhaps more research was needed.

Obviously I knew that in winter it might rain. Or snow. However, I didn't know that, for the second year running, extreme weather would hit hard and early over most of Europe. Further north, snow has covered the continent; down in southern Croatia we have howling bucketfuls of rain. Within this general pattern, micro-cataclysms erupt even more fiercely.

Plied with tangerines, I left my landlady in Gruda. Thunder had rumbled all night but it was not raining when I left. Within half an hour it was pelting. However, this was nothing compared with yesterday. Looking back, I beheld a frightening vision of extreme weather. A vast, blue back monster of cloud had rolled over the whole valley, enveloping the whole area totally. Exactly where the torrent hit me yesterday, it had done it again. The man had said it was an area of extreme weather. I was very, very glad to have escaped it. All day we had only one flash of lightning. I had no doubt that behind me it was continual.

Montenegro arrived. I sheltered in the Croatian border crossing while a storm passed, then sheltered from another one in the Montenegrin post. A third one saw me drinking tea in the café, where the dulcet tones of Eminem oozed from the music system. Ahead, a lake - no, the sea - was visible in the distance until it vanished into the cloud which descended right down to the road. Dripping and cold, I walked down the hill into the new country.

I know nothing about Montenegro. Until yesterday, I didn't know what currency they used: nice to find that it's the euro. I don't know what language they speak, though it doesn't seem that different from what has gone before. Years ago I crossed here on a bus, but nothing from that time sticks in the memory. I know they've got a lot of mountains. Twenty years ago they attacked Dubrovnik in the war. In 2006 only 55 per cent of the country voted for independence from Serbia. They have applied to join the EU. That's about it.

Herceg Novi is part of the Montenegrin Riviera (though not showing many signs of it today). It has a historic old town which I'm afraid got short shrift from me. Tourist information says the battlements have a history of Venetian, Turkish and Spanish ancestry. I found a hotel which was rather grand (though very cheap), then had an embarrassing experience with the lift. It wouldn't go up to the eighth floor. At reception I went in, the doors closed and I pushed the right button. Then the doors opened and I found myself back at reception. Why wouldn't it go up? Finally I realised that reception itself was on the eighth floor. Built into the cliffside, the hotel had eight floors lower down. As I emerged from the lift the receptionist looked down tactfully but she must have been biting back her scorn at the antics of the British hick.

On entering Montenegro, the countryside changes instantaneously; the border must have been fixed at some geological boundary. The trees are much bigger and the pastures look north European. Beyond them, the mountains are bigger too and I realise that I shall have to change my planned route to Podgorica, the capital. Already I have altered my original plan to go inland from Dubrovnik, the shortest route, and now I will have to make further detours. Over the mountains from here, the accommodation will have closed down for the winter. Furthermore, I'm not fit enough yet to tackle them. I will therefore skip the World Heritage Site at Kotor and carry on down the coast as far as possible. Mountains will have to come eventually but I shall try not to think about them.

For lunch, straight out of the oven, I had the greatest cheese *burek* in the world.

At quarter to five, pitch dark, the thunder started again.

DAY 85
HERCEG NOVI TO TIVAT

I've remembered another time I passed through Montenegro. Years ago, tourists were only allowed into Albania in organised groups, which entered through Montenegro. On the way back, the group flew back from Podgorica (then called Titograd) but I left them and returned by train. En route I went through Zagreb, where I bought a shirt for my father, then Vienna, Prague, Bern, Basle, the Black Forest and Paris, staying with people everywhere except Prague. It was convivial.

Almost all the group had gone to Albania out of curiosity, to see what life was like in Enver Hoxha's hardline communist dictatorship. (Answer: grim.) It was an interesting few days, marred only by a journalist who had come in search of a story. Overtly displaying a bible (confiscated), flamboyantly dressed and provocative at every turn, she was eventually told by a number of the group to behave herself. Whether or not she got a story I don't know; I don't read her paper.

A great sliver of sea invades Montenegro, creating ancient harbours and modern tourist traps. The road from Herceg Novi follows one side of this sliver, leading eventually to a large bay. On the other side of the bay, clearly visible a couple of miles away, lies the old city of Kotor. It looks spectacular and well worth visiting, but it's a two-day walk round the bay; then you have to climb a mountain to get out. Instead I took the ferry across the narrow part of the inlet. I hope this is allowed; I haven't taken any other ferries and this was a very narrow stretch of water, but there didn't seem any other solution. After sheltering for an hour in a café I wandered down into Tivat.

It piddled down all morning and this evening great sheets of lightning fill the sky. Doesn't it ever just rain, without the lightning? In decent weather this must all be lovely: docks, moorings and beaches lie round every corner. Tivat's climate encourages exotic plants in the park and flamingos nearby. Above Herceg Novi stands the highest mountain on the Adriatic. Above Tivat, is that a smattering of snow lining the mountains?

First a minus for Montenegro: everyone seems to be smoking. Then a plus: its tourist offices, unlike the offices in every other country in the world, are not only helpful but also accurate.

The TV in my room, which looked pretty ordinary, supplied an amazing selection of programmes. I spent the afternoon in bed watching a documentary about wild chickens in Miami, then *Serial Mom, Footballers' Wives* (always a favourite), a documentary about Charles Dickens and finally BBC World. Why go home?

I'm reading a book by Iain Banks, whom I have always avoided on the grounds that he writes science fiction. From time to time I have been told that this is culturally restrictive of me (not quite the words used - 'bigot' and 'pig' come to mind), but I like to keep my prejudices intact. Anyway, this is one of his non-science fiction novels. He's got a touch of the Aldous Huxleys in that he can't write a paragraph without trying to make a political point. I have found three grammatical errors so far and he seems to have got something seriously wrong about the legal system.

DAY 86
TIVAT TO BUDVA

Outside Budva came an amazing sight. Down the hill before me, descending more slowly than I was, were two rucksacks. Or was it two young people with guitars? No, they were carrying, by God - walking poles! Over the old town of Budva they stopped to look at the view and I caught up with them. Did they speak English?

Hanspeter and Annemarie are walking from Basle to Jerusalem...

It was hard to believe that anyone else was walking and remarkable that I had bumped into them. What's more, they said there was someone else: a 61-year-old Irish woman called Ann who is walking from Rome to Jerusalem. What's going on?

The Swiss couple set off from home three months ago after selling all their possessions; they hope to arrive in Jerusalem in June. They have no address now except email. (People used to have a post office box number, now it's an email.) They walk for a long time each day but stop often and look around. They stay in private rooms, where they cook. Sometimes the rooms are so cold that they use sleeping bags. They also have a tent for emergencies. They are heading for Albania; they don't know whether they will be allowed in on foot but will try it and see. All in all, they are very brave or very foolish.

I wanted to spend an evening with the couple but they were going further than me today. I congratulated them instead on their general intrepidness and on the confidence they must have in each other: confidence above all that they wouldn't fall out irrevocably on the trip. (Why do I have to say things like this? Why can't I just leave it? Some couples do just love each other, for goodness sake.) They smiled politely and we parted and went our different ways.

This morning in Tivat I sat about for a couple of hours until it was fit to go outside. In Budva, they say that the climate may be different because this is the first bit of coastline that sits opposite the clear Mediterranean, without islands or promontories in between. So far it doesn't appear very different. Tonight ferocious storms are lashing the town. Snow lies above and, peculiarly, one lump of snow lay beside the road. The Swiss couple had seen it too. Where did it come from?

I am intimidated even more by the journey ahead. My God, what's that road? Is that the way to Cetinje? It's up a mountain. I checked the map, something perhaps I should have done before. It's 31 kilometres to Cetinje and the climb is over, well over, eight hundred metres high. That's three thousand feet. I'm not sure I can do it. I'm getting fitter, the blisters have gone and the legs don't hurt too much, but I haven't done a climb like this since my heart went wrong last time. Furthermore, I'm short of pills; I hope to pick up some more in Kosovo but meanwhile I have cut out one in four. I may go even further south.

DAY 87
BUDVA TO PETROVAC

The brevity of this entry may be directly related to the quantity of wine drunk. I might not even remember what happened earlier in the day. Blame the pilgrim.

Needless to say, I chickened out of the road to Cetinje. To justify this, another look at the map revealed that the southern route was actually ten kilometres shorter: another fact that I might have noticed before. However, this was cancelled out by walking for only four hours today. The trouble is that there is nothing for the next 25 kilometres so there was no chance of continuing. Instead I walked down from the main road to the shore (so it's up again tomorrow) and asked in the tourist office what they'd got for me in Petrovac.

It turned out that the excellent tourist office had something very nice. I could go to a hotel, they said, but they were very expensive. Instead I could go to the flat upstairs that they rented out for the owner. It was lovely: big TV (British programmes), cooking facilities, warm, nice shower. No contest. Tomorrow is Saturday and the tourist office won't be open but I should just put the key through their window.

Then I met the woman from Ireland.

I offered her a meal and asked if she drank. 'Of course I drink,' she said. 'I'm Irish.' (She said it. I wouldn't dream of saying it.) I bought a bottle of wine and we drank it in my flat. She went out for another bottle but by this time I was flagging. She carried on for a while and was still bouncy but then she went home and I threw the rest away. I know what the morning will be like.

Through talking to Ann, these walks to Jerusalem suddenly became clear. Rome to Jerusalem, you'd think it might have rung some bells somewhere; but sometimes I'm a bit slow on the uptake. I thought they were just out for a good walk. In fact it's a pilgrimage. They're all pilgrims.

Over the course of a few hours I discovered more about Ann than the fact that she liked a bottle of wine. She's extraordinary. There's a husband in Hitchin, Herts, and two grown-up sons who think she's touched in the head. (They may be right.) Some years ago, after a career in computers and with no walking experience whatsoever, she suddenly developed a yearning to do pilgrimages. She has walked enormous distances on various routes. She bears a staff. She too is heading for Albania, very unwisely in my opinion. We exchanged awful experiences - only someone who has done all this can know how dreadful it all is. There were so many of them that it took a long time. It was re-invigorating, a one-off support group.

The pilgrims, of course, have a reason for doing all this. That's an improvement on the rest of us.

Now, after Ann has left, I'm trying to remember the pre-bibulous day. It was more of the same, I think. Sea, rocks, mountains. A small island had a causeway like Mont St. Michel; apparently it's a very exclusive place, whatever it is. Oh, and the coast road is dotted with monasteries.

DAY 88
PETROVAC TO VIRPAZAR

Stay away from pilgrims!

Today was the day to mix a few metaphors: bite the bullet, get the head down, take the bit between the teeth, maybe even gird up the loins. It's no use going further and further south and continually skirting round the mountains, they have got to be crossed. Looking back, it was probably a good decision not to go inland from Dubrovnik, when the weather would have been prohibitive. The alternative, though, has meant short days, detours and losing time. Today was the day to head inland for Podgorica. A big climb of two thousand feet was the first problem.

The other problem was all that bloody wine. Not only was I continually up in the night. I had completely forgotten the resolution about not drinking quantities of stimulants; needless to say, I remembered in the morning. So I set out on the climb with a mild hangover, no sleep and a recurrent anxiety about my heartbeat.

Actually it was all right. But if I ever meet Ann again I will impress on her the need to avoid cheap wine at all costs. It's a bit like sleeping outside and then catching pneumonia; yes, it's cheaper but it's not a sensible economy.

Much simpler is to stay away from pilgrims!

Slowly, very slowly the climb led up to the top of the coastal mountain range. From the bottom, it seemed impossible that those far distant whirls and coils of the road could ever be reached. Gradually, over a couple of hours, they came closer, became a possibility, then were even left behind. No traffic of any sort used this road, not even a bus. The odd church, the odd monastery dots the route but no-one seems to be attending them. Finally the road reached the top.

Over the summit lay a different world. Deciduous trees, their leaves long fallen, spread across the mountain range. In summer it must be very pretty and now it makes for much more interesting walking. After a few kilometres the road reached the edge of the other side. Momentous views stretched away. Far below lay the huge inland lake, Skadar; on the other side is Albania. Far ahead and to the north stand higher ranges of snow-capped mountains. They're impressive. If I wasn't intimidated before, I certainly am now.

The descent seemed deeper than the climb, though as I had started at sea level this was hardly likely. An endless series of steep hairpin bends brought the valley floor. I was pretty tired. It was said that a hotel was still open at Virpazar and this turned out to be true.

The world's greatest pleasure, I have decided - greater even than perfectly timing a cricket shot, never mind those other pleasures - lies in reaching a hotel room, getting into bed with a packet of peanuts and turning on the TV. The converse, however, is that if you don't reach a hotel or if the TV doesn't work or has only Montenegrin channels, the disappointment is crushing. Except for Montenegrins, of course. Yesterday I had a hundred channels and watched about ninety of them. Today there are six, mostly fuzzy, and I'm not watching any of them.

Podgorica. How many people can tell you the capital of Montenegro? For some reason I have no trouble remembering Podgorica, whereas most names on the route I can't remember from one moment to the next: while writing these notes I have had to look up Virpazar three times. The award for the hardest capital to remember goes to Honduras for Tegucigalpa. Does anyone know the capital of Honduras, including Hondurans? How long does it take to remember it? Well, I was walking towards it for a hundred and fifty miles over six days with signposts all along the road; by the time I arrived it had just about stuck in my mind if I concentrated very hard.

According to the TV last night and this morning, most of Britain is covered in snow and the parts that aren't already covered soon will be. Today it didn't rain or snow on me. For the first time, I was genuinely pleased to be here rather than at home.

DAY 89
VIRPAZAR TO PODGORICA

I am very glad to announce that new heights have been scaled in the worst-meal-of-a-lifetime competition. The dinner I had last night was truly disgusting. (The alternative meal was eel pie. Desperate Dan used to eat eel pie but I wasn't that desperate.) Even this dazzling presentation, though, was capped by a boiled egg this morning. I know it had been boiled because it was hot. However, when I took the top off water ran out. The woman who allegedly cooked it was standing next to me at the time. She was unembarrassed. It was the one minute egg. They were nice enough people but they just can't cook.

In Virpazar a book exchange held four English-language books. 1. A book by Anne Enright which I've read. 2. A bad American thriller by Sandra Brown. 3. A romantic novel set in 1952. 4. A Mills and Boon. I took number 2. For a moment, though, number 3 was tempting. The opening page was set on the day of King George VI's death, 6 February 1952. Our schoolteachers, Mrs. Dye and Mrs. Wilson, clapped their hands together and called us over the playing field to hear the news. The King is dead.

Lake Skadar is an extraordinary piece of water, seven kilometres wide in summer but fourteen in winter. Probably fifteen at the moment; in one village a woman paddled a boat to houses where the water reached half way up the windows. The road joins the railway to cross a piece of water and then a causeway across the marshes. At the moment, the marshes and trees are part of the lake. All this leads to a diverse collection of flora and fauna; plenty of herons and cormorants sat around today, though none of the fabled pelicans. The morning was murky, the clouds almost touching the water, the mountains gloomy behind. It was like walking in the mountains of Mordor.

Podgorica approached. Or, at least, the approach to Podgorica approached. From nowhere began a long, straight dual carriageway. Straight? As far as the eye could see, headlights crested the brow of the hill. It was endless. When independence came to Montenegro the town planners saw the opportunity of a lifetime. Building New York must have been the same. No doubt this will all be populated one day by blocks of flats and factories. Meanwhile, it is just a road, leading from nowhere. On the good side, they have built a pavement beside it for walkers. This is the future.

No-one, but no-one, could call Podgorica beautiful. It was built, mostly under communism, to be functional. They are now trying to make at least the ground floors of buildings look more exciting. Knocking the place down would be the only way to make it beautiful.

In cafés now I drink mostly camomile tea. There is a simple reason for this; it's the only tea word I can remember in Montenegrin. Unfortunately I detest camomile tea and the people who drink it. The sooner I get out of here the better.

In the evening another almighty storm hammered down. Apparently it's going to rain for a week.

In poorer countries, no-one ever has any change. Tonight I bought a map for 3.5 euros and proffered a ten-euro note: not an unreasonable offer, one might think. The woman was dumbstruck. Didn't I have anything smaller? She took all the change I had been saving for dire situations (tea and buses). It's a constant battle between shopkeeper and customer to hang on to those coins which you cannot manage without.

More and more signs are in the Cyrillic script and young men kiss each other on the cheeks in greeting. We're a long way south and east.

Day 90
Podgorica to Restoran Hotel Eco Mediteran

Clearly I had missed something about Podgorica. The tourist information put me right:

> AN EXQUISITE GEOGRAPHIC POSITION AND CLOSENESS OF EUROPEAN CENTERS, SPECIFIC AND PLEASANT MEDITERRANEAN CLIMATE AND GEOMORPHOLOGIC DISPOSITION CONTRIBUTE TO THE MULTIPLEX AND CONVENIENT INTEGRATION OF ECOLOGIC SURROUNDINGS.

Be that as it may, it was extraordinarily difficult to find the way out of. Road works didn't help. I went up the wrong road, doubled back, asked around and followed the majority view of two out of three people as to the right road. They were correct. Then I stepped ankle deep in mud.

This is where we head north to avoid Albania. The next town is Kolašin, but that's 65 kilometres away and, according to the tourist office, there is only one place to stay en route. Furthermore, buses on this route stop only to drop people off, not to pick them up, so I couldn't walk some of the way and then catch the bus back or onwards. I find this hard to believe - do people only make one way journeys? - but I'm not keen to put it to the test. Where was the one place to stay?

The tourist office didn't know how far it was or if it was open and couldn't contact them because they don't have a telephone number. Good communications then. The only option was to go there, wherever it was, and find out.

The road led through a gorge up into the mountains; it looks as if a lot more gorge is to come. Somewhere round here is a famous gorge, perhaps the longest in Europe, but I don't think this is it. All the same, it's spectacular already. A few tiny villages, hamlets really, dotted the valley. Dark blue clouds hung over the tops but the rain held off for a while and I wanted to get as far as possible. Unfortunately it was not to be.

The Restoran Eco Mediteran did exist, was open and was keen to welcome me. The downside (well, I discovered several downsides later, but the first one) was that it arrived very early, not long after one o'clock and not many kilometres into the whole distance, which means that I can't possibly reach Kolašin tomorrow. However, the young lad who did the translating said there was no other accommodation for forty kilometres, which I can't possibly do in this terrain and weather. There is nothing I can do, therefore, but wait here. Tomorrow will have to look after itself.

The place here is, well, homely. The dining room is warm and fuggy. Local people look in for a drink or a coffee and everyone knows everyone. In fact most seem to be family. In my accommodation, no man over five foot tall could stand under the sloping ceiling to pee into the toilet. In the shower, the hot tap turns the wrong way so that I scalded myself and have a red mark across my stomach and thigh. All part of the joys of travel.

The son of the house, a law student at Podgorica, unfolded my map to look at my route; then neither of us, of course, could fold it up again. Women are better at folding maps. We tried everything: forwards, backwards, sideways, it just wouldn't go. Later I fought it for an hour in my room. (It gave me something to do in the long wait before bed.) Then, suddenly, it just went right. Easy.

Nero Wolfe, hero of Rex Stout's great crime novels, came originally from Montenegro. He fought with the partisans after the First World War before decamping to New York. My schoolteacher Charles Blackburne gave me Rex Stout to read from the age of eleven and I devoured them through my teenage years and beyond. Stout became the grand old man of crime literature but is now largely forgotten. His non-Wolfe books are largely forgettable, indeed not very good, but the main series are witty, erudite and immensely readable. Like Margery Allingham in the UK at the same time, he needs a reprint every five years to remind the readers of a good plot, wit and good writing.

Day 91
Kolašin (Well, Podgorica Really)

A monumental day.

Scrambled eggs for breakfast yesterday, omelette last night, omelette again this morning. The danger looms of becoming egg-bound. However, that is not monumental (I hope). It rained hard all night, it rained hard all day and at the time of writing it looks like raining all night again. I made an early start.

I walked uphill for thirteen kilometres to the kilometre stone which read 1,009 (though I have no idea where to or where from). I stood inside a tunnel to read the map in the dry. If the signs were accurate it was 32 or 33 kilometres to Kolašin. It was just after ten o'clock. There was rumoured to be a hotel ten kilometres this side of Kolašin but it was just a rumour. If I walked to Kolašin without stopping, uphill in heavy rain, it would take at least seven hours, probably more. It would be dark and I didn't know where I was going.

The spot I was standing on was, I reckoned, exactly half way between Podgorica and Kolašin.

I turned round and headed for Podgorica (downhill). It was the old gambit that I have used two or three times now; I walk half way to somewhere, walk back again and then say I have walked the whole thing. Well, it's exactly the same distance. But it's cheating, of course.

Without stopping, I walked 32 kilometres back to the three-star hotel in Podgorica where I hoped to dry out boots, clothes and self. Including the thirteen kilometres I had walked upwards in the morning, I walked a total of 45 kilometres. It would be hard to imagine a wetter person than I was when I arrived. I emptied the pack and discovered that white bin liners were not as effective as black for keeping clothes dry. Furthermore, in some of the cheaper places the sheets are damp, never mind the rooms. When everything was out and drying I took a heart pill and went to bed. The heart isn't as regular as I would have liked but hasn't misfired completely. It doesn't like this sort of day any more than I do.

The scenery, incidentally, was sensational! On the way up, the river churned through its gorge. Above it, the road passed sometimes through a wide valley, sometimes as part of the gorge. As we climbed, the whole valley grew narrower. On both sides, cliffs enclosed the canyon. As the clouds came down, so the whole edifice loomed more and more threateningly. On a nice day…

Walking back the way you have come is a strange experience. For a start, it always seems much further. Then it all seems completely unfamiliar, even though you walked it the day before. The long straight road into Podgorica from this side was much longer and straighter than yesterday. I sneaked past the Restoran Eco Mediteran hoping that no-one saw me retreating. In the gorge I sang *Oh My Darling Clementine* ('In a cavern, in a canyon') which my father used to sing to me as a small child. Then I sang another medley of early Beatles (*She Loves You, Can't Buy Me Love, I Should Have Known Better*). I tried not to think of the water filling my boots.

Tourist information says that 'It rains in November and December'. They're not wrong. It's a pity I didn't read it beforehand. One point I did note from a few days ago, though. I had asked for rain without thunder, as an improvement on rain with thunder. Be careful what you wish for.

Kolašin has been an important marker, a staging post since first planning the route. I'm still only there in virtual reality but let's hope it really is a milestone. Perhaps real progress can be traced from here.

Day 92
Kolašin (An Enforced Day Off)

The bus left Podgorica promptly for Kolašin but it did not arrive promptly. By coincidence, it was held up at exactly the spot where I turned round yesterday; then it was held up several more times. Beyond the tunnel, huge torrents of water exploded from the mountain into the road. Unfortunately, every time the bus was delayed my seat appeared to be two feet away from a precipice of several thousand feet. I vowed there and then never to take another bus journey abroad. 'A serious accident took place in Montenegro yesterday when a bus toppled into a gorge and all passengers on board were killed or horribly maimed. One Briton is believed to have been among them. His name has not yet been released but he was tall, thin, white, grey haired and a complete idiot.'

Many countries have terrifying bus journeys but the two worst I have known were both in Pakistan; the first led up the Karakoram Highway, the second from Skardu to Gilgit. On both of them you could look over the precipice and see the wreckage of previous buses far below. I remember clutching the seat in front so hard that I could actually see the whites of my knuckles. The bus from Skardu was left on a hill overnight so that it could run down in the morning for a jump start.

Arrival time in Kolašin was very late but it would have made no difference; no further progress was possible today. I wanted information about walking to Berane and accommodation en route. The tourist office was shut; the locals say it's always shut. I walked across the road to book a room in the expensive hotel; not only do they speak English in expensive hotels but they will make enquiries for you. The young man behind the desk spoke English, French and German and, with his colleagues, was about to take a Russian course. The ski season is now packed with Russians and Albanians; the summer season is packed with Israelis, though no-one seems to know why. The young man made some phone calls and roped everyone in for a discussion.

One of the staff comes from Berane and showed me the main road on the map; but it's 84 kilometres and there is no accommodation for the last 62. I showed him the southern route, marked on the map as a main road; he had never heard of it and muttered darkly about rivers overflowing. The main man made another call and discovered that there was accommodation on this southern route after about 33 kilometres. Either way, I couldn't set out today. Tomorrow I have to make a stab at it and, if I don't make it, come back again. A pass is marked as 1,500 metres high, but Kolašin is 1,400 so it should be a gentle climb.

Kolašin will be very busy with skiing in a few weeks' time. It looks, in fact, as if it would be a cheery little number in either winter or summer: hotels, bars, restaurants and shops abound. Today, however, no-one is going out of doors. They say that none of them has ever known anything like it; rain has fallen for 48 hours and is forecast for another 48 hours. The tourist information is right; it rains in November and December.

Suddenly the bar was full of American soldiers, fully rigged out in camouflage gear. Where did they spring from? They were doing what servicemen always do when the weather's bad: head for the bar. Intrigued to know what these chaps talked about, I tried to overhear their conversations.

One of them was saying: 'I know what pressure is...'

Now, these guys, some if not all of them, really do know what pressure is. However, I was reminded of the comment of Keith Miller, cavalier among Australian cricketers who served in the air force during the Second World War. He was asked, when an old man, about the pressure that young cricketers faced today. 'Pressure?' Miller growled. 'I'll tell you what pressure is. Pressure's having a Messerschmitt up your arse.'

I cut my hair and watched TV. Tonight is the first night of sleeping at altitude since the Dolomites.

Day 93
Kolašin to Berane

I think I'm a bit too tired to do this tonight. I'll do it tomorrow.

Day 94
Berane (A Rest Day)

This is two days out of three when I haven't walked, but today there was no option. I must lie down here exhausted and write about yesterday.

The first ten kilometres out of Kolašin were very quiet. Well, they weren't very quiet; the flooding river thundered down the valley and at one point had taken a chunk of the road with it. No traffic came along, not surprisingly.

A clutch of houses surrounded the junction where the road to Berane turned left. The signpost indicated Peć, which is far away over the mountains in Kosovo. But what happened to the road? Instead of the highway indicated on the map it had become a country lane, mostly single track; in six hours I saw about a dozen vehicles. This ought to be ideal walking country.

For some of the time, it didn't rain! The corollary of this is that for much of the time it did rain. However, for the first time in weeks it was manageable, something you got on with rather than a physical assault. So what else could go wrong?

The road climbed. Somehow a misunderstanding had arisen between me and the official altitude in Kolašin because this road climbed for five and a half hours; this is not an ascent of one hundred metres. Up we went, through pastures and small farming villages. Hay ricks dotted the roadside. Activity centres and hiking trails pointed to busy summers. It could almost have been the Alps. Indeed it must be pretty in summer with all the leaves on the trees. Autumn, when the leaves change colour, may be even better. In January the snow will come and cover everything in white. Spring will be heartening, here as everywhere. There is only one time of the year not to come here: now.

After a few hours it appeared that something was wrong with the distance calculations. On the map, the distance from the first junction to the next is marked as 19 kilometres. The top of the pass lies approximately half way, which ought to take about two and a half hours. After two and a half hours it hadn't arrived. After three hours it still hadn't. It came after a hard three and a half hours. To confirm the problem, a sign at the top advertised a hotel, just beyond the next junction, as being 16 kilometres away. The whole stretch is supposed to be only 19!

As fast as I could, I descended. I seem to remember there was a good view at the top but this was no time for views. Towards the bottom, almost every vehicle offered me a lift but I stoically declined. At quarter to five, in the dark, the second junction arrived; it had taken seven hours from the previous junction and the map must have been wrong by at least ten kilometres.

This is where the route takes a diversion. Ahead, the road leads to Peć in Kosovo, which is where I want to go. However, the border crossing is closed; to confirm it, a big cross was drawn over the signpost. It's a two-day detour via Berane.

At this stage I was in a quandary. Should I take the Peć road, where the hotel had been advertised, walk a couple of kilometres off my route in the growing dark and risk the hotel being closed? Or should I head for the motel, two or three kilometres along the road to Berane, which I had been assured, backed up by a phone call, was open? I headed for Berane.

Wherever that motel was, and whether it was open or not, it wasn't on the road to Berane. Instead I had to walk 16 kilometres to Berane. It was pitch dark on 2 December in the middle of Montenegro. Was this how I wanted to be spending my life? It was so dark that I didn't even know if I was going uphill or downhill; a river ran by the road but I couldn't tell which way it was flowing. The plan for the day had been to walk to the motel which should have been about 32 kilometres or twenty miles, with the possibility of continuing to Berane in an emergency. As it was, I walked for almost twelve hours without a break, without even sitting down. The distance was unclear but it was well over thirty miles.

In the old days I would have cursed quite a lot about all this but still got up and walked the next day. Those days are gone. I lay down, took another heart pill, went to sleep, managed to get up later to have a shower then went back to sleep again. Food would have to wait until the morning.

Apparently the mountains here have traditionally been called Accursed.

Approaching Kosovo I took the Albanian phrasebook out of the bag. I can't make head nor tail of it; I can't remember a single word. This is doubly unfortunate because I have finished reading my last book and am in desperate straits. What I have left is the Croatian phrasebook, the Albanian phrasebook and the pamphlet of excerpts by Edith Durham of her travels in Albania which I have read twice already. A bleak few days lie ahead.

Today I did go for a walk round Berane, trying vainly to find the way out towards Rožaje. There are no signposts and, for the first time on the trip, I became irritable with someone other than myself. I asked around. I would like to go to Rožaje, please. No, I do not want to go to the monastery. I would like to go to Rožaje. NO, I DO NOT WANT TO GO TO THE MONASTERY!

Sadly, there is nothing to say about Berane. I covered almost every street and there is nothing to say about any of them.

A fifth day of rain fell. Television pictures are full of floods. The bridge in the centre of town is closed. Storm damage?

DAY 95
BERANE TO ROŽAJE

Sixth day of rain. Or snow.

All night I worried about finding the way out of Berane. In fact it was no trouble. Heading out in the direction I hoped was correct, four separate people indicated the same way. Normally I count on two out of three being a reasonable probability; four out of four must surely be definitive. Signposts would be even better, of course.

Ahead lay what appeared to be a low range of pretty hills. Appearances can be deceptive. After two hours of climbing, the rain turned to snow. After another hour, a ski lift appeared to the right, then a large ski hotel. At the top, a tunnel appeared through the mountain. Some might point out that strictly the tunnel was banned to pedestrians; but I didn't think this applied to me, and anyway there was nowhere else to go. It was 1,300 metres long, though, quite a scary tunnel. At the other end, the road headed downhill.

It did not, however, descend beyond the snow line. In fact the longer it went on the harder the snow fell. After a while it encroached on the road and slush formed; every time a vehicle passed I got heavily sprayed. I lost count of the number of lifts offered: these are generous people and it must have seemed totally mad to be walking in this. I stopped for tea at petrol stations and plodded on.

After the second stop it became cold. Until now, it has been fine to wear just a shirt under the waterproof. In the rain I don't like wearing gloves because they take about three days to dry out. In this weather, though, a lot more clothing will be needed. I shook with cold as I came down into Rožaje.

Ah well, everyone says there's a posh hotel in Rožaje; it's bound to be warm in a posh hotel. Right in the middle of town there was indeed a hotel and it was indeed posh. What it was not was warm. I took the only course of action, asked for the heating to be turned up, went to bed and ate peanuts. Spasms of pain and cold gradually receded. However, when I got out of bed nothing was warmer. The room was cold, the water was cold, the whole hotel was cold, even the tea was cold! They kept going busily off to the boiler to do something about it; nothing changed.

Rožaje is a bustling town, much bigger than I expected. It is the furthest outpost of Montenegro, on the borders of both Kosovo and Serbia. Mosques seem to predominate here. I have absolutely no idea what language I'm supposed to be speaking but instead have had another go at Albanian. The phrasebook is comprehensive and covers football. The phrase for 'penalty spot' consists of three words, the last of which has 21 letters. The final four of those letters are S-H-I-T. Presumably that's what you say to the referee. The phrasebook, incidentally, was geared to Albania, rather than Kosovo, when I went there 24 years ago. It is now, like most of my life, very out of date. It is not necessary today in Kosovo, for example, to say 'Let us drink this toast to your leader, comrade Enver Hoxha.' In fact it might be distinctly inadvisable.

They say that the road to Peć brings a very stiff climb; it is also a long way through high mountains. Can I do it? I have reached the mountains a week later than planned and obviously the conditions may be difficult. Can I make Peć? After that, things may be easier. Tomorrow, however, could be tricky.

KOSOVO

DAY 96
ROŽAJE TO PEJË (PEĆ)

I moan about not having hot water for washing or shaving in the morning. Patrick Leigh Fermor would be hunkered down under his greatcoat in a beechwood forest, taking the opportunity to mug up on a few local dialects. Shaving? A piece of bark would do, or perhaps his trusty pen-knife.

What I want is a piece of cheese on toast, with Marmite spread on top. Last night I ordered a mixed salad. It was perfectly all right, there was absolutely nothing the matter with it; my only problem was that every single item in the salad was pickled. Foreigners are just not like us. They like pickled salad.

And another thing. Every morning I ask for scrambled eggs, which are clearly marked on the menu. Every morning I get an omelette. The man always asks: 'omelette?' 'No,' I say, 'scrambled eggs, please,' pointing to it on the menu. 'Ah yes,' he says. Then he brings an omelette.

Now, about that mountain.

Since first planning to come by this route, I have looked at the map and then looked again. Could I do it? Was there any alternative? The answer to both questions appeared to be no. The only possible outcome therefore was to set out and hope for the best. Last night I wasn't sure about this approach. Today I set out.

Climbing out of Rožaje, I was directed on a short cut up a back road. It was so steep and so icy that further progress seemed impossible. After a while I reached the main road. That was better.

It was a steady climb. Plenty of snow lay beside the road. After a while it encroached on the road despite all the ploughing and gritting. I walked down the middle of the road. The air was completely still and fresh snow lay on every tree: a lovely sight. After a couple of hours the heart was pounding and I realised I was going too fast. I slowed down, took a couple of rests, drank water and set off again at a steadier pace. Looking back, the whole valley of Rožaje was covered in cloud. Above it, the road basked in sunshine and the views in all directions were staggering. I gaped, rested and pushed on to the national border.

The border between Montenegro and Kosovo was in fact a curiosity; the two border posts were nearly two hours' walk apart. Who owns the land in between? Neither border post stood at the top of the pass. From the Montenegrin post a steep incline led to the top, amounting to four hours' walk from Rožaje. From there I began the slippery decline. As it happened, the Kosovan border guards reached me before I reached them; a combined patrol of border guard and police stopped their jeep to give me the usual once over. I carried on down.

It was utterly treacherous. A few miles from the top a clutch of lorries had come to a complete halt on the uphill. They must have been there for days: it was Sunday and no lorries had passed. They were digging and sanding and manoeuvring without much luck. They might have to wait for spring.

Suddenly the mountains were enveloped in cloud and for an hour or two I saw nothing at all. Then the road descended below cloud level and the snow disappeared. Far below, the fields and villages of Kosovo looked like toy farms in a peaceful world, very different from the harsh countryside behind. A huge series of hairpin bends led finally to the valley floor.

The days are rapidly growing shorter; in addition, travelling east brings earlier darkness. The target for the day was Peć (more properly now Pejë, the Albanian title) but I had to stop at a motel a few kilometres short. It was a stroke of luck. The accommodation was adequate, the huge dining room hosted hundreds of customers and the young man from the hotelier family spoke English and almost everything else.

He was born in Sweden of Kosovan parents who had sought refuge there from the mayhem at home. Later they moved to Germany and then, when things improved, they came home. It was a reminder, if one were needed, of the mass slaughter that happened here only a very few years ago. Life may appear normal but it surely cannot be.

A woman came up and asked if I was the American who visited her café in Sarajevo after the war. I had to admit that it wasn't me.

One sign of the recovery in all the new republics is of homes being built in all directions: people are coming home, some are newly affluent and everyone wants to make a fresh start. It has got to be a healing process to help them move on.

There is one way in which no-one in these parts has moved on: smoking. It would not be true to say that everyone smokes. Those who do smoke, however, are living in a different age. It was an age when you smoked over your food - and everyone else's food - and everyone else's lungs. They need a very good dose of political correctness.

Day 97
Pejë to Klinë

Thirty-three years ago I arrived in Peć, having walked from Athens. At this stage, however, it all got too much, I went to bed for a day or two and then I caught a bus out of Peć. As usual, I finished in Scott's flat in Basle to recuperate. I remember nothing at all of Peć (Pejë) but am determined not to get ill there again.

The best way to make sure of this is not to go there at all. It was, so they said, nothing special, so I could skirt the town, stay on the main road and head instead for Prishtinë (Pristina). So I did.

This morning I had another chat with the young man at the motel, who is in a very strange position. He has Swedish nationality but left Sweden when he was five and remembers almost nothing of the language or country. The family then spent eleven years in Germany; he keeps up with friends there and visits once a year. Finally, at sixteen he came 'home' to a country he had never seen.

I solved the omelette question by eating three hard boiled eggs, which might cause other problems, then set out for my first full day in Kosovo. It began with helping to push a car which sounded as if it had suffered a fatal illness. We had several goes at pushing it, without any luck. Then: yes! Success! Smiles all round.

I once pushed a car with John Newcombe, Australian tennis star and Wimbledon winner. It was at Queen's Club, London, one quiet afternoon. A young man came in wanting a push. Only two of us were sitting there: me and John Newcombe. So off we went. Actually I felt a bit superfluous; he could probably have picked it up and carried it if he had felt like it. We were successful, anyway. I doubt, though, whether John remembers the day he pushed a car with me.

In fact there may have been three of us. The other one was a Wimbledon doubles winner whom I knew slightly, but I wouldn't want to drop names. At the time he wanted me to import Australian opals through Germany into Britain; it sounded so dodgy that I, and probably lots of other people, decided against getting involved.

Behind Peć, the huge range of yesterday's mountains dominated the skyline. It would be hard to imagine two days of greater contrast. Yesterday I battled up a mountain and hacked a way through the snow; today I ambled down the flat main road. The farmland is wet and the drainage ditches are being dug but the December sun was balmy and the day passed unmemorably. Tomorrow brings a low range of hills and far ahead lie further snow-tipped mountains. When all this land was ruled by the Turks, their armies must have marched here from Istanbul and thought nothing of it. Or did they? Did they think it was a bloody long way? Then, to make it worse, when they arrived they had to fight people. I haven't got to fight anyone so it ought to be a piece of cake.

Occasional damage from recent wars still litters the roadside. Poignantly, a roadside graveyard commemorated a number of men who had all died on the same day, 14 May 1999. Was it a battle, or was it ethnic cleansing by the Serbs? It won't happen any more, anyway. Kosovo is now almost exclusively Albanian. The road signs are in two languages but on almost all of them one version has been deleted; only Albanian remains.

In London, I went to the Kosovan Embassy to try to find out something useful; when I eventually found the office, however, I couldn't think of anything sensible to ask. The embassy is just a rented office in a block. They were pleasant to me but they couldn't think of anything useful to tell me either. I wanted to know everything about Kosovo but I came out knowing less than when I went in.

Day 98
Klinë to Komoran

Friends!
In Britain, trying to find out more about Kosovo, I came across Elizabeth;

we arranged to meet at Stanford's, the map shop, where she was one of the shortlisted candidates for a travel writing award. Her partner, Robert, is seconded to Kosovo from the British civil service. They have set up a charitable foundation together and Elizabeth does other good works besides. They are the perfect people to know. Elizabeth gave me useful information and said that of course I must stay with them when I arrived in Prishtinë.

Not only are they the perfect people to know, they are also great people. Both have learned fluent Albanian, which not many of the foreign workers bother with. They have numerous Kosovan friends, they are embedded into the culture and customs and above all they really love the place. Something else is remarkable about Elizabeth and Robert: they both have their first books coming out this year. This is a truly remarkable coincidence and feat. Imagine it if they were both trying but only one succeeded; the unsuccessful one would of course be delighted for the other, but still… Elizabeth has a travel book, Robert a tub-thumping novel. I can't wait to read both of them.

Robert has another endearing quality, one which he shares with me: he counts the books he has read. (I have listed every book I have read for the last 54 years.) He takes it further than me in that he makes sure he reads two 'good' books per month in addition to everything else. (I have no such inhibitions; a book is a book.) Like me, Robert reads a certain number of books in the year and then stops, saves up all the half read volumes and tears into them at the start of the new year to get ahead with the target. Ah, kindred souls of sanity.

I walked from Klinë to Komoran. Along the way, schoolkids did what schoolkids do: laughed, joked, said hello, showed off. Drivers pooped their horns. A man told me in German that he had been a fashion worker in Germany but had now retired back in Kosovo and was living on the meagre pension that a poor country could provide. In the evening a politician, campaigning in Sunday's elections, told me in a restaurant that he had seen me earlier on the road. Some people shyly would not speak to me but most were flowing with friendship. They like the Brits because we supported them in the war. Let's hope it lasts.

I caught the bus from Komoran to Prishtinë and will go back in the morning. Elizabeth was still travelling back from Britain so I spent the evening with Robert, swapping tales about books and Balkan history (well, he swapped and I listened) and travel. Elizabeth arrived later. She brought me more heart pills; since I had only two days' supply left this was rather useful. She also brought me a book and today's *Guardian*. Two messages from home have also reached me. First, Simon tells me that England have beaten Australia by an innings. Yes! Second, Tony Spurgeon wants me to be president of Norfolk Lawn Tennis Association. Has he taken leave of his senses? At the moment I can hardly think where Norfolk is; all I am concentrating on is that endless piece of dual carriageway I've got to walk down tomorrow. It's very flattering (or they can't find anyone else to do it) but it doesn't seem like the real world.

DAY 99
KOMORAN TO PRISHTINË

I always thought that if I could make it to Prishtinë I could make it to Istanbul. Now I'm here, I'm not so sure. Still, it's a landmark. A fairly chaotic, fast expanding landmark too, a very busy place bursting with life and commerce and debate. I walked from Komoran, found my way eventually into the city and went to stay another night with my British hosts.

Among her other accomplishments, Elizabeth is writing a book about Edith Durham, whose travel writing about 'High Albania' a century ago makes your hair curl. Apparently more Albanian males than females were always born. Theory had it that this was a process of natural compensation; more male births were needed to make up for the numbers who would always be shot.

In the modern day, Elizabeth and Robert are godparents, or the equivalent, to a Kosovan child. The ceremony involves the godparents in the first cutting of the child's hair. It also involves responsibilities. I asked if this included much shooting. Well, if anyone offends the family's honour…

And then there are other local traditions. For example, when drinking a toast you must look your friend in the eye. Failing to do so brings seven years' bad sex.

A constant stream of visitors of all shapes, sizes and nationalities came to my hosts' door or telephoned, and then we went to a restaurant to eat with a few of them. A political analyst gave us a sample joke about Sunday's election: 'A man takes his wife to the polling station to vote. Because he respects her he does not enter the booth with her but merely tells her whom to vote for. When she emerges he checks that she voted for the right person. She tells him she voted for someone else. "Oh no!" he cries, dumbstruck with horror. He runs to the officials. "My wife voted for the wrong candidate," he says. "Can I correct it?" "Don't worry," they say. "It's all right. We've already done it."'

The restaurant was full of internationals. Until now they have been welcomed because of the independence they brought and sustained. Now there is a danger of outstaying their welcome, of becoming an occupying force. They can even be seen as racist, as they learn no Albanian and look down on the Kosovan people.

In Egypt long ago I met two young Frenchmen, Jacques and Jean-Pierre, travelling to South Africa. We counted the words of English they knew; one knew six and the other knew two, which was not really enough to get them through the continent. Worse than that, of course, was their going to South Africa at all in the days of Apartheid. I saw them last in Kenya after they had survived a jail in Uganda, and asked them to send me a postcard later, just to show they were alive. They never did so perhaps they weren't.

It was a great night in Prishtinë and I will be very sorry indeed to leave. We exchanged contact details and we will meet again.

Day 100
Prishtinë to Ferizaj

The ground came up to meet me.

It was all going quite well, really. Following my two nights in Prishtinë I had plenty to think about and wasn't bored at all. The miles were ticking away and Ferizah was within reach. Then, abruptly, rudely, it all changed.

I tripped on something, a loop of wire or something similar, on the dirt bit beside the road. I went flying - literally head first. Nose, forehead, cheekbone, lips and eyebrows all hit the ground, smack. A bus driver, startled probably by this suddenly tumbling Englishman, slowed, swerved slightly, nearly stopped but went on again. I rolled off the side of the road and sat up. I was in one piece. Nothing was broken. Blood, however, ran everywhere. It used up all the tissues I was carrying. I mopped up as well as I could and recovered from the shock. After twenty minutes or so I got up and walked to the nearby filling station, giving a considerable surprise to two lads chatting in the forecourt as blood oozed all over me.

The filling station had running water. I cleaned up the wounds, applied antiseptic and put a plaster over my nose, then another two around the left eye. The lads, trying to be sympathetic, offered some talc which they had found somewhere and which I didn't like to refuse. Thanks, boys. By the time I came out of the toilet I was passable. Grazes and minor cuts and I would have a black eye. I was glad I didn't have to ask a hotel for a room tonight.

But that made it worse. Through another British couple whom I haven't even met yet I was offered hospitality with a Kosovan family in Ferizaj. I was going to turn up, a complete stranger, somewhat shaken and covered in plasters and bruises. What would they think? Was this how all guests behaved?

Of course the outcome was inevitable. The family of Gani and Ganimete, including Gani's mother and various sisters and nephews, all made me unbelievably welcome. If they were perturbed by my physical appearance they hid it well. According to Kosovan rules of hospitality I was doing them a favour by staying with them: here, close to the centre of Ferizaj, in the house that has been Gani's home for the whole of his life. We talked all evening: football, politics, judo and war. There is much to talk about and much to learn. Eleven people ate the family meal: a sister who is a journalist in Sweden, other sisters who live in the house or nearby and various other blood relations. Everyone wanted to participate, to welcome, to talk and to exchange.

Gani himself has recently returned from a year studying in Leicester, where he made friends with fellow students from all over the world. The only people he did not meet were British. No-one invited him into their homes or socialised with him. That, I'm afraid, is the way we are. It looks pretty pathetic when set beside the hospitality I have received here tonight.

Following his studies, Gani is obliged to work for the Kosovan government for three years. However, if they don't contact him within two months of his return he's a free agent. Currently he is working with the British couple whom I am yet to meet. He's not chasing the postman…

They gave me a bed in the main sitting room because it's the warmest room in the house, where I'm as snug as a bug. Cold weather is supposed to set in this weekend. Kosovo is unseasonably warm at the moment, fifteen degrees this afternoon; normally it's snowing at this time. Revenge is on the way. They say Macedonia is usually a few degrees warmer than Kosovo. I need to get there as soon as possible; then I need to get beyond it to the Mediterranean.

Day 101
Ferizaj to Kačanik

As I walked into Ferizaj yesterday afternoon the temperature was thirteen degrees. This morning, snow lay on the ground. Tonight it's minus thirteen!

We had a discussion around the breakfast table about scrambled eggs and I explained their dearth at all my breakfast tables. No-one understood what scrambled eggs were so I cooked them for the family. I don't know whether they liked them or not but they were very polite about them.

Then I left them the pan to be washed up; that's always the worst part of cooking scrambled eggs.

It was a convivial meal which meant a late start. Gani's brother arrives today from the US so he has taken the day off work. He, mother, sister, nephew and I sat around the table and chatted more. The only problem in the household was that the poor two-year-old screamed whenever she saw my battered old features. I didn't blame her. I wanted to scream myself. I had to be hidden away until she went to kindergarten.

They told me something useful about cooking in Kosovo. No-one starts cooking anything just before the hour. Power cuts always start dead on the hour, so anything you have started is immediately ruined. Beans on toast can be started five minutes before the hour but nothing else. Then, just after the hour, when no power cut arises, everyone starts cooking and there is a huge surge in demand. It's best to start on the half hour and to choose something of thirty-minute cooking duration.

Tonight I am staying with Mary and Alan in Kačanik. They are the first people I have met who understand completely what I am doing. They even understand that in the morning they must take me back to the spot where they picked me up tonight. They're British, they know about these things. I walked through Kačanik and carried on for a couple of hours, through a famous gorge; in fact it's more of a deep valley than a gorge but very pretty nonetheless. By arrangement they picked me up by an enormous bridge and took me back to their house.

This is another couple who are totally assimilated into Kosovan life and committed in the long term to staying here. To demonstrate this, with Kosovan friends they are building a house where each family will have a floor. Meanwhile, the British couple are camping out, to use their term, in another house belonging to the family; in the war this house was a hiding place for refugees. One oddity struck me about the house: there was no mirror to be seen. It is impossible in my experience to shave without a mirror so they eventually found one for me.

It would be hard to imagine a more dramatic change in lifestyle than Alan has experienced. One moment he was working in local government in North Yorkshire; the next, he was seconded to the UN in Kosovo! He said he fancied a change and looked in the job adverts to see what was around. Never could he have imagined where that would take him. Now he works for various bodies, funded in arcane ways by diverse governments and organisations. Essentially he advises on structures, which were totally absent after the war. It's good to know that North Yorkshire local government is now the model for the renewal and rebirth of Kosovo.

After a period of Alan working here, Mary thought she'd have a go as well. At home she was an obstetrician and gynaecologist; sometimes she still is, returning for a spell to keep up with medical developments and earn some money. Here she works in women's health. Both of them speak fluent Albanian. At home they have three grown-up children living in Edinburgh. They also have three of their own parents to think about. Next week they will see them all when they go home for Christmas. Sometimes they feel guilty about leaving their children behind. The children probably think they're mad, as well. They are, however, doing a fine thing.

We had a wonderful evening talking about walking and local government and timber and books and mountains and families and women's health. The Kosovan friends came in and we had tea and popcorn. As I write, it is after midnight.

MACEDONIA

Day 102
Kačanik to Skopje

Before I left home, I said it might take eight weeks to walk from the Brenner Pass to Istanbul. 56 days. Well, 56 days was yesterday and there's still a hell of a long way to go.

It was wonderful speaking English with English-speaking people. I notice, however, that when I have people to talk to I write far less about the journey. Why is that? I can only conclude that there is no time for all that thinking. Far too much of the world's time is spent thinking. It can do no good.

Alan dropped me off where they had picked me up yesterday. It was very cold. Alan and Mary will now spend the weekend packing for the Christmas hols. I envied them going home. However, I don't envy them their life in general; rather, I look at them with awe. I couldn't do what they're doing. For one thing, I don't really like being abroad.

There's another thing, though, about them and about Elizabeth and Robert. Not only did they all come to Kosovo to try to do a bit of good in the world. They came to do it together, each couple united. They will suffer discomfort, put their careers on hold, risk all kinds of problems; but they're in it together. Each couple seem to be in absolute accord. Yes, they fill me with awe.

It is not ideal to cross a border wearing three plasters and sporting various other abrasions and a black eye. The Macedonians didn't seem too bothered, though. The young woman border guard examined my passport and addressed me affectionately by my first name. Down the hill and into the plain, I was able to look back at the mountains. Skopje was cold, but it was a damn sight warmer than Kosovo. I had just got out in time.

Skopje, capital of Macedonia, is a strange town. It was totally destroyed by an earthquake in 1962; the town clock stands still at the time recorded when the earthquake struck. Rebuilt in the communist chic of the 1960s, it still holds old-style monolithic public buildings and a lot of workers' flats. Rebuilt again since independence, it is trying hard to rejuvenate itself with a new breed of more stylish monolithic public buildings. I wandered round some of these buildings and looked up at the fort. Planning the next few days is going to be tricky. I spent a good deal of time thinking about it: fruitless time spent making no decisions at all.

Is Skopje still on the main thoroughfare that people take to Athens from western Europe? By car, bus or train the route always seemed to be the same: Paris, Milan, Zagreb, Belgrade, Skopje, Athens. Bloody boring it was too, most of it. That bit between Zagreb and Belgrade, then Belgrade and Skopje... no thank you. I read a lot of books on trains on that bit in the past.

Linguistically, I was glad to get out of Kosovo; I acknowledge that I struggled with Albanian. However, it's a frying pan and fire situation: I know not one word of the Macedonian language and don't even understand the script. Fortunately I had some tuition tonight with the hotel receptionist, who used to be an au pair in Wembley. She explained the differences between the Macedonian and Serbo-Croat languages. Apparently they are massive and she tried to demonstrate how massive they were; I couldn't understand any difference at all. It seemed likely that my assaults on the language in Croatia and Montenegro would be equally disastrous here, no worse and no better, so I could carry on as before.

I mentioned the two young Frenchmen, Jacques and Jean-Pierre, who spoke eight words of English between them, but I forgot to mention their catchphrase. They tried to persuade me to go to Uganda with them and were highly amused at my reply. 'Pour un français,' I said, 'c'est dangereux. Pour un anglais c'est fatal.' This became their mantra, repeated about every situation in every country.

DAY 103
SKOPJE TO PETROVEC

The tourist information about Skopje says that the motivation for visiting a city is 'detecting the traces of urban history as a common ground constituting the universal quality of all cities. Thus, a cultured person follows Kirkegaard's instructions pertaining to the value of the individual in all the complexity of the social, and Hegel's advice on seeing common destiny in the fragmentariness of the individual.'

Be that as it may, it was freezing in Skopje today and the forecast says that colder weather will be sweeping into the Balkans. Let's get out of the bloody Balkans then.

It's a two day walk to Veles. In fact it's not that far and shouldn't take two days, but there's nowhere to stay en route. I set out purposefully in the morning, found myself walking on a motorway, doubled back and by good fortune happened upon the road to Petrovec. The airport is close by and I walked half way from there to the next village, which had an indecipherable name and was seven kilometres away. Then I walked back to Petrovec; half way and then back will have to count as doing the whole way. I caught the bus back to Skopje. Tomorrow I will catch the bus or train to Veles, walk half way to the indecipherable village and then walk back to Veles. I am no longer even ashamed of such machinations.

The bus driver kept up the great traditions of bus drivers everywhere. He growled, grunted and snarled at me; but he didn't discriminate, he did the same to everyone. By enormous food fortune I had the exact fair, thirty dinars. My next note upwards was five hundred dinars; I shudder to think what would have happened if I presented this to him.

Off the main road a number of cars were parked, their drivers clearly waiting for passengers. Was it a Sunday morning football match? Ah, no, it was a big functional building that came into view. It was a prison, with the high, turreted watchtowers of American prisons in the south. The families must be waiting for Sunday visits, perhaps a visit outside the prison or perhaps home leave. One thing was for sure: they were bound to be kept waiting because no-one had done the paperwork.

Elsewhere, I was sure I saw both a spotted woodpecker and a goldfinch today. Do they have them here? My mother in old age would spend hours at her kitchen window watching the woodpeckers eat peanuts from the holder. I could happily watch them for hours too.

Skopje doesn't have a tourist office, for the obvious reason that there are no tourists. Some people, though, must come here because they have to. In the evening I had another walk round the burgeoning modern buildings of what is a new city. It's all right. It has an old river. It has a castle.

The blotch of blood on my forehead looks worse than when I first fell but the rest is getting better; various abrasions are improving and the swelling around the eye is receding. The cheekbone under one plaster is giving no trouble but the nose under the other one itches continually. I am not an oil painting.

In fact I look a bit like a man I used to know in Manchester. Continually he would go to the pub and come back injured; a speciality of the area seemed to be a bottle, broken off and ground into his eyebrow. 'But you should see the other feller,' he used to say. It took us a while to realise that he did it himself.

I am reminded of the words of Cole Porter in High Society:

> 'Have you heard
> About dear Blanche
> Got run down
> By an avalanche?'
> 'No!'
> 'Game girl,
> Got up and finished fourth.'

Day 104
Petrovec to Veles

This thing about going south and going downhill doesn't seem to have kicked in yet. Overnight, the first snow of the year came to Skopje. Today the first snow of the year came to Veles. How far south do we have to go before it gets hot?

Mind you, four or five days further south would have been disastrous at the moment. Furious storms have lashed Greece, Turkey and Lebanon. Torrential rainfall and gale force winds have caused major damage to property. They might have tickled up a walker too. For once I'm in the right place.

It was a mess of a day, though. This afternoon I thought I had mucked up entirely and fallen short in every possible way. Only later did I realise that I had been rather lucky.

From Skopje to Veles I caught the train - nearly an hour late - intending to walk back from there to the unpronounceable village after Petrovec and then return to Veles. First, I wanted to dump my bag in a bedroom somewhere.

However, the rumoured hotel in Veles closed two and a half years ago. A taxi took me to a motel that stood in completely the wrong direction, in fact back on the road to Petrovec. I left the bag and started walking but unfortunately was pointed towards the motorway. Furthermore, the man told me in English that it was three or four hundred metres when he meant three or four thousand. I am hardly in a position to criticise someone's mistake in an alien tongue but, by the time I returned from the error, I had walked an extra seven kilometres and it was one o'clock in the afternoon.

The decimal point is, of course, easily mislaid. A couple of years ago someone in Walthamstow Council was (allegedly) supposed to order 24,000 daffodil bulbs but unfortunately ordered 240,000. For a period, daffodil bulbs swamped the borough; like everyone else, I acquired some for the allotment, some for the front garden and a bucketful for spares. Daffodils are now everywhere in Waltham Forest. I have no idea if the origin of the story is true but there are certainly a lot of daffodils.

By the time I finally started walking, there was no possibility of reaching Petrovec and making my way back again to Veles, so I decided again to resort to the last refuge of the scoundrel: walk half way and then return. I walked for an hour and three quarters which was almost half way. (If I wanted to claim the morning's superfluous seven kilometres I had distance to spare but opinions must be divided on whether this is legit.) The old road led past a lake on which a large boat serves as a hotel in the tourist season. (But how did it get there? Was it built there?) As the road climbed uphill into the snow, traffic died away. An Italian in a Merc drove on up. Where on earth was he going? Two minutes later he returned and opened his window, which gave some air to his passenger, a small dog; where was the route to the motorway? Tracks in the snow suggested that a previous vehicle had been dug out. Five minutes before my calculated destination of half way, I had to turn round. The snow was just too deep. If I had set out originally from Petrovec I might never have made it.

I pondered on the route which the Italian in the Merc thought he was taking and the illusion that he was travelling on. We have all been given duff directions from time to time. We have all been at the mercy of deluded drivers also. I was once on a bus from London to Athens which got lost before it reached the Thames; it then got lost in Dover, Calais, Paris, Milan, Trieste, Zagreb, Belgrade and all points in between. The drivers did not appear to know which country followed the last. This is something which I do not think I have ever been guilty of. Many times I have been lost, almost always through my own inadequacies; but I don't think I have ever gone to the wrong country entirely.

Belinda's husband, Tim, was once sent to the travel agent to book a holiday in Madeira. When he reached the agency, however, he couldn't remember which country he was supposed to be booking for. He knew it began with 'M' and finished with 'A'... They had a very nice holiday in Menorca.

DAY 105
VELES TO NEGOTINO

Last night I was in the depths of despair. It seemed impossible to reach Negotino today in daylight, let alone Gevgelija in the following two days. I was at the point of giving up. Well, maybe I wasn't really but it felt like it at the time.

This morning I was out of Veles like a rat out of a trap. Then the day went surprisingly well.

Snow lay on the hills and fields as far as the eye could see. It is forecast for Greece and indeed it has already fallen in Athens. (Nice to see signposts for Athens already, by the way.) In the early morning the road was slippery but by the afternoon the tarmac was clear. And it was very, very easy.

The reason? The old road was completely free of traffic because a motorway had been built alongside it. None of this was on my map so it came as a pleasant surprise. It followed the river so it ran downhill. Earlier than expected, Gradsko came along at lunchtime.

This is a wild west sort of a town, a big wide main street full of folks moseying on down; all it needed was a few Cadillacs cruising. I approached a group of men for directions. Unfortunately, looking at my appearance and listening to my pathetic attempts at their language, they directed me to the hospital. 'I'm getting better!' I wanted to tell them. 'These few cuts - pah, you should have seen me five days ago!' I managed eventually to convey that

I wanted to walk to Negotino and they gave me directions so accurate that they could have been Swiss. I'm impressed by a man who tells me it is exactly 1.7 kilometres to a junction.

Actually the most embarrassing aspect of the whole negotiation was that I completely forgot the word Negotino. All morning I had been saying the word to myself and remembering it without difficulty. Then, at the hour of need, it completely deserted me. It's not even a difficult word but the age thing just crashed in. Humiliation knows no bounds when you get old. They say it helps to do crossword puzzles.

Over to the left, a big bridge had been washed away. On either side of the river, people stood looking into the abyss. There has been a lot of water.

In the afternoon a scooter pulled up beside me and a truculent man in a woolly hat dismounted. He asked what I was up to and demanded to see my passport. Since he was pretty scruffy and showed no ID I asked who he was and he said he was an observer of some sort: he kept an eye on things in the area. He claimed that this was like being in the police. At least, that was what I think the conversation was about; since it was conducted in German it may have been about football or fancy dress.

Eventually I let him have the passport but I stood very close lest he should try to make off with it. He asked a whole lot of questions, all the usual ones but with a few extra touches of malice. He wanted to know how I contracted my head injuries and he wanted to know if I had a job in England. Finally he was satisfied. No problem, he said. No problem in Macedonia. No, I thought, except for you.

All these officials seem transfixed by my visa for Belarus. Yes, it takes up a whole page in the passport. Yes, it's still a hardline communist state. As it happens, I was there for one night on my train route to Lithuania but I wish I had never been. In a few months my passport comes up for renewal so I shall be rid of it.

The quasi policeman was a bullshitter anyway. He said it was twenty kilometres to Negotino when I knew it was only ten.

Outside Negotino, in the gathering dark, came one of the most extraordinary sights of my life.

A massive, multitudinous flock of starlings had assembled in the sky. Thousands, no, millions of them converged: swooping, swirling, sweeping across the skyline, forwards, backwards, sideways, moving as one. They were like a vast cloud, constantly changing, joining and re-joining, breaking off and re-gathering. They looked like a solid entity, so close together that it seemed they must be touching. How do they all go in the same direction? How do they know which way the others will go? It was the largest group of birds I had ever seen and I stood and gaped. I wished my mother could have seen it.

On the BBC tonight the sports presenter made an interesting gaffe while speaking of some US sports star 'who stated he was gay in 2007'. No, Sean, it's 'who stated in 2007 that he was gay'. We don't believe he was gay only in 2007.

Pedantry rules.

Day 106
Negotino to Demir Kapija and Beyond

On that trip to Lithuania, also in December, on the first morning I went out of doors wearing a normal pair of jeans. Within seconds I was back indoors again. I ran indoors and put another pair of jeans over the top of the first pair; then I dared venture out again. For the rest of the trip I wore two pairs of jeans and was very snug.

The first time I ever experienced real cold was in Cut Bank, Montana, where I stayed with my friend Carol. On stepping outside the door, I was amazed by what happened to the inside of my nose: it froze! It was like having a small, sharp knife stuck up each nostril. Carol, incidentally, had previously taught in Alaska for a year. On the way back from school her pupils used to buy a bottle of Coke, take the top off and tip it upside down. By the time the liquid hit the ground it had frozen; the children picked it up and ate it as an iced lolly.

It wasn't as cold as that today but it was cold. It was also a mess.

The distance to Demir Kapija was twenty kilometres and it was uneventful. From here, however, the day took a knockback. The plan was to leave the bag in the promised hotel, walk on a good way and then walk back. However, there was no promised hotel. For ages I sat about, not doing any of the sensible things or even working out what they were, completely flummoxed. It was four hours for a train on to Gevgelija, seven hours back to Negotino. Buses went regularly to Negotino but not to Gevgelija. For some reason I couldn't even get a cup of tea. No-one spoke English, which is of course my problem not theirs. For an hour and a half I just sat there like a lemon.

Then, by an amazing coincidence, the waiter from my hotel last night in Negotino turned up. Our conversations were all in German so I was never too sure what was going on but he said that the restaurant across the street might do me a room; for five hundred denars, about eight euros, was I interested?

In the restaurant the young man, Alexander, spoke English, contradicting my earlier view. He showed me the room, which was absolutely freezing. He fetched a heater. Over hastily, I agreed to stay. Only afterwards did I look round. It wasn't the lack of sheets on the bed that was the problem; it was more the toilet block with broken window. I won't go into details.

Anyway, dumping my bag there I went off at speed in the direction of Gevgelija. The old road became a dirt road beside the railway line, through a dramatic canyon and into open farmland. The road itself was a sheet of ice and I trudged through the snow at the side. Actually it was very good fun. If only I had made a decision - any decision - earlier I could have gone a long way this way. After an hour or so, though, I had to turn back before it got dark.

By the time I reached town I had at least made a decision about the room: I couldn't stay there. I resolved to take the train back to Negotino and return in the morning to carry on. However, just as I reached town a man approached me, asked if I was heading to Gevgelija and said a taxi driver was just going there. Did I want to go with him?

Very quickly I went back to the restaurant, apologised profusely, explained about the lift, insisted on paying some of the money and made my way. They were fine about it. I was extremely relieved, to say the least.

This is not the shortest time I have ever been in a hotel room. (No, I have not hired one for an hour for an assignment.) In India once I was on a train when I was overcome with the need for a toilet. The train facilities did not seem adequate for my purposes. Just then, the train drew into a town where a large billboard advertised a smart-looking hotel about fifty metres from the station. Perfect. I left the train, walked (delicately) to the hotel and booked in. Having hastily done what was necessary in the toilet I was able to look round the room. No, no, this was not Ok. I was not fussy but this went beyond being fussy. I went back to the man at the desk, thanked him, returned the key, apologised, told him please to keep the (very small) money and returned to the station. The train was still there and I continued on my journey!

DAY 107
GEVGELIJA

Failure.

This was the day I failed to walk the whole distance.

In the morning heavy snow fell. Gevgelija ground to a halt. There was no chance of walking anywhere for the time being but I asked around for advice on the route back towards Demir Kapija. Was there an alternative to the motorway? Well, no, there wasn't. This would have made life difficult even without the snow. Everyone agreed: there was no alternative. What about cyclists? We run them over, said a taxi driver.

To my great surprise, Devgelija had a tourist office. The very, very nice young woman was just as surprised to see me as I was to see her. 'We don't get many tourists,' she said. Not only did Gelvgelija not receive many visitors, but the tourist office was tucked away where you would only come across it by accident. She was delighted to see me. I asked her too about the road to Demir Kapija. Was there any alternative to the motorway? No. Could I walk on it? 'Yes, of course. How else can you go there?'

Just in case all progress in any direction was impossible, I asked about trains into Greece. She rang several numbers but soon gave up. 'They sell the tickets,' she said, 'then they go home'. She said that the trains tended to go at different times each day and that the decrepit state of the railways was due to potential privatisation. I went up to the station, a truly unwelcoming venue for travel, and found a nominal time for travel south if all else failed.

Next I walked up to the motorway. The whole surface was covered by closely compacted snow and ice. It was clearly lethal and under no circumstances was I going up there. Not only was it certain that a vehicle would skid into me or vice versa but one could only imagine the conversation with the boys in blue. 'Where are you going, Mr.' - looking at passport – 'Mr. Jeremy?' 'I'm walking towards Demir Kapija then walking back again.' 'So you are needlessly endangering the lives of yourself and others for what exactly…?'

It really looked as if I was going to miss a section for the first time, so something else was needed: perhaps some equivalent of the distance I wasn't going to do, to find an equal punishment or at least a form of atonement. Putting on the balaclava for the first time, I set out into the countryside. Bogdanci was ten kilometres away. Yesterday a sign towards it had led from the motorway so it looked as if it might be vaguely in the right direction. Actually it turned out that it was at ninety degrees to the right direction, but it's all a distance. With some difficulty I walked there through the ice and drifting snow, failed to find anywhere for a cup of tea and walked back again.

That was it. From Demir Kapija to Gevgelija is 52 kilometres. Last night I may have walked ten kilometres. Today I walked twenty. I'm still 22 kilometres short. This may be due to circumstances beyond my control but it still hasn't been done. I would like to say that twenty kilometres in today's conditions were worth forty in any other, but that way lies a slippery slope. It's failure.

Tomorrow, weather permitting, I hope to progress into Greece. Yesterday Greece enjoyed a national strike in protest against austerity measures. Today those measures were due to go through parliament. Just to underline how things stand, the Greek government has, out of the blue, decided to ban trade unions from negotiating with private employers! What? So what are unions for? In this case, why not make them illegal altogether? Why do governments think they have the right to interfere in the workings of a private organisation? Would they apply similar legislation to an employers' association?

GREECE

DAY 108
GEVGELIJA TO POLYKASTRO

'Please hold the door in order not to be taken by the wind.' It was good advice for leaving the hotel in Polykastro because the wind howled all night. One might think it was also good advice for life.

It was hard work ploughing up through the snow from Gevgelija to the border; then the whole area between the two border posts was a massive sheet of ice. If you break your leg in No Man's Land, which government do you sue?

Not the Greek one if possible. Riots have broken out in Athens against the government's austerity measures; hundreds of petrol bombs are being flung in all directions. I have to admit though - and this is unworthy - that my first reaction on watching it on TV was to notice that the rioters were wearing t-shirts. It's warm in Athens now.

Greece certainly has more money than it did yesterday. For my first two cups of tea they have gathered in four and a half euros, by far the most expensive country since Holland. I like to think that I have done my bit for the economy.

'Welcome to Macedonia,' said the signs. Haven't I just left Macedonia? Ah, yes. 'Welcome to Greece. Welcome to Macedonia.' This is the Macedonia that lies within Greek borders. From time to time an independence movement rises up to demand unification. Most people think it won't happen.

First, a book exchange in the hotel in Gevgelija nearly brought me to a halt. A book exchange is, I'm afraid, more of a book acquisition when I'm travelling. However, I wanted two books out of this one. (*The Book Thief* by Markus Zusak and a Val McDermid I haven't read.) I felt too guilty to take two without leaving anything so I had to read four hundred pages of *The Girl With The Dragon Tattoo* overnight. It's a good book, although it's hard to see what all the fuss is about. It would be really nice to read a crime novel or watch a television series which was not about the serial murder of young women.

A day of bleak countryside, studded with fields of solar panels, led into

Greece and the town of Polykastro, administrative capital of the region. Here I bumped into a man who claimed to own all the hotels in town. He welcomed me to one of them. Then he gave me some advice. Take the bus to Thessaloniki, he said. It costs five euros. The combination of the weather conditions and Greek drivers makes it far too dangerous to walk. For the next day or so, he said, while I was under his wing, he was responsible for my safety. 'After that I don't care what happens to you.'

It is 33 years since I was last in Greece. I can remember four words of the language: please, thank you, yes and no. Suddenly, out of nowhere, two more have come to me: good morning and good evening. Thanks to a classical education I can remember the alphabet but the only word I can remember of ancient Greek is *thalassa*, the sea. Tonight I tried to buy a phrasebook but the bookshop was shut; I haven't yet worked out the opening hours. Until I get one, I will have to manage on six words.

In the last 33 years Greece may have changed. At that time I was walking from Athens through the countryside into what is now Kosovo. In those days, hospitality in the villages seemed universal and I had great difficulty paying for anything. In a shop I would ask for biscuits or chocolate and the woman would decline payment; in a café someone would buy my coffee. It was hard to reciprocate. I often tried to give something to the children but if the shopkeepers saw me doing so they would give me something else. Finally I got the children to write their names and addresses on postcards, which I eventually sent them from Britain. This seemed to satisfy everyone's sense of hospitality and no more gifts were proffered.

One day I suffered an incident of acute embarrassment. Walking up to a house which appeared to be a taverna, I asked if I could get a meal. Of course, they said. I sat down and, while I was waiting, I realised that it was not a taverna at all but a private house. I was mortified, apologised more than profusely and offered to leave immediately. They just laughed and insisted on giving me the meal.

Two other memories remain of the countryside on that trip. First, one night I was kept awake by the noises of tortoises mating; outside my tent there was a lot of rustling and a lot of squeaking. Second, no matter where I slept I could never avoid the local goatherd; I would seek out the most obscure of places, somewhere that surely no human being had ever trodden, but it made no difference. One night I found the perfect spot, half way up a mountain, miles from human life. Next morning at six o'clock a goatherd was unzipping my tent and laughing. He was absolutely delighted to find me inside the tent and wanted an early morning chat. Above all, he wanted to see me gather up my things and pack them all into my rucksack. How would they all go in? We shared my biscuits and water while I packed; all the while he was simply delighted. We said our farewells on the best of terms.

Speaking of rucksacks, today I managed to leave my rucksack undone after a stop, probably while taking the balaclava out. Idiot. Later, I had a count up and seemed to be missing a banana, half a bar of chocolate and a granola bar. It could have been a lot worse.

DAY 109
HALF WAY TO THESSALONIKI

Christmas is coming and everything is gearing up for it. Yesterday in a supermarket the canned music played the Greek version of *O Come All Ye Faithful*. It was overwhelmingly nostalgic. When I was three years old my father took me to the carol service at Gayton Thorpe where they played *O Come All Ye Faithful*. I remember the service and I remember coming home to tell my mother about it.

On the tapes, they mix up carols with modern Christmas songs. The best of the modern songs is, I'm afraid, that corny old chestnut, *White Christmas*. (Why don't the television schedules put on the film *Christmas Eve*, with George Raft, any more?) After that comes John Lennon's *Happy Christmas/ War Is Over* and then Shane MacGowan and poor Kirsty MacColl singing *Fairy Tale of New York*.

Once at a party I approached Shane MacGowan for some information. He was drunk, of course, and nearly insensible but his minder gave me the information I wanted. On my social work training course was a woman called Deborah, who was the partner of a band member of what later became The Pogues. Years after we trained, I heard tragic news about Deborah; she had a baby and then, unexpectedly and inexplicably, she died. I wanted to know what happened to the child. The minder said the child was loved and cared for and doing well.

Outside Polykastro, a police car passed me, travelling north. Ah ha, I thought, I bet I see you again soon. Two minutes later it had turned round and was beside me, wrong side of the road, lights flashing. The usual questions. Among them, where did you sleep last night? I hope I didn't make trouble for my friend the hotelier, who had given me not a shred of paperwork and was clearly involved in the national pastime (not my words) of tax evasion. The police moved on.

Once upon a time I worked as a postman in Windsor, Berks, England. Work began early and I had to leave home by bicycle at four thirty in the morning. Frequently I was stopped by the police. What did they think I was doing at four thirty in the morning on a bicycle: escaping with the swag? Why did they stop me rather than any passing cars? They were bored.

In that job my 'walk' for delivering mail in Windsor was number eighteen, the High Street and Peascod Street area. This walk was twinned with number one, which was the castle; when one postman was away the twin should be able to cover. I looked forward to delivering postcards to the queen and asked about being trained for it. Somehow it was always going to happen, it would be next week or next month; but somehow it never did.

Through the unremittingly bleak countryside of northern Greece I walked for seven hours. In the last hour the climate changed; the snow slithered away and the air grew warmer. Out of nowhere, a hotel appeared at a road junction. Which way do I go tomorrow? I'm none too sure, but that's tomorrow. Football from England is on the lounge television and a cup of tea is in my hand.

DAY 110
THESSALONIKI

The last time I was in Thessaloniki was so long ago that the colonels were still in power in Greece. On the train from Athens I met a student who said that, for the price I was going to give the youth hostel, I could stay with him instead. So I did. It seems insane now to have stayed with a complete stranger but in those days you did that sort of thing. That night he took me round the university and showed me all the big black cars of the secret police, watching, waiting.

Next morning the student was ill. He asked me to make him some chicken soup, which he said was the only thing that would make him better. On vegetarian grounds I refused to make chicken soup. I said I would gladly go out and buy the ingredients for vegetable soup. He didn't like it but had little choice in the matter. I made the soup.

He had second helpings. Very soon he began to feel better.

Before I left that afternoon, he said he had made two discoveries about life through my visit. The first was that vegetable soup was very nice. The second was that an Englishman would go to the trouble of making him soup; he hadn't thought that an Englishman would do anything for anyone. With that backhanded compliment following me, I left Thessaloniki.

Now I am as far south as the route goes; from here it's all east and a little bit north. The time difference has also kicked in. Greece is an hour further on than the rest of mainland Europe, so we have an hour more daylight in the later afternoon.

At nine o'clock on Sunday morning the cafes were full and everyone was jovial, laughing, jesting, knocking back the coffee. Everyone? Well, it was all men, of course. I wonder where the women were before Sunday lunch…

The long drag into Thessaloniki was interminable, through suburbs and scrap land and more suburbs. It used to be said that the second largest Greek-speaking city in the world was Melbourne. Surely Thessaloniki must have overtaken it by now? It was hard to know whether I had reached the centre, but at least this was the railway station, with hotels along the street. This is comfortable living. I bought a *Guardian Weekly* and failed to buy a phrasebook at the station bookshop. The *Guardian Weekly*, reporting from the elections in Kosovo, has a quote from Ardi, whom I sat opposite at a meal eleven days ago.

DAY 111

THESSALONIKI TO LANGADAS

There are two things I would definitely not want to have been doing on this Monday morning. The first is commuting to work in Thessaloniki. The second is commuting to work in London.

Never have I seen so many cars as in Thessaloniki. For a country in the depths of financial crisis, Greece has a lot of motor vehicles. Maybe it's even worse when they're not in the depths of financial crisis. Greece does not have the world's most patient collection of drivers, however, and you take your life in your hands.

London too has ground to a halt today. *BBC World* shows pictures of shrouded airports and thousands of stranded passengers. It's the coldest winter for a hundred years. Tomorrow, Alice and Mimi are scheduled to leave for Christmas in Lapland. It's hard to believe that this chaos could assail them twice in succession. Last year they were stranded by train and plane on the way to Switzerland. Eventually they got there and we had a lovely time; but there aren't many alternative routes to Lapland.

Probably there are sights to be seen in Thessaloniki: museums, old buildings, shops, all that. I sought the exit, however, only to find that leaving was just as interminable as arriving. I got lost, couldn't find any way out that didn't involve walking on the motorway, then clambered down a hillside and got found again. By this time I was short tempered. Then the motorway went on a nice flat route straight through the hills but the old road followed a long curvy detour over the top. I had only the vaguest clue where I was going but finally arrived at a crucial junction. Decisions, never my strong point, had to be made immediately.

The choice lay between the southern route, where there might be accommodation because of the lakes beside the road, or the northern route, where there might be accommodation because of the motorway. Either choice brought a long diversion. For no particular reason I chose the northern route and ended in Langadas, the largest town before Kavala, four or five days away.

It's a nice little town with a crummy little hotel. The landlady knows a few words of English and one of them is money. She does not know the English for 'Oh, two of the lights in your room have gone, I'll replace them straight away.' As I write, I have sought refuge in a young people's bar where the Vodafone people are about to approach me to buy their product.

I sat here feeling, as I said to myself, like a right prat due to not having a phrasebook and knowing only the same six words of Greek. Then I laughed out loud at the thought of my friend Mike, playing a tennis match for Norfolk, berating himself for being a right prat and missing an easy shot. Except that he didn't say 'prat'. 'YOU GREAT PRIRTLE!' he cried out loud at himself. Or perhaps it was PRYRTLE. Either way, the whole team was convulsed. Afterwards he was asked about it in detail; indeed he has been asked about it regularly in the ensuing thirty years. What exactly is a prirtle? It is not a creature known in Norfolk. He originates in Derbyshire so perhaps it is something growing in the hills. It has passed into legend and I chortled yet again into my tea at the thought.

As it happens, I did manage to buy a phrasebook today. However, it's in Greek. This is not, perhaps, surprising as we're in Greece but it is designed for the Greek person wanting to travel in Britain rather than the British person wanting to travel in Greece. It is unbelievably difficult to work backwards. If, for example, I want the Greek word for 'bedroom', I want to look up the English equivalent; but I can only look up the English equivalent if I already know the Greek word for it... I look like continuing with the same six words as before.

Langadas is not far enough for the day but it was unclear where the next accommodation would be. Every day I think the next day will be a big day; almost every day is much too short.

Tomorrow will be a big day.

Day 112

Langadas to Apollonia

What a huge day.

But first, what was this coming towards me?

Maybe an hour into the day, I could barely believe my eyes when a young couple with rucksacks advanced on the other side of the road. Did they speak English? Fluently. Unfortunately their business card, containing their email address, became stuck to my shirt later and totally illegible but I think their names were Kevin and Martha.

'Where are you walking to?' I asked.

'Austria.'

'Oh. I've just come from there.'

They were from Linz. Four years ago they set out round the world, travelling slowly and, I would guess, working here and there. Her parents had joined them in Canada, his in Turkey, but apart from that they were alone.

They had decided to conclude their trip by walking home from Istanbul to Austria.

And they were camping, by God.

For the last week they had not had a hot shower. (I had already told them that they must like each other a lot.) Last night they completely ran out of food when they found that the local shop had closed for the night; a local butcher gave them his own meal to share between them. They're heading for Albania to avoid the worst of the weather. I think they, like the previous walkers I met, may be in for a bad surprise when they reach Albania but I didn't like to disillusion them. All I could do was stand back and gape in awe. I told them they were tough guys. They're aiming to reach home in the spring; that's another four months of sleeping out. In the cold.

Beside the motorway, and accessible via a broken fence to the minor road, a couple of food vans did a brisk business. One of them gave out information to all and sundry. He was a walking tourist office: he even had brochures. He advised me that nothing lay ahead on this side of the lake for 35 or forty kilometres and I should cross to the other side, on the old road to Istanbul, where I was more likely to find accommodation. In particular, at Apollonia I would find the Spa Hotel, open all year, right on the main road. The area held thermal baths, Alexander the Great had stayed there and so could I. 'You've saved my life,' I told him. 'Just trying to help,' he said modestly.

He was very kind. The only problem was that there was no hotel of any description in Apollonia.

In the afternoon I came across something terrible.

To reach the other side of the lake, a long detour lay in a big curve. On the way, a strange cry, something like a young kitten, stretched softly upwards from the roadside hedge. I followed it. In a metal container lay three baby animals, their eyes still not fully open, mewling piteously. What were they? At first I thought they were puppies. Too big. Piglets? Maybe. In fact they looked like boar. Someone had left them there to die miserably.

I tipped the container on its side so they could at least get out, though this probably did them few favours; they needed to suckle, not forage for food. There seemed nothing else I could do. What kind of person can do this?

It was a long way to Apollonia. A billboard announced very early that we were entering the municipality of Apollonia. Ah, so it was a big place, the administrative centre of the region. I walked the last hour in the dark, unworried and planning a long soak in those thermal baths.

It's a crossroads. It has a couple of cafés. That's Apollonia.

To cut a long story short, I took a taxi to find a hotel. Local opinion said I should go back five kilometres to a hotel. No thank you, I don't want to go backwards, and anyway it was shut. The alternative was to go onwards for 25 kilometres, so it was an expensive day too. I will retrace the steps tomorrow.

The town of Stavros lies beside the sea. *Thalassa*! It's a cheery little place, full of cafés and souvenir shops and cheap hotels, some of them even open. I have eaten but I may have to go to bed dirty because I'm too tired to take a shower. At Apollonia I took a heart pill. The chest is tight and the heart isn't absolutely regular. But look at it this way: the Austrian couple are sleeping in a tent!

On the subject of Alexander the Great, didn't Robin Lane Fox write the definitive book about him? I was at university with Robin Lane Fox, though he wouldn't remember me. He used to bowl slow left arm.

Incidentally it was a beautiful, spring like day. Who needs a bed? The Austrians are probably complaining of the heat.

DAY 113
APOLLONIA TO NEA KERDILLIA

I was sorry to leave Stavros. The bakers were opening, the cafés were full, even the souvenir shops were pulling down the blinds though it's September. A few kilometres took me to the main road, then I walked back through pleasant woodland towards Apollonia. A village called Rendina was half way so I turned round and walked back again. That would have to do.

Up at Rendina the clouds had sunk to the road. Back at sea level the sun was still shining. The afternoon, however, brought the exact opposite as a sea fret rolled across the water and enveloped the whole coast line. It was like Cromer in Norfolk; the rest of the country can be bathed in sunshine but Cromer is covered in mist. Sometimes it's the other way round. They do different up there.

I carried on eastward. Asprovalta is a bustling town, a centre of the northern tourist industry, a seaside resort full of hotels and shops and restaurants. Should I stop here? No, it was too early. I could put in another three hours to Nea Kerdillia, which looked just as big on the map and where

I was assured there would be accommodation…

The afternoon was beautiful and it was hard to believe that a couple of weeks ago it was minus eleven round here. Today the sun shone and the road ran beside sandy beaches. If it weren't for that nagging feeling that arrives in the afternoons (where am I sleeping tonight?) I might even have thought I was enjoying myself. Sun? Sand? Sin? Sangria? Two out of four.

There was, of course, nowhere to stay in Nea Kerdillia and I had just missed the two-hourly bus back to Asprovalta. In a café the very helpful young woman, and the rest of the clientele, tried their best to give me good news. What they couldn't provide, however, was anywhere to stay. The enveloping mist suddenly swamped the village, and the bus, when it did turn up, was so warm and cosy that it was tempting to stay on it all the way to Thessaloniki. But I got off in Asprovalta and will return tomorrow.

Until now I have laboured under the misapprehension that Thessaloniki was next door to Istanbul. It's not. It's hundreds of miles. Looked at on a map of the world, it's next door to Istanbul. Looked at by a pedestrian, it's a depressingly long way. As I said to the Austrians yesterday (Where are they now? Have they had a shower yet?), I want to go home. I want a proper cup of tea. Yet there is all this bloody road in front of me.

On another matter, twice yesterday I dropped the little bank wallet that contains my debit card. The second time, someone picked it up and gave it to me, otherwise I might not have noticed. I must be crazy. Without that debit card, I'm destitute. I amaze myself with my incompetence.

Among other things, the wallet contains my probation officer ID card from 26 years ago. Some years later they issued us with fresh cards and I returned this one when I left. However, they never asked for the first one back. I confess that I have sometimes used it for photo ID, even though I am no longer a probation officer; it's the only photo ID I carry. In the process I have probably committed a crime. In addition, I have pretended to be someone with no grey hair.

The phrasebook I bought is unfortunately a waste of money for me but I'm sure it's very useful for Greek people visiting Britain. For example, they can understand it when English-speaking people say 'She was on call and couldn't go out drinking with the others' and 'The hotel organises a pub crawl on Saturday nights.'

Now a couple of grizzles about local conditions. In the supermarket today the pocket dictator known as the manager called out something to me. At first I ignored him, not knowing it was me he wanted. Then, when I realised, I still ignored him. He wanted me to leave my rucksack at the entrance while I went round his shop. No thank you. Just because I've got a rucksack it doesn't mean I'm a thief. And it's on my back where I would have to be a contortionist to put a bar of chocolate inside. He didn't like me but he was happy to take my money.

Then there are those graffiti artists who think it's clever to paint all over the road signs so you can't read them. They need a good smack. A few years ago I wrote a court report about a graffiti artist who, having had previous warnings, was eventually sent to prison. It's a strange occupation. This young man was risking his life painting tube trains in the middle of the night. It's utterly selfish. Someone always has to clear up after them, either their paint or their body.

DAY 114
35 KILOMETRES BUT NO PROGRESS

From my window a bus could be seen leaving for Nea Kerdillia. Should I run for it? There wasn't time. It might have made a difference to the day.

For the second time I walked to Nea Kerdillia, this time in a blanket of mist. The plan was to count these kilometres in the distance towards Kavala, press on, catch a bus to Kavala and walk back tomorrow. It seemed a good plan.

Past Macedonian tombs, a large and no doubt famous stone lion, over a river and on towards Kavala. From the junction for Drama (not a crisis, ho, ho) I walked for a mile, decided it was the wrong way, came back, decided it was right after all and walked the same road again. At the next junction I realised there were no buses on this road so I couldn't pick one up further on. I walked back for the second time, hoping no-one could see me. If I could get a bus to Drama, I could get another one to Kavala and walk back as planned. Ten minutes before I reached the bus stop, a bus sailed past me.

Feeling more self-conscious by the minute, I took another bus back to Asprovalta. I had walked 35 kilometres, half way to Kavala if it had been in a straight line, but I was back where I started. Furthermore I had to face the abuse of Greece's rudest bus driver. He shouted at me, he shouted at everyone. Perhaps he was having a bad day, or perhaps he was in the wrong job.

Then I lost my glasses. I can't read without them. They're only convenience glasses, straight off the shelf for a few quid, and they continually fall off my nose, but they come everywhere with me. I put out an all points search but no-one had seen them. This was the last straw for the day. I went to the optician to try to buy a new pair but the optician was closed.

Then I found them again.

What a day.

23 December. My father's birthday.

Day 115
Kavala

Think of the positives, I told myself at eight o'clock in the morning. What positives was that? Well, you're healthy and wealthy enough to be making a complete prirtle of yourself in eastern Greece. Most people wouldn't be able to say that.

Those were the positives.

It was stated authoritatively that a bus would leave for Kavala at eight o'clock. Needless to say it didn't. A couple of young lads pointed out on the timetable that one might leave in a couple hours. I wasn't taking a chance on that. I followed their example and caught the bus to Drama.

The lads seemed to be on their first day out alone. Out of school, nervous, giggling, they couldn't believe the bus would actually take them to Drama even though it said so on the front. (I know that feeling.) Then they kept asking questions about Drama of the other passengers: was it a big place, did it have shops, was it nice? A young man in front of them went and sat elsewhere; but they were just young lads, having fun on their harmless adventure.

At Drama another bus left immediately for Kavala. Perhaps it should be recorded that the bus crew were very friendly and helpful.

I'm actually very pro-bus. Not only do I use them all the time but some of the best days of my life were spent playing cricket for Northenden bus depot in Manchester. We played in the Wednesday league, composed of teams who could get time off during the week - various bus depots, the police, Manchester taxis, Failsworth Co-op. It was fiercely competitive cricket. Manchester taxis turned up one day with someone they had found working in a restaurant; the previous winter he had played for Bangladesh.

My mate Derek, who worked at Northenden, took me along to play for them. In those days I was very badly dressed. (Not just in those days.) Derek gave me a couple of his old inspector's uniform jackets. Shorn of the gold rings, they served as my best jackets for over twenty years and I still have them today.

One of the team was our friend Jim (not his real name), who became unwillingly famous for an exploit one day when he turned up early for work.

Finding that he had a couple of hours to spare, Jim went off to see a girlfriend. Now, this might have been perfectly normal behaviour except for two things which unfortunately combined to undermine him. First, he wasn't really supposed to be seeing this woman. Second, he took his bus with him.

This too might not have been disastrous but, yes, you guessed it. When the time came to return to work, the bus wouldn't start... Stuck outside his girlfriend's house, riding an illicit bus which he had used as a taxi, Jim had to ring the depot to get the mechanic out. Within minutes, of course, everyone in south Manchester knew where he had been and why.

What a spectacular place Kavala is! An ancient city with an old fortress, it resembles Monte Carlo in that it is wedged between mountains and sea and every square inch is built on. There the resemblance ends. The inhabitants of Kavala have a hundredth of the money of the inhabitants of Monte Carlo. No, not that much.

Three years ago Belinda and I were on holiday in the area and went to watch the tennis in Monte Carlo. Not having tickets for the main court, we watched the doubles. Belinda never had much time for the behaviour of sports people (except for Nadal, of course). As the players went through their stupid rituals, touching hands between points, signalling behind their backs or whispering through closed fists she grew steadily, rapidly speechless with fury. After an hour I thought she might climb down on to the court and smack their bottoms for them. We had to leave.

Dumping my bag in a hotel in Kavala, pausing only to check that the TV had *BBC World* (yes!), I set off to cover as many kilometres as possible to fill in for yesterday. Fifteen kilometres out, fifteen kilometres back; that should just about cover the whole distance. I took the pleasant coast road through the villages, where the local population could be identified from the newsagents' stalls: *Time Magazine*, *The Economist* and *Uncut* dominated. It was growing dark when I returned to Kavala.

Father Christmases are bobbling everywhere on buildings now and everyone seems to be wearing Christmas hats. At work I always used to like Christmas Eve. Most people went home at lunchtime but I would stay until four or five, drinking tea and catching up with paperwork. When the traffic died down I would travel to wherever the family Christmas was that year.

The court always has to sit on Christmas Eve and Boxing Day to deal with the overnights. Boxing Day court duty is never short of volunteers from the Probation Service. It's always the women, desperate to get out of the house, who come forward. There is also no shortage of defendants in court on Boxing Day. Christmas in the family is not always as peaceful as it is made out to be.

I was Father Christmas once. Walking down the street where I lived in Holloway at the time, I was approached by a desperate woman teacher. 'You've got to be Father Christmas!' she cried. 'Our Father Christmas has let us down! You've got to do it!'

I protested my total inability and unsuitability for the part but she wouldn't listen. It wasn't a question of whether I wanted to do it or not: I had to. So within minutes I was decked out in the gear, seeing a succession of children and telling them the best stories I could think of. Afterwards the teachers gave me a large bottle of sherry which I later gave away. I never saw any of them again.

These days, of course, you would need a police check before you could even breathe the idea.

DAY 116
ONWARDS FROM KAVALA

Happy Christmas! (Again.)

When I worked with people in prison I used to talk to them about Christmas. Christmas in prison is a difficult time, with too much time to think, reflecting on Christmases past and future. The problem is that everyone thinks of Christmas as a golden time, whereas in reality it often isn't; but when someone is in prison you can't really say to them 'actually your home life was shit so there's no point getting sentimental about it.' Of course, they could easily say the same to me. The difference is, though, that I think all my Christmases were just as good as I remembered them to be.

A few years ago I went for a walk on Christmas morning round the farm tracks. In a belt of trees, something clattered. I took no notice; it sounded like a pheasant. Then it clattered some more, in fact a commotion sprang up. What was going on?

The pheasant rose into the air with something hanging off the back. What could it be? It was a weasel. It must have made a lunge for the pheasant just as the bird rose from the ground. What would happen? The pheasant rose to about fifty feet up and the weasel decided that discretion was the better part of valour. It dropped to the ground and ran off into the trees.

Not knowing whether there would be buses on Christmas Day, I set out to walk twenty kilometres from Kavala and then walk back again. I'm feeling guiltier and guiltier about this method of covering eastern Greece but I will count that as being forty kilometres towards Xanthi. In fact there was a normal bus service so I could have walked forty kilometres and then caught the bus back to my comfortable hotel with *BBC World*, but it was too late by that time. I went beyond a village with a long name beginning with a P, then came back. Tomorrow perhaps I will manage to walk in a conventional manner across the continent.

The day was uneventful. Out of Kavala, past the old city and under the amazing ancient viaduct (aqueduct?) leading to the castle, out past the football ground and eventually threading between the oil refineries and the motorway. The old road is itself a major highway and not a problem to walk down. On one side lie the hills, on the other side farmland. It was warm and until the last hour was comfortable enough.

Last night I burst a blister on one foot but today the other foot has become painful and I limped back into Kavala. To add to the minor woes, my stock of glucosamine is low. Some time ago I increased my daily dose from one tablet to two, but now I have had to revert. It's hard to say whether it's a consequence but my knee hurts.

If you didn't know it was Christmas, this would be a normal day, wouldn't it? I managed not to get maudlin about it all.

This is the last page of my notebook. Before the first half of the trip, Emily gave it to me to keep a record. Since at that stage I didn't know if I would last the week (and nearly didn't), I never imagined that the book would not be big enough. I have bought a flimsy exercise book to do the rest.

I haven't been keeping a close record, but at a conservative estimate of eighteen miles per day I may have walked 1,200 miles in this second part of the trip and over 2,000 overall in 116 days. When I walked from New York to California I did 2,650 in 105 days. Why the decline in speed and distance? I'm getting old.

Day 117
Paradis to Porto Lagos

There must be a lot of places called Paradise but I can only think of the town in Robert Parker's last novels. Parker, dead now, was a supreme journeyman of American crime novels, an artisan who could give two lessons to virtually all British crime novelists. First, be funny. Second, write better.

The bus deposited me in Paradise, the village sixteen kilometres from Xanthi, and I walked into town. Xanthi, huddled between barren, scrubby hills and the plain leading to the sea, is famous for museums, churches, markets, music and the old city. A clutch of hotels suggests that a number of people come here to look at it all. I set out to cover the 56 kilometres to Komotini by tomorrow. After an hour I realised that the alternative route was only fifty kilometres; but by that time I had done five or six kilometres and was going like an express train. Conditions were perfect: a big wide main road, flat, straight and traffic free. Furthermore, the scenery was nothing to write home about, which always helps. Before I knew where I was, I was in Porto Lagos. I caught the bus back to Xanthi and will return in the morning.

At exactly three o'clock this Boxing Day morning I awoke with a start. I knew exactly why I had woken. At three o'clock on Boxing Day morning, two years ago, a life was cruelly taken away.

DAY 118
PORTO LAGOS TO KOMOTINI

It would be hard to imagine a more depressing spot than Porto Lagos at eight o'clock on a winter's morning. It was barely daylight. Rain fell slowly. The village (well, the clutch of buildings) has a small port but nothing moved in it. On one side is the sea - but it's a sea composed of estuaries and marshes, not a beach to paddle in. On the other side is a large, flat lake. That's a stupid thing to say - obviously it's flat - but no hills or greenery lead down to it. Marsh and bog lie all around. Clearly the area is a sanctuary for birds; whole flocks of herons rose, twenty at a time, and one pelican joined them. Within six hours I had done twenty miles and was in Komotini.

In the midst of all this desolation, I came across a very large dead dog. In itself this is not unusual; I do see a lot of dead dogs unfortunately. To be killed on a wide straight road like this, however, when cars arrive approximately five minutes apart, would have to be very unlucky indeed.

The dogs that are still alive howl uncontrollably at me from behind wire fences.

Worms and insects at the roadside distress me. Irremediably they head for the middle of the highway. 'Don't!' I cry silently at them. 'Your chances of survival are minimal!' They have to be left alone, though. If I moved them back to the edge they would only set off again. Some instinct has told them they must cross that road and nothing I can say or do will stop them.

I looked for the beautiful side of Komotini but, wherever it was, it eluded me. They clearly wanted some aspect of culture to boast of, but all they could dream up was a museum of art folklore. If that's the best they can do they're struggling, frankly.

Be thankful for small mercies, though. Everywhere else in Europe is suffering disastrous weather conditions. Paris, Brussels, London, Moscow, Romania, Italy: disaster has struck all of them. The only sliver of moderation in the whole continent appears to be here. Well, that's a welcome change. Can it just last for another week and a half, please?

Yesterday something sharp appeared in my sock. I pulled it out. It was a toenail. Today I had a hunt round to find out where it had come from, but it was a fruitless search. Assuming that it wasn't someone else's toenail, I have lost one; but under all the plasters it is hard to be specific. It doesn't seem to hurt, anyway.

When I took money out of the cash point a statement appeared unbidden. I have been avoiding a statement lest it conveyed bad news, but I seem to have much more than I thought! Oh well, then. I had been depressed until now.

DAY 119
KOMOTINI TO SAPES

Winter has returned. A couple of miles out of Komotini I had to dress. On went the fleece under the waterproof jacket; on went the waterproof trousers. I need to find my gloves. Apparently it snowed here last week. A retired sailor stopped me for a chat. He said Turkey was very cold. Greece is none too warm either.

At the moment the days don't fit with the schedule. I'm fit enough and desperate enough now to want to make good progress but it's impossible to do that and find accommodation. From Komotini to Alexandroupoli is 65 kilometres. That's comfortable in two days but I'd like to do more. In the event I did less than that today. Sapes was only 28 kilometres but it had a fine little bus station. Catching a bus at a bus station, rather than out on the road, is a major advantage; for one thing they don't drive straight past you. All the bus stations are great. New, clean, bright and shiny, they boast a shop and canteen. They're indoors, of course, which helps. Someone authoritative is on duty who probably speaks English and is helpful. Unlike the bus stations of almost every other country in the world (try New York, for example) they're positively inviting. So I caught the bus in town rather than walk any further today.

Lately I seem to be accumulating things which make the pack heavier again. Yesterday I had to buy more shaving soap; it may be my imagination but it seemed to weigh a ton. Today I took out the Greek phrasebook, lifted it half way to the bin and then took it back again. Some time, a Greek tourist may call at my door in England and want to know how to book a second-class return ticket to Edinburgh. It would be a shame to be unable to help because of throwing away the phrasebook.

As it happened, I remembered a second word of ancient Greek today: *agora*, market place. You see it nowadays advertising grocery stores.

Again I reflected on those people who learn languages without seeming to try. My friend Howard only has to look at a language to learn it. Scott is the same. It's not just languages, of course. I knew someone called Tim who won a classics scholarship to Cambridge. I don't know whether he worked for his scholarship but I do know for a fact that all he was interested in was cricket, hockey and rugby. At university I knew someone called Cliff who did nothing but play cricket and football but happened to be a mathematics genius. He used to infuriate the other mathematicians. All day they would be working while he was on the sports field; then he would come in and immediately know the answers to all the problems. To him they simply weren't problems. He got a First, of course.

Forty years later I saw Cliff again. To my amazement he had become an academic and gone off to teach in California. I asked him if he kept up with cricket and football. No, he barely followed them at all. Sacrilege! I asked him what his leisure pursuits were instead. Well, he said, he sued the American government. What, all the time? Yes, pretty much. He sued them for endangering his wellbeing through going to war in Iraq or contributing to global warming. I asked who won these encounters. 'We called it a draw,' he said. He did win quite a lot of money off them, though. By this time he needed it because with each performance in the law courts he became less employable in the universities, so that he now taught in the University of Tumbleweed, New Mexico, or somewhere similar. It was just a shame that he had given up cricket and football. He was a tricky leg spinner and an elusive inside forward, as we used to call them in those days.

I caught the bus to Alexandroupoli and will return in the morning.

The scenery today? Mmm. Not a lot of scenery.

As usual, lots of cars offered me lifts. One of them was quite literally tied together with string.

Day 120

Sapes to Alexandroupoli

I was finally mugged today.

With hindsight, grumpiness because of a bad night under a bloody duvet was disproportionate. I caught the 7.45 bus to Sapes, severely lacking sleep, and set off on the 37 kilometres via the old road to Alexandroupoli.

Indeed it is old. A roadside information board described the Romans building the road, their first outside Italy; then it was used by Alexander, the Persians, the Turks and everyone else. It's the Via Egnatia. All the towns along the route began as staging posts and are set a day's march apart, generally 45 to sixty kilometres. So that's who's to blame for these inconvenient distances! Perhaps they were on horseback; otherwise they must have walked faster than I can. Komortini to Alexandroupoli is 65 kilometres!

After a productive stretch of road in the morning, all the traffic went on to the motorway and I was just thinking that the highway had become empty, climbing into completely unpopulated hills. Then a car pulled up opposite me.

At first I assumed it was another offer of a lift and declined politely. Then one of the two young men in the car got out and came over to me. He said he wanted my passport. It was ludicrous to think I would have given him my passport even if I was carrying it, which I wasn't. He grew nastier and buffeted me. Now he wanted money. I shrugged him off and started walking. The other one got out of the car and joined in. They jostled me.

I was thinking reasonably clearly and pulled a five-euro note from my back pocket. Obviously they wouldn't be satisfied with five euros but I wanted them to go in the direction of that pocket, which contained sixty or seventy euros and might make them think it was all I was carrying. They wrestled me, took the money and ran off. I headed down the hill towards the motorway. When they drove off I returned to the road. It didn't occur to me that they would come back.

This time they went straight for me and flung me down. I didn't know what they wanted but I don't think they did either. 'What do you want?' I kept shouting at them in English. Neither appeared to have a weapon. One raised a fist but didn't hit me. They knew they wanted something out of my pockets but I was fairly well wrapped and they couldn't get anything. We wrestled. Then they heard a vehicle, an engine; in fact it was a man on a scooter. They went off.

Like a fool I never thought of taking their car number; at the time I was more interested in self-preservation. This time I did head for the motorway because they would obviously be back. Scrambling over rough ground, looking behind me from time to time, I eventually reached the hard shoulder of the highway. For a time I walked down the motorway itself. A few cars hooted at me but they were the least of my worries.

Was I frightened? Yes, of course I was. In the past I have been attacked a few times at work, but that wasn't on a deserted road in Greece. I was angry and humiliated and felt stupid. An hour later, I suddenly broke into a heavy sweat.

When I used to work with criminals I occasionally asked them what right they thought they had to take other people's money. I felt like asking these two the same. Yes, I had more money than them. Did that mean they could assault and rob me?

Beside the motorway I eventually managed to find barriers or walls to walk behind, then finally climbed a hill and came down through olive groves and fields to the old road again. It was hard work and slow going but strangely enough I made good time for the day, completing the 37 kilometres in eight hours. On the old road a series of villages materialised. I cheered up with a Fanta and a packet of Doritos and followed the increasingly busy coast road into town.

Alexandroupoli is a city rather than a town, a fast-growing modern metropolis with a new medical university on the edge and a variety of tourist and business activities. It's on the sea. Ferries go to islands. It's near Turkey. They say that life here has plenty of activities but is a lot quieter than in Athens or Thessaloniki.

My hotel landlord rang his friend, the chief of police, on hearing of my experiences. We all agreed that without the car registration number very little could be done.

Instead the landlord had a long chat. He runs 25 kilometres every day except Friday. He goes to the gym. He thinks Greeks should work more and play less and tells his young staff that all they seem to want to do is have fun. (True, probably.) This afternoon he told them it was necessary to work and work throughout their adult life. When they had done that, he said - he had a look at my passport - when they reached the age of 63 they could have fun walking across Europe!

He found information for my route tomorrow and showed me his large collection of specialist teas. He made me a cup from one of them, which I'm sorry to say was revolting.

I want to go home.

DAY 121
FERES AND THE BORDER

For a proper cup of tea I walked into the airport. Inexorably I was drawn to the ticket sales counter in Departures. A long queue caused me to withdraw again. That was a close shave.

In the morning I was a bit nervous after my experiences yesterday. Whenever a vehicle drew up near me I shied away, and when the road was clear of traffic I grew edgy. By the afternoon it had worn off.

Feres, 29 kilometres from Alexandroupoli, is the last sizeable town before the border. In the early afternoon a place like this is a ghost town; the shops have closed until four thirty, the bars and restaurants are desultory, the supermarket is open but there are no customers. Later the town comes to life. By the time it dies down again I am long asleep.

I left the bag in Feres and walked onwards for nearly an hour, which I hoped was half way to the border, then walked back again. Tomorrow I'll catch the bus to the border and start walking into Turkey.

The day was cold and clear. Darkness fell as I approached Feres from the east. Now, a couple of days after Christmas, the days are definitely growing longer but, travelling eastwards, it is more noticeable in the morning than the evening. The sun set over Greece for the last time. I like Greece and the Greeks but I'm not bloody coming back here.

However, I'm not going anywhere else either if I can help it so they shouldn't take it personally.

In the journey east, mosques seem to proliferate. Am I right in thinking these are mosques? How do they get on with the Greek Orthodox? It's remarkable how religions seem to fall out. Not only between religions but within religions they don't seem to like each other: Protestant and Catholic, Sunni and Shia. The most remarkable thing is that they all believe in the same god: Christians, Muslims and Jews all have the same deity. It's only in the coming of the prophet that they have a difference of opinion which entitles them to kill millions of people.

I discovered when walking in the US that they're all wasting their time, of course. Only fundamentalist Baptists can enter the kingdom of heaven.

One day somewhere in the mid-west I was stopped by a Baptist minister who insisted that I stayed the night with him and his wife. This chap spoke six languages and was stupid in all of them. He believed that seven years of plenty would be followed by seven years of famine, that the Antichrist was coming with 666 stamped on his forehead and that he would come first in the US because it was the newest of the great nations and was a land where the rivers had been spoiled. He believed that a highway was built between Beijing and Baghdad. Above all, he believed that only if you were born again and took Christ into your heart in the Baptist Church could you enter the kingdom of heaven. It wasn't even enough to have been a Baptist all your life, you had to be born again. I believe this is called exclusivism. It doesn't matter how good you have been all your life, you can't get to heaven without being a born again Baptist. Heaven is full of Baptists and no-one else.

So the rest of them are wasting their time.

TURKEY

DAY 122
KESAN

The border held a few problems.

A bridge marks the border between Greece and Turkey, with both nations standing guard over it (a very, very boring job), and no-one is allowed to cross it on foot. Why not? What's the difference? Ours not to reason why. All travellers have to cross in a vehicle.

The Greek border guard explained the situation but told me not to worry, he would hijack a car. Accordingly, he approached the second car, occupied by two Greek men, and asked them to take me across. They agreed straight away. In the circumstances this was rather noble of them since I could have been anyone, but in the next few minutes we were of use to each other. Well, they were far more use to me than I was to them but I tried to do my bit.

The passenger in the car worked in Germany for an American company and spoke English, German and Turkish as well as Greek. He was on his six-monthly visit home and had a busy day ahead. First, the two men were entering Turkey briefly to buy white goods, much cheaper over the border. Then he was partying for New Year's Eve. Finally, the night ended with a drive to Thessaloniki for the daybreak flight to Frankfurt. Not a very full flight on New Year's Day, one might imagine.

We crossed the Greek border section without difficulty and they bought so many duty free cigarettes that some had to be attributed to me. I bought them a sandwich for helping me out. Then we continued to the Turkish section and the fun started.

First, it was decreed that I had to buy a visa. Can this be right? I didn't have much choice. The visa man invited us to his cubbyhole and gave everyone a sweet as a sign of the nation's hospitality. Thanks, mate. With the aid of my translator we got through that, but then their car was hauled to one side.

The car was emptied and the cigarettes inspected closely. Vehicle documents were microscopically examined. Everything was spun out tediously. By the standards of a communist country of the 1970s this was lightweight, but by any other standards it was heavy duty. Apparently the whole business becomes very swift indeed, in fact doesn't even get started, if you offer them a backhander; but my friend said that under no circumstances was he doing that. So they take a random selection of vehicles and hold them as long as possible.

Once across the border, we said our farewells and the two men went off shopping. The first signpost held a welcome surprise: it wasn't 43 kilometres to Kesan as advertised but only 27. The same surprise seems to be true of several other days ahead. The 27 uneventful kilometres through rolling farmland brought Kesan, or rather the shopping mall strip outside town. To my astonishment, the supermarket Migros have a store here; I hadn't realised they operated anywhere outside Switzerland. Cheap and friendly accommodation was waiting at a crossroads and I went off to Burger King, whose chips in Turkey were just as disgusting as their chips in Britain. I bought the English-language Turkish newspaper, which presumably is a front for the CIA.

In Turkey, the dogs don't seem to be locked in or chained up, and most of them seemed to fancy putting the frighteners into me. Crossing the road to avoid one such monster, I unfortunately missed talking to the only long-distance cyclist I have come across so far. He waved a cheery greeting but was gone.

Day 123
Kesan to Malkara

Happy New Year! (Again.)

I have made one New Year resolution which I shall definitely keep. I am never, ever, ever going to do one of these things again.

Steve Redgrave said, after winning his Olympic gold medal, that if anyone ever saw him in a boat again they should shoot him. Later he got back in a boat. There are no worries on that score with me. I'm not doing it again. I wouldn't mind a walk from Westacre to East Walton to pick blackberries or up on the farm tracks behind Tumbley Hill sheds. I wouldn't even mind going to Switzerland, after a good rest, for a stroll or two and then a raclette and a beer. But I am not waking up in some dive hotel on a main road putting a new collection of plasters over the toes and wondering how far it is today and how I will make a fresh fool of myself in some foreign land. No thank you.

The Linda Hotel, on the junction at Kesan, was patronised last night by me and a clutch of very young women, girls really, staying there overnight for the New Year celebrations. They all went out to a club somewhere. I assumed they would be coming in noisily at various stages of the night - after all, it was New Year's Eve - but as it happened they all crept quietly in at six o'clock, when I was getting up. Shortly afterwards, the call to prayers came from the mosque. I don't think any of them made it.

From Kesan to Malkara was not far, barely fifteen miles, but at the moment the days are falling like this into inconveniently short segments. Or perhaps I am winding down. No accommodation could be found in Malkara so I caught a bus to Tekirdag. This is a rather drastic solution since it is still two days' walk away, but it does give me three nights in the same place as I catch the bus back to where I was and walk on from there.

I'm trying to train myself to remember the place names in the face of overwhelming difficulty from the ageing process. Malkara I can remember because of Malky Mackay who used to play for Norwich. Tekirdag is giving me a bit more gyp. We haven't had a player called that at Norwich.

On the map nothing much shows itself between Malkara and Tekirdag and it was reassuring to reconnoitre from the bus. I'm still a bit nervous about deserted roads and this morning the road climbed into isolated hills where traffic was sparse. I found myself looking around a few times and hastening on. Then a man drew up his car on the other side of the road, which does spook me, walked to the car boot and took out an axe! He was, of course, not in the least interested in me and went off to chop wood.

The road is fast, big, wide and straight, runs between modern towns and has a substantial hard shoulder for me to walk on. Even early on New Year's Day there was enough traffic to make my fears ridiculous; but the land itself is open and empty. Neither the towns nor the scenery will lend themselves to graphic descriptions over the next couple of days.

I came in and watched a documentary about Mark Chapman and the death of John Lennon. It was, as always, unbearably sad. My friend Nigel had his thirtieth birthday on the day John was shot. (They call him Lennon now. He was never Lennon. To us he was John.) Ever since, Nigel has been unable to enjoy his birthday properly. On the day of the murder, I was going into Brunel University on my social work training course. I asked if they would cancel the training for the day since it was impossible to work; they declined but understood my position, so I sat outside the door all day listening to the radio until the course finished.

Since I'm going to be sleeping here for three nights I can do all my washing for what I hope will be the last time.

Day 124
Malkara to İnecik

My friend Monica was on holiday in New York in the 1970s and sitting in a café one day when John and Yoko walked in. All the tables were occupied so they asked if Monica would mind sharing with them. Er, not at all! They sat and chatted for half an hour, then John and Yoko left as quietly as they had come in.

When I worked in pubs in London in the late 1960s, the Apple HQ was in Savile Row. Between shifts in the pub I used to walk round London and sometimes went to Savile Row to see if anything was going on. Girls were always sitting on the Apple doorstep; eventually they would be invited in for a cup of tea. One day I stood on the pavement and watched through a downstairs window as John and Yoko gave an interview. That was the closest I got.

My three heroes have always been Dashiell Hammett, George Best and John Lennon. All three behaved rather badly at times. Each, though, enhanced my life to such an extent that it would be difficult to imagine it without them.

I worked once for a man called John Lennon. Bad luck for him having the same name but far worse luck for other reasons for those who had to work for him. The children's home in Norfolk was a good place when my friend Eric ran it. However, after various disputes with the authorities he left and they got John Lennon in. He wasn't a bad man, just inadequate. He couldn't run the place so he got a couple of thugs in to help him cover the traces.

A few months later I handed in my notice and wrote a fifteen-page typed letter to the Director of Social Services describing the abuses the two thugs had committed. The letter was ignored. The deputy director, to whom it was assigned, happened to belong to my squash club, so some time later I grabbed him in the changing rooms and asked what the hell he thought he was doing, why they hadn't even interviewed me about my allegations. He was evasive, pretending they couldn't get hold of me. I was still working at the home for a month after my resignation!

Those were the bad old days when everything was swept under the carpet in Social Services. Some years later, however, the police came after these thugs and I contacted them. Mysteriously, all the relevant papers including my letter had been destroyed in a fire at County Hall. Like a complete fool, I had lent the only copy of my letter to a colleague, who despite numerous requests had not returned it. Many years later I bumped into him at Paul Foot's funeral and gave him a piece of my mind. The letter might have helped the police prosecute. Later, one of the thugs in question was sent to prison in any event but it would have been nice to help.

The other thug fancied himself as a squash player; eventually, while we were working together, he had to ask me for a game. He then made the mistake of betting £1 with Ian, one of the children in the home, that he would take one game off me. Ian, of course, immediately reported this to me. Now, I was never a great squash player but I could play the game and knew what the standards were. Huh, I told Ian, you should have bet him a fiver that he wouldn't win a point, never mind a game. I played him and beat him 9-0, 9-0, 9-0. For good measure we played a fourth game and I beat him 9-0 in that one too. Then we played a fifth. By now I felt sorry for him, always a mistake, and let him have a point. 9-1.

Thirty years later, the fury is still there. Recently I met Ian, who has done very well in life, and we went over old times and the scandal of the thuggery.

Anyway, today I walked from Malkara to İnecik. Contrary to my earlier impressions, it's amazing country for walking. The road falls in great swoops and sweeps, over rolling farmland with steep climbs and descents like the prairies in the US. At one time this area would all have been brown in winter. Now, as in England, winter wheat has been sown everywhere and the land is a patchwork of colours. İnecik is a village with two mosques. Tomorrow I will walk out to here and catch the bus back to Tekirdağ. Why do it in that direction when I could easily catch the bus out and walk in the right direction? Because I can't pronounce İnecik and don't want to humiliate myself on the bus.

Day 125
Inecik to Tekirdağ

A barrel-shaped, tattooed and very gregarious Texan gas worker has taken Tekirdağ by storm. He already knows everyone by name, has exchanged mobile numbers with all and sundry and gets invited to parties whenever he's not working. He's one of those charismatic figures we would all like to be. He likes it here. I asked him what he missed about home. 'I don't miss anything,' he said.

He and his buddies are all returning from their Christmas break. They work, probably very hard, for a petroleum company. They all seem to be from Texas. I base this on the fact that when they talk together I can't understand a word they say.

As far as I can tell they do speak English, unlike most people in Texas who speak Spanish. It is said that the US conquered Texas in 1840 and took it from Mexico but that Mexico has now taken it back.

For the last few days I have been lucky with the weather but today was cold, wet and miserable. The cloud came down so far that at one stage all visibility vanished and I thought I might have to turn back. Then the cloud lifted, fell again, lifted again. It was only 23 kilometres so I did it without a break and caught the bus back to Tekirdağ.

The scenery, when visible, is rewarding. Substantial hills have to be climbed and bigger hills loom to the south. The view over Tekirdağ is dramatic. The town itself has been here for centuries, based around the port and the ferries to the islands. Ships dock right in the middle of town. Like all the Turkish towns so far, Tekirdağ has doubled or tripled in size in the last twenty years, but the centre and waterfront are relatively unchanged. A short walk away, an enormous new Carrefour shopping complex contrasts absolutely with the street market outside and the dwellings around it. I went to goggle and drink tea out of little glasses. It was still raining outside.

DAY 126
TEKIRDAĞ TO MARMARAEREGLISI

(Split it into two. Marmara is because we're now on the Sea of Marmara. Then think of it as almost the French for church. Change the 'e' to an 'i' on the end. Bob's your uncle!)

Greece is talking about building a fence along the Turkish border. Apparently 120,000 Turks crossed into Greece last year. It would give the border guards something to do, patrolling the fence instead of standing still looking at nothing on the bridge. They would have to make a reciprocal arrangement though to stop the Greeks getting into Turkey, otherwise one lot of sentries would be standing there doing nothing while the other lot madly patrolled the perimeter.

One thing they could all start patrolling for is litter. The detritus by the side of the road is appalling. Of course it happens everywhere – fly tipping is scarcely unknown in Britain - but the whole of the country here is marred by debris. It began in Kosovo and has grown steadily worse. Everything goes out of the car window. Then, as if that weren't enough, hundreds of people drive out and dump whole carloads of household waste. Most of it is plastic bottles and cans (the manufacturers of Red Bull have a lot to answer for). The other day I watched an elderly woman leave two very large plastic water bottles by the side of the road outside her village. There they would stay. No-one would come for them, no-one would re-cycle them, they would be there until the next millennium. Waste disposal lorries are in operation and there are plenty of dustbins, but everyone dumps by the roadside.

A strong, cold wind blew from the north, making my nose run and threatening to blow me into the traffic. The road came down to the coast and followed the sea.

After a while the housing development was almost continuous. Some of the houses had been built twenty years ago and hadn't lasted in the sea air but many more were new. Further from the sea, houses are built on waste land wherever it is available, with no gardens or cafés and only the occasional shop. The houses are fine in themselves but it doesn't look an attractive place to live.

According to my map I walked 47 kilometres today, but I didn't. According to the signposts I did little more than 35 but that isn't right either. The truth lies about half way between the two. Four hours after finishing, the heartbeat is still too fast. Perhaps I should have done less today; but I want to get there and get home. Furthermore, it's too cold to stop. I really didn't mean to be here in winter.

The Texan appeared again. Last night he went out to try to meet a woman, which he said is difficult here. I don't fancy his chances. Furthermore, if he does meet a woman, I don't fancy his chances of getting home again.

Oh dear. I've finished reading my last book. Tomorrow it's the Turkish phrasebook.

DAY 127
MARMARAEREGLISI TO SELIMPASA

I'm going home tomorrow

I'm going home tomorrow.

Some days pass easily and without pain, others are long and difficult. Yesterday was the one, today was the other. Yesterday passed without thought. At one moment it was two hours, at the next it was eight. Where did all those hours go? What did I think about? I have no idea, except that for some reason I spent hours singing *I Never Felt More Like Singing The Blues*. 1957? 1958? More than fifty years ago, anyway. The Tommy Steele version or the Guy Mitchell version? I don't know.

Tommy Steele used to play squash at my club in Manchester in the 1970s. When he was touring in Manchester he always played squash with Dennis Tueart, the City and England footballer. I never saw him sing live but I saw him play squash. I saw Tueart perform live many times, needless to say, in that wonderful City team (Peter Barnes, Colin Bell, Dave Watson, Asa Hartford etc).

Today was admittedly a struggle. After a bad night in a bad hotel (imagine camping) and into a headwind, the hours passed slowly. The plan was to do 29 kilometres to Silivri and then see how the land lay. At Silivri I dumped my bag in a hotel where the young man was rather stern towards me until he discovered what I was up to, after which he was overcome with hilarity. 'And would you walk to China if you were asked?' he enquired. He said the airport, my target for tomorrow, was a long way off. I knocked ten kilometres off the distance, catching the 303 bus back from Selimpasa to Silivri. It will take me back tomorrow to continue.

Silivri came as a surprise. On the map it seems insignificant but it has over 100,000 inhabitants and is expanding so fast that between starting and finishing this sentence it will have grown some more. The town centre, round the harbour, is active and relatively untouched by the traffic thundering past on the dual carriageway. From the main road, myriads of passengers are catching buses in all directions.

As I write at the meal table, a guitarist is weakly strumming and humming in one corner. I do detest these people interrupting your meal with their caterwauling. Apart from me only one couple is eating here and we will probably be racing each other to the door. The waiters are joining in the songs so perhaps they'll give us a tune. I was on a Russian boat once across the Mediterranean where it was traditional for all the crew to perform, but that was different. They were good.

Strange aches and pains are breaking out in my legs and feet. Sometimes one leg or the other will nearly give way completely. It's time to stop walking.

Virtually all the world's hazelnuts are grown in Turkey. I am eating them as fast as I can.

I haven't managed to get hold of any more copies of the English-language newspaper but the copy I read was interesting on the perennial headscarf issue. My knowledge of this is gleaned only from the work of Orhan Pamuk (a good writer but oh, such heavy going). Turkish society seems to labour under an extraordinary dichotomy. None of the women on TV or in business life would be seen within a hundred miles of a headscarf. In the interior, however, exactly the opposite seems to rule.

I won't count any chickens but I'm due to finish tomorrow and I'm still in one piece. Usually I get ill at this stage. I have had sunstroke in Nevada, snow blindness in Switzerland, an infected toenail in Canada and general ague almost everywhere else. I don't look like being delayed this time either; I once had to wait five days for a flight in Mexico City (five books, six films in those five days). I must try not to blot the record by walking under a bus tomorrow. Actually the volume of traffic on the dual carriageway means that may be more easily said than done.

Day 128
Selimpasa to Istanbul (Suburbs)

The Istanbul suburbs stretch nearly to Hook of Holland.

I never really wanted to go to Istanbul. I've been there before. Years ago, before we knew about global warming and aeroplanes, I went there for the Easter weekend, flying out on Good Friday and back on Easter Monday. I've seen the Blue Mosque and it's very nice. I've eaten lots of delicious food and I've bought enough spices in the fantastic covered market to last a lifetime. I don't need to go back.

So this is more about travelling hopefully than arriving. Now I am about to travel back again. I write sitting in the airport where priorities suddenly, indeed dramatically, feel a lot different from those of the past few weeks.

I feel safe now. I feel looked after. It's not that I have felt generally unsafe: apart from the incident in Greece I have never felt in danger at any time. But here, I can speak English without feeling guilty or ashamed and I don't have to make a prat of myself in any other language. I don't need to worry about where to spend the night. I don't have to put on my waterproofs. I don't have to think about dehydration. Nutrition is not an issue. Am I strong enough to climb that range of hills today? Will that dog bite me? Are England winning the Ashes in Australia? How can I combat the depression every morning when I wake up and think of the day ahead? What did that shopkeeper just say and how do I answer? Can I arrive before dark? Is my toe turning septic?

Already, as I sit drinking my last cup of tea made with lukewarm water, I can hardly remember what was so difficult. If my legs didn't still ache and if I wasn't in need of a shower I wouldn't remember the hell that was this morning, and every morning.

It's 6 January. Can this really be on the same trip as walking down the Brenner Pass on 16 October? At that time I didn't know if I would last the week - and I very nearly didn't. I haven't kept a close record of the miles but it's probably about 1,500. Added to the first 'half' last year that makes about 2,300 or 2,400. Before I started, people looked up the distance and said very discouraging things about it. They were right.

In some ways I have been lucky. Certainly I have been lucky lately with the weather, though it often didn't feel like it at the time. Winter came late to Montenegro and Kosovo. Then winter came early to Greece and Turkey, blasted them to pieces and went away again. I wasn't lucky earlier on but that's forgotten about now.

I was lucky, a year ago, to have very good friends to stay with in Switzerland. I was lucky to have the right company over that first Christmas period. This time I have already forgotten Christmas but before that I was very lucky with the British and Kosovan company in Kosovo. First it gave me something to anticipate, then it gave wonderful conversation and hospitality and finally it gave me something to think about afterwards.

I write haphazardly, waiting for the plane. What's it like, people ask occasionally, to walk a long distance? What does it feel like to arrive at your destination? Well, I don't really know. Every minute of every day is hell, leavened only by occasional views, the odd joke and intermittent company. No-one would do it for fun. You do it to get to the other side.

Going home will, as usual, be a total anti-climax. Nothing will have changed. I won't be any different and nor will anyone else. Every minute I'm away I want to be at home, but as soon as I'm at home I shall probably want to be away again.

One difference this time is that I haven't failed as I normally do. I fail to reach my objective, I get ill or I just get too fed up to continue. This time I have, by and large, succeeded. There have been a few double ups and double backs which the purist would disapprove of but I have, with the exception of 22 kilometres in Macedonia, covered the whole distance between Hook of Holland and Istanbul.

I would really, really like Patrick Leigh Fermor to know about it but I don't know him or have any access to him, I don't know his state of health and I don't even know if he has died while I've been away.

Today I walked for five or six hours from Selimpasa into Istanbul. It gradually became the most dangerous walk of my life. Forget the mountains, deserts, snow blindness and sunstroke. The roads into Istanbul gradually became impossible. Furthermore, it must be the world's largest city. According to the map, the city would not be reached for several hours; but an extraordinary, gargantuan expansion has enveloped all the surrounding townships. Vast building complexes stand erect on all sides. More are being constructed every day. At one stage a very long climb from the sea led to the joint pinnacle of a Ramada Inn and a mosque, bookending another large new complex. Roads arrived at every step from all sides. An endless dual carriageway, busier than any motorway, led further and further into the city. Often there was nowhere to walk. No footpath or pavement lay beside the road and it became more and more impossible to carry on. Eventually I gave up. This is Istanbul. I never said I would walk to the centre. The suburbs will do. Take me to the airport.

Of course, I shouldn't be catching an aeroplane. I haven't been in one for years and have certain principles about flying. I am breaking them all. This is an emergency. I want to go home!